The Book
of Jewish Belief

The Book of Jewish Belief

Louis Jacobs

Behrman House, Inc.
Publishers & Booksellers   New York

for My Granddaughter Noa

ACKNOWLEDGEMENTS

I am indebted to Dr. Barry Holtz and Hannah Grad Goodman for their careful editing;
to Karen Rossel, for reading and copy-editing the manuscript;
to Ralph Davis, for his consultation and expertise;
and to Maris Engel, for her photo research.

PROJECT EDITOR: Arthur Kurzweil

BOOK DESIGN: Marsha Picker

LIBRARY OF CONGRESS CATALOGING IN PUBLICATION DATA

Jacobs, Louis.
    The book of Jewish belief.

    Includes index.
    1. Judaism. I. Title.
    BM561.J29 1984   296   84–320
    ISBN 0–87441–379–6

Contents

1. What is Judaism? *1*
2. Belief in God *10*
3. The Torah *19*
4. The Mitzvot *29*
5. The Chosen People *38*
6. The Bible *46*
7. Talmud and Midrash *56*
8. Rabbinic Literature *67*
9. Jewish Philosophy *77*
10. Jewish Mysticism *86*
11. The Sabbath *96*
12. The Festivals *105*
13. The Synagogue *115*
14. Tallit, Tefillin, Mezuzah *124*
15. The Dietary Laws *132*
16. Jewish Movements *140*
17. The Holocaust *149*
18. The State of Israel *157*
19. Love Thy Neighbor *166*
20. Compassion *174*
21. Benevolence *180*
22. Justice *187*
23. Holiness *196*
24. Jewish Ethics *203*
25. Marriage and the Family *212*
26. The Messianic Age *221*
27. The Hereafter *230*

Definition

When one is asked to define Judaism, one is really being asked to state in a single sentence what is special about the Jewish religion and how it differs from every other religion. And yet since Judaism does have many things in common with other religions, it will not do to try to describe only the differences. To do this would be to leave out some of the most important aspects of the Jewish religion. Thus the two distinctive ideas in Judaism are the special role of the Jewish people and the Torah as the will of God.

But belief in God is also essential to Judaism, so that it would be quite wrong to say only that Judaism is the religion of the Torah or the religion of the Jewish people. The best way of defining Judaism is to say that it is a religion that centers around three tremendous ideas —God, Torah, and Israel. Within these three we can find the total set of teachings that is Judaism. A chapter in this book will be devoted to each of these ideas in detail. Here we shall only state the basic ideas themselves.

God

There are religions that have no belief in God—some versions of Buddhism, for example—but Judaism is not one of them. From its beginnings Judaism has had as its central theme the belief that there is a Supreme Being, the Creator of all things, who loves His creatures and with whom His creatures can communicate in prayer and worship. It is true that in modern times here and there, Jews are to be found who say that they subscribe to a secular Judaism, that is, a Judaism without God. They mean presumably by this a Jewish way of life based on Jewish ethics and on Jewish practices, but with no religious dimension. All we can say is that if by Judaism we mean the way of life as it has hitherto been understood, it cannot by definition be "secular." All the great classics of Judaism are unintelligible without the strongest belief in God, even though there have been differing views about what God is. God appears on practically every page of the Bible, as He is behind all the discussions of the talmudic rabbis who strive mightily to grasp His will, and as He is ever-present in the prayerbook, the Passover Haggadah, the poems and songs and philosophical treatises of the Middle Ages. G. K. Chesterton was right when he said that God is not the chief character in the Bible, He is the only character.

"Judaism is a religion which centers around three tremendous ideas— God, Torah, and Israel."

The Torah

Moreover, the God in whom Jews believe is not an absent God who created the world and then left it to its own devices, indifferent to its fate and unconcerned with how people conduct themselves. As Judaism sees it, God has conveyed His will to humanity and this will is to be discovered in the Torah (which means "teaching," what it is that God would have us do). Judaism, in other words, is a religion of *revelation*. Revelation suggests that God has appeared to people and spoken to them, and the record of all this is found in the Bible and in elaborations on the Bible by the great Jewish sages. Needless to say, by "appearing" and by "speaking," we do not mean that God can be seen by the physical eye or that He has a physical mouth, tongue, and lips by means of which He "speaks."

Revelation, as understood by Jewish thinkers, is a communication from God to certain people, the nature of which is bound to be a profound mystery but which led them to an unshakable conviction that God had made the communication and that it expresses God's will. This does not mean that it is easy to know exactly what the Torah contains. There has to be a constant search for authenticity, for deeper appreciation, for recognizing the true. Baḥya Ibn Pakudah in the Middle Ages compared it to a letter sent by a king to a subject he loves, telling how he wishes to be served. By the time the subject receives the letter, some of its words may have faded and the writing none too clear, requiring much effort for it to be deciphered. Yet if the

> *"Revelation refers to a communication from God to people, the nature of which is bound to be a profound mystery."*

(Babylonian Talmud, tractate Berakhot 5a)

"R. Zera said: 'Come and see how a human being differs from the Holy One, blessed be He. When a human being sells a valued article to his fellow, the seller is distressed (that he was obliged to sell it in his need for money) but the buyer is pleased. But with the Holy One, blessed be He, it is otherwise. He gave the Torah to Israel and he was pleased; as it is said: "For I give you good doctrine; forsake not My teaching" (Proverbs 4:2).' "

(Babylonian Talmud, tractate Berakhot 6a).

"R. Naḥman ben Isaac asked R. Ḥiyya bar Abba: 'What is written in God's *tefillin?*' He replied: 'And who is like Thy people Israel, a nation one in the earth?' (I Chronicles 17:21). Does, then, the Holy One, blessed be He, glory in the praises of Israel? Yes, for it is written: 'You have recognized the Lord this day' and: 'The Lord has recognized you this day' (Deuteronomy 26:17–18). The Holy One, blessed be He, said to Israel: 'You have made Me the unique object of your love in the world, so I shall make you the unique object of My love in the world.' 'You have made Me the unique object of your love in the world' as it is said: 'Hear O Israel, the Lord our God, *the Lord is One*' (Deuteronomy 6:4). 'I shall make you the unique object of My love in the world' as it is said: 'And who is like Thy people Israel, a nation *one* in the earth?' (I Chronicles 17:21)."

subject loves the king and is convinced from the handwriting that the letter is really from the king, he will be undeterred by the labor of deciphering it. Indeed, he will be glad that it has not been given in an easy manner because the very obscurity provides mental exercise and a chance to demonstrate love and loyalty strong enough to be put to the test.

In its narrow meaning, the Torah is the Five Books of Moses. But more broadly, Torah refers to the entire body of Jewish teaching, even to the future words of a Jewish scholar.

Israel

Together with belief in God and in His Torah, Judaism believes that the people of Israel, the Jewish people, has its special part to play, because the Torah was given to Israel. It is important to say "given *to* Israel" not "given *for* Israel." The Torah, which refers to God's will, is for all people—not only for Jews. In that case, what do we mean when we say it was given to Israel?

The answer is twofold. First, God used the Jewish people to be the vehicle for communicating His will. Second, because of this, Israel has greater responsibilities and a far richer course of action in trying to fulfil that will. To take a simple example: "Thou shalt not steal," though addressed in the Ten Commandments to Israel, is a rule for all people. It is as wrong for a Gentile to steal as it is for a Jew. But the Torah tells us in much detail how honesty and integrity are to be pursued, and much more is demanded of the Jew. The observances, such as the Sabbath and Festivals are peculiarly Jewish and are binding upon Jews alone.

For Jews, religion is not separate from daily life, but is integral to every aspect of existence.

Differing Emphases

While, then, Judaism embraces these three ideas—God, Torah, and Israel—the ideas themselves are so full of significance and so open to interpretation that inevitably some Jews stress one over the others. It has been said, and with some truth, that Orthodox Jews today place the emphasis on the Torah, Reform Jews on God, and Conservative Jews on Israel. There is also the question of personal temperament. Some people are especially fired by the idea of God; they are "God intoxicated." Their greatest religious joy lies in serving God; in thinking about Him and the way His wonders are revealed in the universe. Other people, in honesty, find it hard to think of themselves as being near to God, some even find the idea frightening. But they do enjoy studying the Torah, carrying out its laws, considering it a privilege to be Jewish and to live Jewishly. Again, there are those whose hearts are full of love for Jews, who admire the achievements of their people, and find fulfilment in working for this people and through them for humanity as a whole.

The talmudic rabbis remark that just as no two human beings have the same physical features, they also differ in their mental and emotional states. That is why we ought not to be disturbed by differences in emphasis among believing Jews. Each person, said a Ḥasidic master, must discover his own way in Judaism and then live by its light and be true to the religion by being true to himself. It is only when one of the three ideas is totally excluded that Judaism is distorted. A Judaism without God is no Judaism. A Judaism without Torah is no Judaism. A Judaism without Jews is no Judaism.

The Principles of Faith

In the long history of Judaism, various beliefs have been held by Jews and have become part of Judaism. But it was not until the twelfth century that the great teacher, Maimonides, laid down thirteen principles of the faith, which he and many later Jewish teachers saw as essential to the totality of Judaism. Here, too, there have been varying interpretations and emphases, which will be considered later in this book. These are Maimonides' principles, though not in his own words (they were originally in Arabic, the language used by intellectuals of his day in Islamic lands).

"Each person, said a Ḥasidic master, must discover his own way in Judaism and then live by its light and be true to the religion by being true to himself."

Maimonides' Principles of Faith

1. God is the Creator of the universe.

2. God is One.

3. God has no body, form, or likeness.

4. God is eternal. There was never a time when He did not exist, and there will never be a time when He will cease to exist.

5. One must pray only to God.

6. God revealed Himself to the prophets.

7. Moses is the greatest of the prophets.

8. The Torah was given by God to Moses.

9. The Torah is eternal; God will not change the Torah, nor will He allow the Torah to be superseded.

10. God knows all the thoughts and all the deeds of people.

11. God rewards those who keep His laws and punishes those who disobey them.

12. God will send His Messiah to usher in a new and better world.

13. God will revive the dead.

Challenge and Response

A careful look at Maimonides' list shows that he emphasizes these principles because they were being challenged in his day. The sixth principle, that Moses is the greatest of the prophets, seems almost certainly to be aimed at the claim Islam makes for Mohammed. It is as if Maimonides is saying: If no Hebrew prophet was greater than Moses, how can the Islamic claim be justified? Maimonides' third principle, that God has no bodily form, seems to be aimed against the Christian doctrine that God was incarnate in Jesus. Maimonides' ninth principle, that the Torah will never be superseded, refutes the claims of both Christianity and Islam that a new religion has taken the place of Judaism. How can this be, implies Maimonides, since both these religions acknowledge that the Torah was given to Israel at first. To suggest that God later revealed another religion is to believe that God is like a human being who changes his mind.

Thus, Maimonides' principles are a kind of manifesto of Judaism. Maimonides did not invent these principles. He found them in the ancient Jewish sources and simply saw fit to place the stress on these for reasons of religious policy. They are not so much a bare, formal statement as a significant response to the challenges presented to Judaism in Maimonides' day. Later teachers similarly drew on the vast range of Jewish beliefs to stress those ideas that needed to be stressed in their time. (Maimonides' principles and their implications will be discussed later.)

But Others Disagree

Not everyone took kindly to Maimonides' attempt. There were those who argued that a neater formulation would reduce the principles to three: (1) God is the Creator of the universe; (2) The Torah was revealed by God; (3) God rewards and punishes people. In these three principles, it was held, all the others are included, since once we believe that God gave the Torah and He rewards those who keep it and punishes those who do not, it follows that the beliefs it contains are binding upon Jews. Others opposed Maimonides for a different reason. They held that the very attempt to formulate principles of the Jewish faith implies that these principles are more important than others, whereas in the traditional view, the whole of the Torah, as God-given, is important in every one of its parts.

In the fifteenth century, Don Isaac Abarbanel argued that Maimonides treats the Torah as if it were a secular science. In every human science one must first state the axioms, its essential principles, and then go on to show how its details follow logically from these premises. But the Torah is not a human science—it is a divine communication, and it is pointless to try to reduce it to three, or thirteen, or any other number of basic principles. It is all God-given and all equally divine and equally important. Again, others, like

Jewish tradition says that Jews have a special role in the world and that the Torah reveals God's will to them.

Moses Mendelssohn in the eighteenth century, disagreed with Maimonides' principles of faith because, as they saw it, Judaism asks us to obey the laws of the Torah but does not tell us what to believe. This position is sometimes described as the view that Judaism has no dogmas. Much nearer the truth is the view that Judaism does have essential beliefs (what kind of a religion would it be if it had no firm beliefs?) but that they have not been too rigidly defined, so that there is room for differing interpretations. On Maimonides' principle regarding the resurrection of the dead, for example, there are many interpretations.

A Rabbinic Formulation

For all that has been said up to now, there does seem to be a need for a short, clear statement of the nature of Judaism, not necessarily embracing the whole of the faith but at least, providing a handle by which the Jewish religion can be grasped. In this connection, a famous talmudic passage (*Makkot* 23b–24a) deserves to be quoted in full.

    The passage begins with the statement that God gave to Moses on Sinai 613 commands, and goes on to state, however, that various prophets sought to "reduce" them to a more manageable number. "Reduce" does not mean that the prophets sought to exclude any of the 613, but that they stated certain basic ideas from which all the rest followed. First, it is said, King David in the Book of Psalms reduced them to eleven basic ideas when he said in Psalm 15:

> Lord, who shall sojourn in Thy tabernacle?
> Who shall dwell upon Thy holy mountain?
> [i] He that walketh uprightly, and [ii] worketh righteousness,
> And [iii] speaketh truth in his heart;
> That [iv] hath no slander upon his tongue,
> [v] Nor doeth evil to his fellow,
> [vi] Nor taketh up a reproach against his neighbour;
> [vii] In whose eyes a vile person is despised,
> But [viii] he honoureth them that fear the Lord;
> [ix] He that sweareth to his own hurt, and changeth not;
> [x] He that putteth not out his money on interest,
> [xi] Nor taketh a bribe against the innocent.
> He that doeth these things shall never be moved.

Thus in this, the "gentleman's psalm," as it has been called, the ideal of the Jewish gentleperson is put forward for emulation.

The talmudic passage continues that the prophet Isaiah later reduced them to six principles (Isaiah 33:15–16):

> [i] He that walketh righteously, and [ii] speaketh uprightly;
> [iii] He that despiseth the gain of oppressions,
> [iv] That shaketh his hands from holding of bribes,
> [v] That stoppeth his ears from hearing of blood,
> [vi] And shutteth his eyes from looking upon evil;
> He shall dwell on high.

Faith is the cornerstone of Judaism. Faith implies trust in God and reliance upon Him for guidance.

"Judaism does have essential beliefs, but these have not been too rigidly defined."

Then the prophet Micah came along and reduced them further to three great principles (Micah 6:8):

> It hath been told thee, O man, what is good,
> And what the Lord doth require of thee:
> [i] Only to do justly, and [ii] to love mercy, and [iii] to
>   walk humbly with thy God.

And then Isaiah again reduced them to two (Isaiah 56:1): "Thus saith the Lord: [i] Keep ye justice, and [ii] do righteousness." Finally the prophet Habakkuk came along to reduce them all to one great principle (Habakkuk 2:4): "But the righteous shall live by his faith." In this passage it is implied that various programs of good behavior (note that in the main these are ethical rather than purely "religious") set the tone for a sound Jewish life, are what Judaism is all about. It is further implied, if Judaism has to be based on one great idea, it is that of "faith" (Hebrew: *emunah*). In this context, faith means trust in God, reliance on Him to guide us correctly. From trust in God, all the rest will follow.

"Judaism is the religion of doing the will of God."

Ashkenazim and Sephardim

Jews fall into two major groupings, the Ashkenazim and the Sephardim. *Ashkenaz* and *Sepharad* are biblical names denoting two nations. In the Middle Ages these names were applied, respectively, to Germany and Spain. Thus the Ashkenazim are the German Jews (including, nowadays, French, English, East European, American and other "Western" Jews); the Sephardim are the Spanish Jews (including Portuguese, Italian, Turkish, Greek, Moroccan, Arabian and other "Eastern" Jews). The division has existed for more than a thousand years. In the State of Israel today there are two Chief Rabbis—one for the Ashkenazim, the other for the Sephardim.

While the basic practices of Judaism among the two groups are, of course, the same, there are numerous minor variations in ritual. For instance, the Sephardic *Haftarot* (the weekly prophetic readings) often differ from those of the Askenazim. The Sephardim eat rice on Passover; the Ashkenazim do not. Customs originating among German Jews, such as reciting Kaddish for parents and observing Yahrzeit, were followed, until recently, only by Ashkenazi Jews. A problem that faced the Rabbis was what happens when a Sephardi man marries an Ashkenazi woman, or vice versa; which rituals should be followed in their home? The consensus is that the husband's status is determinative.

(Babylonian Talmud, tractate Shabbat 88a).

"A certain Galilean preached in the presence of R. Ḥisda: 'Blessed is the All-Merciful who gave a threefold Torah (i.e., the Pentateuch, the Prophets and the Hagiographa) to a threefold people (i.e., Israelites, Priests and Levites); to a third-born child (i.e., Moses, born after Miriam and Aaron) on the third day (the people prepared themselves for the giving of the Torah for three days) in the third month (the month of Sivan).' "

The God the Jews believe in is not an indifferent, absent God who created the world and then left it to its own devices.

A Summary

This introduction to our inquiry can be summed up as: Judaism is the religion of the Jewish people, who believe in the One God, Creator of heaven and earth, who loves all His creatures and who has chosen Israel by giving them His Torah so that they, and through them humanity, may have His presence dwell among them. Judaism is a practical religion, concentrating more on correct action than on correct beliefs. Yet it would be a gross distortion to view Judaism as having nothing to say about belief. For a religion of action without any beliefs is not a religion but a set of mechanical observances. A non-Jewish writer's definition of Judaism is not far off the mark. "Judaism," he writes, "is the religion of doing the will of God." He does well to place the emphasis on action, but it is an emphasis that has always grown out of Judaism's belief that God is and that the actions conform to His will.

2
Belief in God

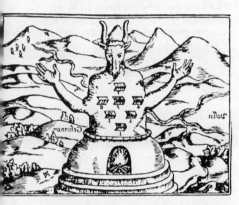

The pagan god Moloch, to whom children were sacrificed by fire, represents the conversion of Jewish children to other religions. The name *Moloch* is a distortion of *melekh*, the Hebrew word for *king* used to refer to God.

The Existence of God

It is striking that biblical thought takes the existence of God for granted. The biblical authors never doubted that there is a God. The truth is that in biblical times nobody doubted the existence of beings above human creatures who were called gods. But the biblical authors taught that the pagan gods were unreal and that to worship them was an abomination. Their argument was really one for nonexistence of the many gods the pagans believed in. They were saying in so many words: "You are mistaken if you imagine that there are many gods. Such a belief is nonsensical. There is only One God and He is the sole Creator." It is only in comparatively modern times that atheists were to be found, people who denied that there is a God. When that happened, it became necessary for believers in God to argue against the atheist. The argument has taken many forms but in essence it amounts to a demonstration that belief in God is more convincing, makes better sense of human life, than any rival philosophy.

Why Jews Believe in God

The majority of Jews believe that there is a God because that is what they have been taught by their ancestors. Nevertheless, when called upon to defend this belief they are able to show that it is not blind and unthinking. On the contrary, if we consider theism, the belief in the One God, and its rival, atheism, it is easy to see why theism is to be preferred. Consider what life means if there is no God. Everything just happened—how no one knows, and no one can possibly know since, in the atheistic view, there is no explanation. Somehow it has to be maintained that atoms and molecules just came together in particular combinations to produce not only the material universe, but the human mind (including the mind of the atheist!), all beauty and art, all music and goodness, all science, all philosophy, all the kindness and generosity of which people are capable, all the protests against evil and the struggle for justice, righteousness, and compassion. In the atheistic premise, there is no ultimate meaning to human life. It is just there. Now, no human being behaves as if life had no meaning. Every one of us tries to make sense of things, to be as rational as we can, implying that the universe is reasonable. But how can the universe be reasonable unless there is mind in the universe, and how can there be mind in inanimate matter? That is why theists speak of the Mind that is behind all existence and this Mind is what is meant by God.

But There Is Suffering

So convincing is the argument that no one would ever doubt the existence of God if not for one fact: the existence of evil and suffering in the universe. If God exists and if His glory is to be seen in the workings of the Mind that is behind the universe, how and why could such a Being tolerate all the pain, misery, and anguish that is often the lot of humanity. For the Jewish people, the argument against God's existence was presented with terrible force when six million innocent people were murdered by the Nazis. Why did God allow such horror?

Whole books have been written by theists about this tremendous problem. When all is said and done, the believer falls back on faith that somehow, in a way not to be fathomed in this life, all the evil and pain ultimately serves the good. The very protest against evil suggests that the universe makes sense (otherwise, what is the point of protesting? A child who hits a chair after knocking his knee on it is behaving irrationally). But we can obtain faint glimpses of how it can all make sense. For instance, if there were no evil to overcome, how could human beings ever develop their characters, how could heroism and generosity and skills be possible?

The poet Browning uses the illustration of a checkerboard with black and white squares. One person says it is a black checkerboard with white squares, the other says it is a white checkerboard with

Many have asked: Where was God?

The Gods of the Ancient Near East

The chief pagan male god in the ancient Near East was *Baal;* the word means "lord" or "master." The ancients believed that there were many Baalim, each attached to some special place or event in the history of the people he was supposed to protect. The word *Baal* also means "husband," and the female goddesses were considered the spouses of the various male gods. In the temples there were often to be found the god's throne, his bed, a lamp to illumine his darkness, a cupboard in which his clothes were kept and other furniture. The pagans thought their gods had to be appeased when they were angry—by gifts or sacrifices, even child sacrifices, especially of the first-born child. Worshipers of *Moloch,* a Canaanite god mentioned in the Bible, "passed their children through fire" to placate him. Rain to make the earth fruitful was thought to be a gift of Baal. In order to encourage fertility, the worshipers patronized temple prostitutes. The sun, moon and stars were also worshiped.

In the monotheism of the Bible, the One true God demands purity, justice and righteousness from his adherents. Every form of idolatry was strictly forbidden. At least in the later parts of the Bible the term used for the gods is *elilim,* which really means "nonentities." That is to say, it is not that the gods are evil or unworthy of human worship but that they do not exist at all; they are only figments of the imagination.

Is a zebra white with black stripes or black with white stripes? This riddle reflects Judah Halevi's belief that a simple shift in viewpoint can change the world we see and experience.

"There is so much wisdom evident in the spider's web that it is extremely hard to believe it just came about of itself."

black squares. The Jewish thinker Judah Halevi said much the same thing. He noted that there is so much wisdom evident in the spider's web, so wonderful that it is extremely hard to believe it just came about of itself. Yet, Judah Halevi remarks, the web is used to catch flies, so that there is evidence of lack of wisdom, at least from the point of view, as it were, of the flies. Yes, Judah Halevi says, that is indeed a difficulty. But should not the wisdom seen in the spider's web keep us from stating that there is no Mind behind the universe? We are, to be sure, left with a problem but problems can be solved. The alternative presents the biggest problem of all: how could wisdom have emerged from raw matter?

The anguish of believers when confronted by the agonies suffered by good people is the theme of the biblical Book of Job, which states the problem in matchless poetry. (Since the book uses poetic imagery throughout, it is a very difficult book to read.) It is not a cold, philosophical investigation, seeking to provide a clear answer. It seeks rather to create a mood, to "ring a bell" so that readers may say: "Yes, this is how I feel, this does give me a glimmer of light, reducing but not removing the torment of my soul."

Here is the story of Job in brief (there is no real substitute for a careful reading of the book itself, even if only in translation). Job is a good man. He is described as "one that feared God, and shunned evil." He is pious and generous, ever ready to help life's unfortunates. But then tragedy of the most horrible kind strikes. His children are killed in a series of accidents. He loses his wealth. He is afflicted with a loathsome disease so that even his wife cannot bear to come near him. From a happy, serene, prosperous man of faith, Job is reduced to a quivering wreck of a man. He had been led to believe that sin is the cause of all suffering and his friends hint strongly that Job suffers because he is a secret sinner of the worst kind. Job cannot accept this. He knows that while he may have sinned, the pain he suffers is more than could have been required as atonement. Why, then, has it all come about, is the question he hurls at God, protesting that God, in whom he still believes, must justify Himself.

It is noteworthy that when God does eventually speak to Job "out of the whirlwind," He does not offer Job a reasoned argument but challenges Job to explain the mystery of creation. God asks: Where was Job when the universe was created? How can Job hope to fathom the wisdom of the Creator? How does Job explain the marvelous ways in which the sun, moon, and stars revolve around the earth? Could Job have created the smallest of God's creatures or the hippopotamus and the crocodile?

What are we to make of God's response? The Book of Job seems to be saying that to grasp the ways of God, a human being would have to be divine. The human mind is simply too limited. It is incapable of fitting the mysterious universe into a neat and tidy scheme in which everything makes sense. The reference to the hippopotamus and the crocodile is highly revealing. These strange creatures are not those we might have created had we been creators. But that is precisely the point. We are not and never can be creators of worlds. Job eventually bows in submission. He has not found an answer to his problem, but has learned to live with it because he has experienced God directly. God has spoken to him and has made him aware how awesome is life.

The truth is that a religious attitude involves far more than intellectual agreement that God exists. It involves feelings of dependence on God and an appreciation of our insignificance, and yet of God's concern for us. It involves the kind of emotions we have when we see an awe-inspiring sunset or other wonders of nature like lofty mountains, mighty seas, the Grand Canyon, the starry sky at night, lightning and thunder. It is the feeling expressed in William Blake's poem:

> Tiger! Tiger! burning bright
> In the forests of the night,
> What immortal hand or eye
> Could frame thy fearful symmetry?

That is to say, not only *could* we not have created a tiger or a hippopotamus or a crocodile, we *would* not have created these weird and wonderful creatures even if we had the power. It is a frightening as well as a beautiful world in which we live, a world of risk, and terror, and strangeness—but a world shot through with wonder and delight. It is a world which, in the words of Isaiah, is full of God's glory.

The Nature of God

The term "God" is just a word. To have any significance we must apply it to the Being we designate as the Creator of the universe and we tend to speak, in this connection, of Mind. But when we try to describe the nature of God, we find that we are using human terms

"Once we try to describe in any detail the nature of God, we find that we are using human terms for Him."

The sight of a vast desert, a majestic mountain, a magnificent rainbow, or a crashing sea evoke feelings expressed in the special blessings found in the Jewish tradition. There is even a special blessing for a sunrise: "Blessed are You, Lord our God, King of the Universe, who created the work of the Beginning."

for Him and we realize they cannot be applied to Him. For instance, when we speak of Mind, unless we are naive, we cannot believe that God has a brain or any other physical parts like our brains. So the use of descriptions, or attributes, as they are called, of God must be treated with caution. The same applies to our speaking of God as a person. This can only mean that He is not less than a person. He is real and brought human personality into existence. As for His true nature, this human beings can never know.

That is why the great Jewish thinkers tell us that we can never know God as He is in Himself, but only as He is manifested in the universe, that is to say, by His tremendous acts that can be observed. Maimonides gives this illustration. We see how a child grows in its mother's womb. This is an astonishing marvel, a full human being growing for nine months to emerge into the world with all its limbs functioning immediately, and with the means for satisfying all its needs. If such care and love had been given by a human being, we would certainly say he is good and kind. Consequently, we are permitted to say that God in His manifestation (that is, in the way He appears to us) is good and kind, without suggesting that we are trying to do the impossible, to grasp His complete or true nature. If I knew Him, I would be He, said a famous Jew. Hence, the Jewish tradition allows us to say certain things about God provided it is with a realization of the futility of trying to pin down in human language the Creator of the universe. In this spirit we can examine some of the ideas of Judaism about God.

> *"To postulate that there could be other gods is to suggest that God is not in control of every part of His universe."*

Freedom and Foreknowledge

A remarkable illustration of how Judaism tolerates freedom of thought and a variety of opinions is provided by a debate among the medieval philosophers. The topic was how God's foreknowledge can be reconciled with man's freedom of choice. If God knows before a man is born how he will behave, how can that man be free to do otherwise? Alone of those great thinkers of the Middle Ages, Ḥasdai Crescas holds that, because of God's foreknowledge, man only appears to be free. But Crescas is in difficulty. If man is not really free to choose, how can he be deserving of reward when he leads a good life and how can he deserve punishment if he is evil?

Gersonides, on the other hand, teaches that man is really free to choose and that freedom of choice is, indeed, incompatible with God's foreknowledge. In order to safeguard man's freedom, Gersonides is willing to compromise on God's foreknowledge. God knows everything there is to be known, but man's freedom of choice, by definition, is not something that can be known, even to God. This very bold position does not really satisfy the religious mind, since it implies a kind of ignorance in God.

Maimonides, therefore, argues that man is free and yet God has foreknowledge. How can these two propositions be reconciled? Maimonides replies that God's knowledge is God Himself. We can have no more understanding of God's knowledge than we have of the nature of God Himself. In other words, there is a mystery here that we must not expect to understand, since man cannot fathom the secrets of the Infinite. Even for Maimonides, generally considered to be the foremost rationalist among Jewish thinkers, there are some things we must accept on faith. This, too, is *reasonable* because it is irrational to imagine that the finite human mind can grasp God's nature.

God Is One

The doctrine that God is One is formulated in the *Shema*, which may be described as Israel's declaration of faith. This verse, more than any other, has been used to express the special meaning of the Jewish religion. The Shema ("Hear") occurs in the Book of Deuteronomy, chapter six, verse four. The usual rendering of the Hebrew is: "HEAR, O ISRAEL: THE LORD OUR GOD, THE LORD IS ONE." What precisely does "One" mean here? First, it means that there is only one God, not many, as the pagan religions supposed. The Shema is thus a protest against idolatry, the worship of the pagan gods.

But implied in the word "One" is a further and very far-reaching idea, spelled out particularly by the Jewish thinkers of the Middle Ages. "One" is understood not merely as "one among many," but also in the sense of "unique." In a sophisticated view of what Judaism says about God, the meaning is not merely that there is only one God (though, theoretically, there could have been more); rather, Judaism is saying: God, being God, can *only* be one. If God is understood as the sole Being who brought *everything* into existence, it must follow that even theoretically there cannot be any other gods! For to postulate that there could be other gods is to suggest that God is not in control of every part of His universe. Thus God, as Judaism understands Him, is not *a* Being among others. He is the *only* Being and is the Source of all that there is.

The artist Michelangelo, in his painting on the ceiling of the Sistine Chapel, depicts God in finite terms, hardly approaching the Jewish concept of the Divine.

God Is Eternal

Arising out of this is the further idea that God, being God, always existed and always will exist. Since He is the Source of existence, it makes no sense to speak of existence without Him. Some years ago

An ancient fossil records the intricacies of God's design. Evolution is not an argument against the existence of God; it is a way of understanding the world He continuously creates.

some theologians were fond of speaking of "the death of God." It is not too clear what they meant by this statement; perhaps they meant that people no longer believe in God, a very dubious proposition. Be that as it may, it is nonsense to say that God did once exist, but that He no longer does. A God who can vanish into nonexistence could not have been God even before His demise. The Book of Deuteronomy expresses the eternity of God in the wonderful phrase: "The eternal God is a dwelling-place, and underneath are the everlasting arms" (Deuteronomy 33:27).

This implies that the human craving for permanence can be satisfied because God, the Creator, is eternal. God is real and ever-present in the world, which is not a meaningless conglomeration suspended in a void, but which rests securely on "the everlasting arms" of the Creator.

God Is All-Powerful

Traditionally, Judaism has understood God to be all-powerful. He can do anything He chooses and nothing can prevent Him from so doing.

A Paradox

The problem has been posed: Can God create a stone which even He cannot pick up? If we say He cannot, then He is not all-powerful. If we say He can, then, again, He is not all-powerful because there is something He cannot pick up. It is easy to see the fallacy in this type of argument. Since there cannot possibly **be** a stone which God cannot pick up, to ask whether or not He can create one is to talk nonsense. It is as if we asked the equally nonsensical question: Can He will Himself out of existence? He cannot, but that is because there is no meaning to the words "will Himself out of existence," and not because there are limitations to His powers.

Amulets

Those who believe in the power of amulets to ward off evil believe that besides the names of God mentioned in the Bible, there are numerous other divine names, formed by combining letters of the Hebrew alphabet. These combinations, they believe, have been handed down secretly from generation to generation and can be used by the writers of amulets. For example, a divine name, which often appears on amulets, is *kera satan,* formed by combining certain letters. Although the name is supposed to have supernatural power, kera satan also has a meaning which makes it even more powerful. The two words can mean: "Rend Satan asunder" (i.e., "Tear the Devil to bits so that he can do no harm"). Thus, amulets are thought to make a direct assault on the powers of evil. For instance, in amulets to protect women in childbirth from the evil deeds of Lilith, the expression is used: "*Hutz* Lilith" (i.e., "Be gone from here, thou female demon with evil designs on the mother-to-be"). Undoubtedly, many Jews have believed in the efficacy of amulets. But Jews of note, including Maimonides, did not believe in them, or if they tolerated their use, they did so only because of the psychological relief they gave to those who believed in them.

This belief follows from God's creation of the universe. Since He brought into being all the power there is, He must be all-powerful. However, we must be careful to grasp this idea for what it is. It does mean that God can do the impossible, if by impossible we mean impossible for us. He can do things we cannot possibly do; He can cause water to boil without heat, to take a simple example of what we would call a miracle. But He cannot do the *absolutely impossible,* not because His power is limited but because there cannot be any such thing!

God Is All-Knowing

Judaism affirms that God knows all. In the language of the Bible, His "eyes are open upon all the ways of the sons of men, to give every one according to his ways, and according to the fruit of his doings" (Jeremiah 32:19). With very few exceptions, this has been understood by the Jewish teachers to mean also that God knows all future happenings. And this raised one of the most stubborn problems in Jewish thought, widely discussed in the Middle Ages: That is, since God knows before a person is born exactly how he will behave during his life (which is presumably what is meant by saying that God knows all future events) how can we be free to choose our way of life? It will not do to reply that we are not free to choose, since the idea of freedom of choice is also basic to Judaism; otherwise what meaning can there be to all the admonitions to do this and to refrain from doing that? In the technical language of the medieval philosophers, how is God's foreknowledge compatible with human freedom?

Maimonides, for all his mighty attempts to make everything in Judaism seem perfectly reasonable, has to admit here that we simply do not know the answer. Maimonides suggests that we cannot, in fact, know the answer, since the problem touches on God's knowledge, which belongs to the nature of God as He is in Himself, and even the faintest notion of this is completely beyond finite humans. The good Jew, declares Maimonides, even though incapable of understanding, will hold fast to both beliefs: that God has foreknowledge *and* that we are free.

The majority of Jewish teachers have been content to leave it at that. But one or two thinkers have tried to provide us with some slight idea of how God's foreknowledge can be squared with human freedom. According to these thinkers, it is a mistake to say that God knows now how a person will behave in the future. If He did, a person could not possibly be free to do otherwise. No, we should say rather that God sees into the future; that is, God is beyond time and He observes what we do when we do it. It is our *future* acts that God sees now. This is far from clear. How can God see *now* acts that will take place in the *future*? It is suggested that God sees, as it were, the whole of time *at once.* This illustration is given: Suppose a person stands at the top of a deep gorge and looks down on a number of people passing along the floor of the gorge one by one. From the point

Rabbi Akiva said, "Everything is foreseen and freedom of choice is given." Jewish sages have said that even the falling of a tiny bird from its branch is part of God's intimate relationship with His universe.

of view of those on the floor of the gorge, they walk along one at a time. But from the point of view of the one at the top of the gorge, they all appear simultaneously. From our point of view, there is past, present, and future. But from God's point of view past, present, and future are all one and He sees every act, whether in the past, present, or future, as happening *now*.

At the most, this gives us only a very faint glimpse into how the problem can be resolved. It is in an area such as this that faith comes into the picture. We cannot know all the answers and must learn to appreciate that the human mind is severely limited when trying to think adequately about the nature of God. The Ḥasidic master, R. Naḥman of Bratslav, went even further. He argued that if a person has no difficulties whatever in conceiving of God it is because he has an inferior conception of God. The God who can be fully grasped by the human mind would not be God at all. Or, as it has been put, instead of trying to get the Heavens into our heads, we should try to get our heads into the Heavens.

Ethical Monotheism

"The God who can be fully grasped by the human mind would not be God at all."

The attitude of Judaism has been described as ethical monotheism. *Monotheism* is the belief in the One God in the way we have tried to describe it in this chapter. For monotheism to be Jewish, the word "ethical" has to be added. Judaism would not see much significance in the belief in God as the Supreme Being unless it made demands on us to lead a good life. That is what we mean by God's concern for us and what the great Hebrew prophets meant when they declared that He desires righteousness, justice, compassion, and holiness from the men and women He has created. There have been philosophers who worked out a system of ethics without any belief in God, as there have been a few religious people who have led pretty poor ethical lives. Judaism, however, insists that there can be no religion without ethics and no ethics without religion; or, better, that unless ethics and religion are wedded together, neither constitutes the Jewish way, which is *ethical monotheism*.

3

The Torah

The Meaning of Torah

The word *Torah* has an interesting history. The root of the word is *yarah*, meaning "to shoot," i.e., at a target. When someone shoots at a target, he is trying to direct an arrow, and so the root meaning of the word Torah is that of "correct direction" and hence the word means a "teaching," a "doctrine," or a "law" (the Greek translators of the Bible rendered Torah as *nomos*, "law"). In the Bible, the word generally refers to a particular law or doctrine, or to a set of such laws or doctrines. But eventually the term referred to *the* Torah, the Torah of Moses (the Five Books of Moses, the Pentateuch. It is in this sense that we speak of the Scroll of the Torah, containing the Five Books of Genesis, Exodus, Leviticus, Numbers, and Deuteronomy) as the *Sefer Torah*, the "Book of the Torah." Later still, the term Torah came to mean the whole of the Bible and eventually all the explanations, elaborations, and extensions by the sages of Israel, so that in this sense the Torah means the whole of Jewish teaching, the total picture of what God wishes us to do.

"Torah means the whole of Jewish teaching, the total picture of what it is that God wishes us to do."

The Written and the Oral Torah

In rabbinic literature there are many references to the two parts of the Torah: (a) the *Written Torah (Torah she-bi-Khetav)* and (b) the *Oral Torah (Torah she-be-al Peh)*. The original idea here is that, together with the laws and teachings recorded in writing in the Pentateuch, God conveyed to Moses on Mount Sinai by word of mouth (not in a written document) all the explanations of the written word. For instance, the Written Torah states it is forbidden to work on the Sabbath but gives almost no indication of what constitutes "work." The definition is given in the Oral Torah, now found, according to the traditional view, in the Talmud and in the rabbinic literature generally. Or, to take another example, the Written Torah speaks of buying and selling houses and fields, but gives little indication exactly how property is transferred from one person to another. This, too, is in the Oral Torah.

    At first it was forbidden to write down any of the Oral Torah because its very essence is its flexibility. A written text is bound to become too rigid. Recorded in one particular age, it cannot offer guidance for conditions and situations that arise later. But eventually,

The Hebrew root of the word *Torah* means "to shoot"; the Hebrew root of the word *sin* means "to miss." A basic Jewish attitude toward life is seen in the metaphor of shooting at a mark—and sometimes missing (Jasper Johns, *Target with Four Faces*, 1955).

"A written text requires interpretation and reinterpretation as new challenges present themselves."

though the actual date is none too clear, the rabbinic teachers decided that the Oral Torah, too, must be recorded, lest it be forgotten. Thus, the writing down of the Oral Torah was really a concession to human limitations. That is why we have written (and now printed) texts of the Oral Torah, such as the Talmud and the *Midrashim*. Nevertheless, since it is impossible to know these works without a good deal of instruction verbally communicated by teacher to pupil, the dynamic principle behind the Oral Torah is still preserved. One cannot simply *read* the Talmud. One must be introduced to its intricacies by a competent teacher.

The concept of the Oral Torah signifies much more than a set of oral teachings existing side by side with the teachings recorded in writing. It is told of the renowned rabbinic scholar, David Hoffmann, that when he was a little boy, his teacher told him of the doctrine of the Written and Oral Torahs. Little David Hoffmann asked his teacher the obvious but very penetrating question: "Why could God have not made up His mind? If He wanted to give the Torah in writing, why did He not give it all in writing; and if He wanted to give some of it orally, why did He not give all of it orally?"

The truth is that a written text, compiled in a given age and referring to the conditions of that age, requires interpretation and reinterpretation again and again as new challenges present themselves and as new conditions obtain.

To take an example from writing itself: When printing was invented, a number of questions arose, such as, is a Sefer Torah that is printed, instead of written by hand, fit for use in the synagogue? Has a printed book any sanctity? The written name of God must not be erased—would the same prohibition apply to the printed name of God? The Jewish authorities deal with this kind of question, to which there could be no answer in the Written Torah because printing had not yet been invented when the Written Torah was compiled. Applying the principles of the Torah to new situations is also an intent of the Oral Torah. Therefore, whenever some new interpretation of a biblical verse or some fresh insight into Jewish teaching is given, even by a contemporary Jew, if it is in line with the truth of Judaism, it becomes part of the Oral Torah and, therefore, part of the Torah.

The Torah Scroll

The Sefer Torah ("Book of the Torah") has to be written by a skilled scribe on parchment manufactured from the skin of a kosher animal. In the Book of Exodus we read "that the law [Torah] of the Lord may be in thy mouth" (Exodus 13:9). The Rabbis took this literally—the Torah must be written on skins from an animal whose meat may be taken in the mouth, i.e., which Jews may eat. The idea behind this appears to be that only that which is pure and wholesome is suitable for holy writ. Implied here, perhaps, is the idea that unworthy means should not be adopted when pursuing worthy ends; the ends do not justify the means. A special type of black ink is used to form the

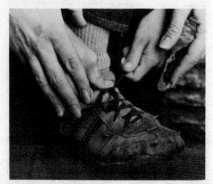

The Oral Torah transmits stories, incidents, and explanations that are not part of the Written Torah. Upon returning from a long journey to see his teacher, Rabbi Leib Saras said, "I did not see Rabbi Dov Baer of Mezeritz to learn from him interpretations of the Torah text, but to note his way of tying his shoelaces."

Only a skilled scribe is permitted to produce a Torah scroll.

letters. Lines are ruled, so that the letters stay in a straight line, and the columns are similarly neatly laid out. The columns are sewn together so that they form a long continuous scroll. Some especially pious scribes immerse themselves in a bath of natural water (the *mikveh*) as an act of purification before writing any of the divine names. The completed scroll, if written properly, is a work of art with clear, shining script. It usually takes a scribe about a year to complete a single scroll. If even one letter has been written incorrectly the scroll is unfit for use but, unless it forms part of the divine name, the error can be erased and then written correctly. If the scribe makes a mistake when writing the divine name, the whole column must be removed and buried (generally in the grave of a scholar or very religious person).

Seven of the letters (*shin, ayin, tet, nun, zayin, gimmel,* and *tzadi*) are to be written with little "crowns" (*taggin*) to adorn them. Among other things, this represents the "crown of the Torah," the privilege, akin to royalty, enjoyed by students of the Torah and those who keep its teachings. There is a tradition that some of the letters must be written very large and others very small. Although various conjectures have been made (i.e., that the small letters may have been inadvertently left out by the ancient scribes and then put in in the small space left), the reason for the tradition is still not completely clear. But these small and large letters allow for numerous interpretations in the spirit of the Midrash. For instance, the tradition has it that the letter *ayin* of Shema and the letter *dalet* of Eḥad ("One") in the first verse of the Shema have to be written large. These two letters taken together form the word *Ed,* "witness," yielding the thought that whenever the Shema is recited, testimony is being given to the Oneness of God.

שעטנז גץ

The letters with crowns appearing in the Torah scroll.

Some words have to be written with dots over them. Again the reason for this is uncertain but may either suggest that there is a question whether these words should appear in the scroll or, conversely, whether they should be emphasized, much as we today use italics. Neither vowel points nor musical notations may be written in the Sefer Torah, but they are traditional and are found in the printed versions. The musical notes represent the various melodies to be used when the Torah is chanted. Since they are not written in the Scroll, the reader of the Torah in the synagogue has to be familiar with them beforehand. In some congregations, woe betide the reader who gets the vowels or notes wrong! The reader will be loudly corrected by the more knowledgeable members of the congregation and be compelled to repeat the word correctly. The musical notes are really a kind of commentary to the text. For instance, on the Hebrew word for "but he lingered" (Genesis 19:16) the Hebrew note is *shalshelet*, a wavering, drawn-out note, so that the congregation can almost see Lot hesitating before he commits himself to leaving the doomed city which was his home.

Rabbinic Midrash provides interpretations of particular words, letters, and modes of writing of the Scroll. A good example is provided in the midrashic comment on why the very first letter of the Torah is a *bet* (*bereshit*, "In the beginning"). The letter *bet* is closed on three sides but open toward the left, the Torah being read from right to left. This is to remind us that what is beyond space and time (above, below, and behind) is a mystery too deep for us to penetrate, but we are expected to look toward the future, secure in our trust in God. Similarly, the last letter of the Torah is *lammed*. When this is added to the first letter the word *lev*, "heart," is formed. This yields the thought that the Torah is unending, its final letter leads back to its first letter, and that God wants the heart, which represents human goodness, inwardness, and compassion. A Midrash tells us that the Torah in Heaven was written in black fire on white fire (in another

Rabbi Akiba

A typical story about love for Torah is that of Rabbi Akiba. During the Roman persecution of Jews and Judaism at the end of the first century, the Romans decreed that whoever taught the Torah would be put to death. Akiba continued to teach and when warned of the danger, answered with his famous parable: A fox wished to entice fish out of the water onto dry land, and he pointed out the dangers they faced in the water. "O fox," they replied, "they say you are the cleverest of beasts. Verily you are the most foolish. If we are in danger, as you say, in water, our natural element, how can we survive on dry land, which is so completely foreign to our nature?" The Torah is frequently compared in rabbinic literature to life-giving water. The Torah is the Jew's natural element. There are, to be sure, risks in living the life of Torah, but without it there is no life. Akiba was eventually caught teaching the Torah and sentenced to death by torture. Akiba was seen smiling as he suffered martyrdom. This smile on the face of the saint dying for love of the Torah expresses Israel's hope and trust that Judaism is an undying faith and that ultimately the Torah will win out.

version in letters of white fire on a background of black fire). God's revelation in the Torah partakes of the unfathomable (the black fire) as well as the perfectly intelligible (the white fire). Moreover, the letters are letters of fire. Fire provides us with heat and light but it is dangerous to draw too near to it. The Torah warms our souls and illumines our eyes, but we must keep at a respectful distance. We must never imagine that we have mastered all the Torah and we must not treat it with over-familiarity as if it were no more than a human document.

The Love of Torah

Since the Torah is the Jew's way to God and since it consists of God's communication to the Jew, it is considered God's most precious gift to His people. Israel's delight in the Torah expresses itself in many ways. There is even a festival, *Simḥat Torah*, when the annual reading of the Torah is completed, in which there is merrymaking and rejoicing because we were privileged to receive the Torah. In the prayer recited just before the reading of the Shema in the morning, joy in the Torah is expressed in words that could have been written only by a Jew full of appreciation of what the Torah means as his people's chief joy:

With abounding love hast Thou loved us, O Lord our God, with great and exceeding pity hast Thou pitied us. O our Father, our King, for our fathers' sake, who trusted in Thee, and whom Thou didst teach the statutes of life, be also gracious unto us and teach us. O our Father, merciful Father, ever compassionate, have mercy upon us; O put into our hearts to understand and to discern, to mark, learn and teach, to heed, to do and to fulfil in love all the words of instruction in Thy Torah.

The Torah Is a Blueprint

In a remarkable rabbinic passage it is said that before He came to create the world, God first looked into the Torah, which existed even before the creation of the world, much as an architect consults his blueprint before beginning to build. This is a poetic way of saying that the world is so constituted that it all fits in with the teachings of the Torah. When we observe the laws of the Torah we are "in tune with the infinite"; in accord with God's plan. Some people fail to see this, imagining that the Torah and its laws are frustrating to human development. They tend to look upon the Torah as being like the Victorian nanny who said: "Go and see what the children are doing and tell them not to"! As Judaism sees it, the very opposite is true. The Torah is intended not to interfere with, but to promote, human well-being and growth. It teaches people how to realize the best in themselves, how to lead worthy, dignified, noble lives, in the process of which they come nearer to God.

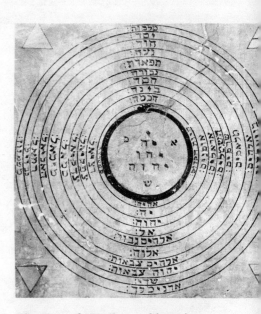

The view of Torah as a blueprint is often reflected in the kabbalistic diagrams charting the structure and course of the universe.

The Love of Torah

One of the Rabbis sold all that he had so in order to devote himself entirely to the study of the Torah. He gave up his riches, saying: "I sold that which was created in only six days (the material universe) in order to buy that which was created in forty days (the Torah, given to Moses during the forty days he spent on the mountain)." The rabbi quoted the verse:

> Many waters cannot quench love,
> Neither can the floods drown it;
> If a man would give all the substance of his house for love,
> He would utterly be contemned.
>   (Song of Songs 8:7)

The love of the Torah is more precious than anything the material world has to offer. Throughout Jewish history literacy and learning have been greatly prized. Pious Jewish parents always longed for their children to be learned in the Torah. No one could hold any position of leadership and trust in the ancient Jewish community without being learned in the Torah. A library of Jewish books, however small, was considered essential in every Jewish home.

But the Torah Is Not to Be Worshiped

Yet for all the love and regard Israel has for the Torah, it is never allowed to become an object of worship. God alone is to be worshiped; the Torah is no more, though no less, than the instrument by means of which He is worshiped. That is why Judaism speaks of the love of God and of the fear of God, as well as of the love of the Torah, but never of the fear of the Torah, since "fear" denotes worship. Some Jewish teachers, anxious to avoid any suggestion that the Torah can be an object of worship, even forbid bowing to it. Nowadays, it is the custom to bow to the Torah, but only in respect, not in worship.

The Study of the Torah

"More important even than the practice of Torah is the study of Torah."

More important even than the practice of the Torah is the study of the Torah, according to the traditional rabbinic teaching. On the basis of the verse in the Shema, "and thou shalt teach them diligently unto thy children, and shalt talk of them when thou sittest in thy house, and when thou walkest by the way, and when thou liest down, and when thou risest up" (Deuteronomy 6:7), the Rabbis urge that schools teach the Torah both to children and to adults so that from childhood to death, a Jew engages in the study of God's word. Not every Jew can be expected to devote all his time to study of the Torah, but every Jew is expected to devote some time to it each day, no matter how busy.

The ideal is not for the Jewish community to be a community of rabbis but, as far as possible, a community in which learning is a joy and a privilege for each, according to his capacities. In former times in Eastern Europe there were brotherhoods that met daily to study with a teacher. The members of these brotherhoods were small businessmen, artisans, coach-drivers and the like, who recognized that the Torah did not belong to the rabbis but was the heritage of all Israel. Ideally, this total devotion to Torah study, expressed in the verse addressed to Joshua, is applied to every Jew: "This book of the law [Torah] shall not depart out of thy mouth, but thou shalt meditate therein day and night, that thou mayest observe to do according to all that is written therein; for then thou shalt make thy ways prosperous, and then thou shalt have good success" (Joshua 1:8). In many Jewish communities, no person is more respected than the student of the Torah. Jewish parents had boundless joy if, in answer to their prayers, their children grew up to be Torah scholars.

Study and Practice

The Talmud (tractate *Kiddushin* 40b) records a debate that took place in the town of Lydda over 1,500 years ago as to which was greater, the study of the Torah or its practice. The debate concluded that study is greater because it leads to practice. The meaning of this strange conclusion (if study is greater because it leads to practice, it follows that practice is greater!) is that in study of the Torah there is *both* study and practice. In other words, study leads to practice and study *is itself* the practice of Judaism. Of course, the Rabbis did not see much point in study of the Torah without Jewish observance. The scholar who behaves contrary to the Torah in daily life cannot have allowed the Torah to be much of a guide.

In prewar Poland, young married men, who were supported by their fathers-in-law so that they might study the Torah without financial worries, spent some time each week begging at doors, not for themselves but for the poor. Far from considering such conduct demeaning and unbecoming to scholars, they held it to be the necessary demonstration that Torah study inspired compassion and action.

The principle, therefore, was that one should interrupt study to do good deeds, if they could not be carried out by others. Yet in the hierarchy of Jewish values it is study that occupies the topmost rank. The *Mishnah* (*Peah* 1:1) states this emphatically in the full spirit of rabbinic Judaism: "The following things are those for which a man eats the fruit of the reward in this world with the capital of the reward stored up for him in the World to Come: Honoring parents, performing acts of benevolence, and bringing peace between man and his fellow. But the study of the Torah exceeds all of these." In the traditional scheme, the study of the Torah is greater even than prayer. The Talmud (tractate *Shabbat* 10a) tells of a rabbi who rebuked his colleague for spending too much time over his prayers when he could have been studying the Torah. The rabbi declared: "They leave aside eternal life to engage in temporal existence," meaning that important though prayer is, it consists chiefly of requests for things in this life—health, wealth, and so forth—whereas Torah study belongs to that which is eternal and beyond time and place.

> *"In the hierarchy of Jewish values it is study that occupies the topmost rank."*

The Scope of Torah Study

The main topics of Torah study in the Middle Ages were the Bible and the talmudic literature. Early on, however, kabbalistic (mystical) and philosophical studies were added, at least by some students. Maimonides, for example, holds that it is an important part of Torah study to attain correct ideas regarding the physical world and to have correct opinions regarding God and humanity. Thus Maimonides allows the concept of Torah to embrace both physics and metaphysics. Later commentators on Maimonides try to explain this away, but a plain reading of what the famous teacher actually said leads to the conclusion that if he were alive today, he would not only advocate a course of study in modern physics and in philosophy at university level, but would treat this as part of the obligation to study the Torah. Similarly, the historians considered the study of the Jewish past to be part of Torah study.

"In ancient times it was held to be a religious duty for each Jew to write by hand his own Torah scroll."

For modern Jews, therefore, the scope of Torah study is wide enough to satisfy almost every taste. And there are excellent works in English for those unable to master Hebrew and Aramaic, the original languages of most of the sacred texts. Every Jewish home should have a number of Jewish books which are regularly studied. In ancient times it was held to be a religious duty for each Jew to write by hand a Sefer Torah. Some pious Jews still carry out this duty literally, spending a good deal of their leisure time in carefully copying column after column of the Sefer Torah until eventually the whole scroll is complete. However, the fourteenth-century authority, R. Asher ben Yeḥiel, ruled that since the purpose of the obligation is to have a scroll from which to study and since a major part of Torah study involves the reading of postbiblical works, it is far better to purchase a large number of Jewish books and to have a good Jewish library.

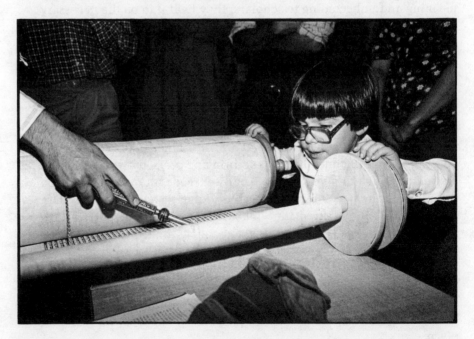

How to Study the Torah

There is an old rabbinic saying that one can study the Torah only from a text to which the heart is attracted. The person who is particularly interested in the Bible should concentrate on biblical studies; and so on through the whole range of studies. Nevertheless, the ideal is to become familiar with as much of Jewish learning as possible. Some students study one text in depth while reading others in a less profound but more comprehensive way, so that eventually they become expert in one field but also knowledgeable on many other matters.

With the rise of modern critical scholarship, a new problem presents itself. Nowadays, a host of scholars have subjected the Bible, Talmud, and the other classics of Judaism to much critical and historical analysis so that the texts are given frequently other than the traditional interpretation. To give but one example, the traditional view is that King David wrote the whole Book of Psalms, and the study of the Psalms was based on this view. When one studied the Psalms one was examining a text believed to have been conveyed directly to King David by means of the holy spirit, that is, by divine inspiration.

The verdict of modern scholarship is that the Book of Psalms is a composite work, namely, a collection of writings by various authors operating at different times, and this new concept is of immense assistance in grasping the meaning of this marvelous book. As a result, it is far harder, nowadays, to think of directly grasping the mind of God through sacred Scripture and other sacred works. The new view seems to demonstrate that human hands had far more to do with what has emerged than the traditional view would allow. For all that, it is possible to study the Torah with critical aids and yet in a devout spirit. The point is that, as the Rabbis declare, truth is God's seal, so that in studying the Torah we search for the truth, and must avail ourselves of every aid now available.

In its broadest sense, Torah includes all of human learning. The Talmud informs us, "Lunar diagrams hung on the wall of Rabban Gamaliel."

Students of the Torah

One of the glories of Jewish history is the astonishing dedication to Torah study by generations of keen students. For example, the famous Lithuanian Yeshiva (academy) of Volhozhyn attracted thousands of the finest young minds from Europe and even from the United States. The students used to divide themselves into groups, one sitting down to study as soon as the other left for home, so that there was no hour of the day or night when the voice of the Torah was not heard within the walls of that Torah institution.

In the eighteenth century the Gaon of Vilna is reported to have studied the Torah for at least eighteen hours a day during the whole of his life. If you come across a photograph of R. Joseph Rozin of Dvinsk in Latvia you will notice that he wore his hair very long. This

"The Gaon of Vilna is reported to have studied the Torah for at least eighteen hours a day during the whole of his life."

was because he was so devoted to Torah study that he had no time even to go to the barber. In talmudic times it was stated that a scholar must not enter an unclean street because it is forbidden to think about the Torah in an unclean place and a scholar cannot help thinking about the Torah wherever he goes. The second-century scholar Ben Azzai, we are told, once preached a sermon extolling the virtues of marriage, even though he himself never married. When his companions accused him of hypocrisy, of not practising what he preached, Ben Azzai retorted: "What can I do? My soul is in love with the Torah!" To this day there are people so devoted to the Torah that they never allow their minds to be distracted from it. Of course, such total dedication is possible only for the very few, but these few are a constant reminder of the power of the Torah, its depths and the joy it can evoke.

Let a passage from *Ethics of the Fathers* (Chapter six) be a summary of what has been said. "R. José b. Kisma said: I was once walking by the way, when a man met me and saluted me, and I returned the greeting. He said to me, Rabbi, where do you come from? From a great city of sages and scholars, I replied. He said to me: If you are willing to come to live in our town, I will give you a million gold dinars and precious stones and pearls. But I said to him: Even if you were to give me all the silver and gold and precious stones and pearls in the world, I would not live anywhere else than in a home of the Torah."

4
The Mitzvot

Mitzvot Commands

Torah and *Mitzvot*—this is the usual combination of Jewish observance, *Torah* referring to the teaching as a whole and to its study; *mitzvot* ("commands," singular *mitzvah*) to the particular observances. The crucial idea behind the concept of mitzvot is that the conduct of a Jew is governed by commands of God, so that at every step of life, the Jew is brought into contact with God. In general, these commands are found in the Pentateuch, the Torah. Some people find distasteful the whole idea of regulating life by commands, even by divine commands. In their view, religion ought to be spontaneous. The truth is that a command does not interfere with free human response, since Jews are not compelled to carry out the mitzvot, but do so of their own free choice. God does not issue commands in a tyrannical way in order to exercise His power over His creatures, but because He loves them and guides them in the way of life best for them.

In *Ethics of the Fathers* it is said that the word ḥarut, "engraved," describing the tablets of stone on which the Ten Commandments were recorded, can be read as ḥerut, "freedom." The mitzvot are, indeed, "engraved" in the hardest of stone; they are to be obeyed come what may, but, at the same time, they offer us freedom. On the face of it this seems contradictory. How can observant Jews be free if restricted by the mitzvot, by the many obligations and the many restraints? Perhaps Rabindranath Tagore's illustration can help. Tagore discusses, though in a non-Jewish context, the relationship between freedom and self-discipline. There can be no freedom to do what one really wants without the sacrifice of other freedoms, a sacrifice freely undertaken. For instance, if a person wishes to be a doctor, he must sacrifice time and effort. There will be many a sleepless night and much giving up of anything that interferes with his ambition. Tagore gives the illustration of the violin string. Before the string is fixed in the violin it is free. It can move in any direction. But it is not free to sing. When it is fixed in the violin, it is no longer free to move in any direction. But for the first time it is free to sing.

Positive and Negative

The talmudic rabbis divide the mitzvot into two categories, positive mitzvot and negative mitzvot. The positive mitzvot—*mitzvot aseh* ("do")—are the commands to do something, such as to give charity, to

At every stage of life, a Jew is brought into contact with God.

keep the festivals, to pay workers promptly, to love one's neighbor, to affix a *mezuzah* to the doorposts of the house. The negative mitzvot—*mitzvot lo ta'aseh* ("do not do")—are the commands to refrain from doing something, such as not to steal, not to bear false witness, not to eat pork, not to speak evil of others. In a sense, even the negative mitzvot are positive commands. There is a *positive injunction* to refrain from certain acts. That the aim of both positive and negative mitzvot is to promote holy living can be seen from the benediction recited before carrying out a mitzvah: "Blessed art Thou, O Lord, King of the universe, who has sanctified us with His commandments and has commanded us to. . . ." Naturally this benediction is recited only before carrying out a positive mitzvah since an act is involved, and one does something. There would be no meaning in reciting this benediction over a negative mitzvah: "who has commanded us not to do . . .," since it is a command to refrain from an act. We carry out, in a sense, the command not to steal, all the time, without any special effort, unless there is a special temptation to steal.

Person to God and Person to Person

Another rabbinic classification of the mitzvot encompasses the mitzvot between a person and God, obligations of a spiritual nature, such as to offer prayer to God or to keep the Sabbath; and mitzvot between two people, obligations to one's fellow human beings, such as to help others and not to trick them or defraud them. To put it another way,

The positive mitzvot are commands to *do* something, such as "to keep the festivals." Acquiring a palm branch and citron are mitzvot in preparation for the festival of Sukkot.

Cheating a friend during a card game is forgiven by God so long as the wrongdoer first asks his friend's forgiveness.

Judaism knows of religious conduct and of ethical conduct, though it should be noted that even the "ethical" mitzvot are more than rules of conduct between people. They are also divine commands, so that by behaving well to others we are also bringing a *religious* dimension into our lives.

In a famous formulation, the talmudic rabbis say (*Yoma, Mishnah* 8:9) that on *Yom Kippur* God pardons sins committed against Him ("between a person and God") provided there is a sincere resolve not to repeat them, but He does not pardon offenses committed against other human beings ("between two people") unless the injured party has been appeased. If, for example, we have insulted someone, we must first make our peace with him by asking his forgiveness; it is not enough to ask for God's forgiveness on Yom Kippur.

Reasons for the Mitzvot

Another division of mitzvot includes those for which the reason is obvious (such as to be honest, not to kill, to be careful not to cause harm to others) and those for which the reason is far from evident (like the dietary laws, animal sacrifices in Temple times and blowing the *shofar* on *Rosh Hashanah*). The Rabbis use two biblical terms to denote these two categories. The mitzvot whose reasons are clear are called *mishpatim*, "judgments," while those whose reasons are not clear are called *ḥukkim*, "statutes," meaning something laid down by God which we observe without questioning its rationality. The medieval thinkers used two other terms for them—"rational" mitzvot and "traditional" mitzvot, which we could never have invented by our own reasoning, but which we know from our tradition.

Should we try to discover the reasons for those mitzvot which do not seem reasonable? Many Jewish teachers say we should not, that it is enough that God has commanded them, and that He knows why. It is an impertinence, they argue, for human beings to try to

"It is not enough to ask God to forgive us on Yom Kippur. We must first ask forgiveness from the person whom we have wronged."

A Ḥasidic Proverb

Unlike other distinguished rabbis, Rabbi Israel Salanter would often pour only a very small quantity of water over his hands for the ritual washing before meals, even though the Talmud advises that as much water as possible should be used. Those who witnessed Rabbi Israel's conduct were astonished that he should be content with the minimum requirements of the law. "Yes," said Rabbi Israel, "I know that it is a mitzvah to use a good deal of water, but have you noticed that the poor servant girl has to bring in the water from the well outside in the bitter cold? I am not anxious to perform special acts of piety at the expense of the poor girl's toil."

The Light of the Sabbath

Such a simple mitzvah as the kindling of the Sabbath lights on the eve of the Sabbath receives many interpretations; all of them are legitimate interpretations of Jewish ideas. Originally, there was no special mitzvah at all of kindling Sabbath lights. All that was required was that the home be well lit to create the proper Sabbath atmosphere. Strictly speaking, then, if the home is already well-lit—nowadays, for instance, when we do not need the Sabbath candles to illumine our homes—there would seem to be no need for the Sabbath candles. But in the Middle Ages it was felt that there is much significance in having special lamps or candles for the Sabbath.

Once this custom was introduced, the Jewish teachers began to read all kinds of beautiful ideas into it. At least two candles should be kindled, they said, corresponding to the two different phrases about the Sabbath in the two versions of the Ten Commandments: "Remember the Sabbath" and "Keep the Sabbath." Since light represents spiritual illumination, when Jewish mothers lit the candles they prayed to have children who were both spiritually and physically healthy, and would bring spiritual light into the world.

"Many modern Jews would think not so much of the reasons for the mitzvot as the effects of the mitzvot on their lives."

explain why God chose to command this or that, as if the human mind is capable of fathoming the divine mind.

Other teachers, especially among the medieval Jewish philosophers, argued that the motivation for trying to discover why God gave these mitzvot is, on the contrary, religiously sound. First, they declare, God is not arbitrary. He does not issue commands without reason, merely to test our obedience. Hence, unless we can see reason in the mitzvot we may conceive of God as a dictator Who forbids us to raise questions. Second, if we know why we keep the mitzvot we shall keep them better. Third, in order for Judaism to present itself to the outside world as a rational religion, its rules must be seen to be wise. Maimonides devotes a large part of his *Guide for the Perplexed* to suggesting reasons for the mitzvot. Some of his reasons are very convincing, such as his view that the pig must not be eaten because it is a dirty animal and to eat its flesh increases the danger of illness, or his hint that the sacrifices in Temple times were a concession to those who identified religion with the offering of animal sacrifices, allowing them to offer sacrifices in a controlled manner, rather than in idolatrous orgies.

Such a simple mitzvah as the kindling of the Sabbath lights on the eve of the Sabbath receives many interpretations, and all of them are legitimate interpretations of Jewish ideas. Originally, there was no special mitzvah of kindling Sabbath lights. All that was required was for the home to be well lit, in order to create the proper Sabbath atmosphere. Strictly speaking, then, if the home is already well lit—nowadays, for instance, when we do not need the Sabbath candles for illumination—there should be no need for them. But in the Middle Ages it was felt that there is much significance in having special lamps or candles for the Sabbath.

Once this custom was introduced, the Jewish teachers began to read all kinds of beautiful ideas into the rite. At least two candles should be kindled, they said, corresponding to the two different versions of the Ten Commandments: "Remember the Sabbath" and "Keep the Sabbath." Then again, light represents spiritual illumination, so that traditionally when Jewish mothers lit the candles they prayed to have children who were healthy spiritually as well as physically, who would bring spiritual light into the world. Moreover, the human soul is "a lamp of the Lord" so that the Sabbath lights remind us that we have immortal souls, that the soul lives forever and that Sabbath bliss is a foretaste of the spiritual delights in store for the righteous in the Hereafter. Yet again, the Torah is light and the mitzvot the means by which that light is spread to banish the darkness. Just as a belief in God as Creator is expressed by the observance of the Sabbath, so, too, knowledge of the Torah needs expression. We live in a physical world and require concrete symbols if our religion is not to be too abstract to influence our lives. The light of the Torah requires the lamps of the mitzvot.

Many modern Jews are less concerned with the *reasons* for the mitzvot (they accept the critical view that many originated in primitive taboos) as they are with the *effects* of the mitzvot. The prohibition of certain animals for food, for instance, whatever its origin, has served the cause of holiness by making the Jew aware, even when eating, of the religious side of existence. According to this view, the mitzvot are divine commands, because this is what has been revealed in the historical experiences of the people of Israel.

Taryag

The Talmud (tractate *Makkot* 23b) records a sermon preached by the third-century Palestinian teacher, R. Simlai, in which he said that God gave 613 mitzvot to Israel; 248 positive mitzvot, corresponding to the limbs of the human body (counting the joints of the fingers and so forth as "limbs"), and 365 negative mitzvot, corresponding to the days of the solar year. R. Simlai implied that the mitzvot embrace all of our being and the whole of our years. In the Middle Ages, various attempts were made to list these 613 by counting all the dos and don'ts in the Torah. Actually, in doing such a counting, we would discover that there are more than 613, and that people have tried to distin-

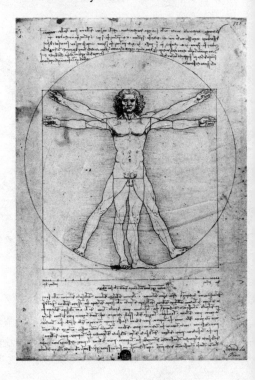

The 248 positive mitzvot are said to correspond to 248 parts of the body, reflecting the view that the mitzvot embrace all aspects of human activity.

"The deeper significance of the taryag *is that each person is expected to keep as many of the mitzvot as possible."*

guish between the *main* mitzvot, which are counted, and secondary mitzvot that need not be counted. Be that as it may, the term *taryag* (formed from the Hebrew letters *tav* = 400; *resh* = 200; *yod* = 10; *gimmel* = 3, total = 613) came to be used for the totality of the mitzvot. The observant Jew is said to keep the *taryag mitzvot*.

It must be noted, however, that the idea of taryag is only a generalization. It is simply not possible for anyone to keep all the taryag. Many of these mitzvot belong to the Temple worship of ancient times which no longer exists. Since one mitzvah is to return an article that you have stolen, it can be performed only by a thief—and since another of the mitzvot is not to steal, the person who carries out the one must previously have disobeyed the other! The deeper significance of the taryag is that each person is expected to keep as many of the mitzvot as possible. A second-century Palestinian teacher (*Mishnah, Makkot,* end) put it this way: "The Holy One, blessed be He, wished to bring merit to Israel so He gave them much Torah and numerous mitzvot."

Rabbinic Mitzvot

Although the command to perform mitzvot is found in the Torah, there are a few special postbiblical, rabbinic mitzvot, one of which is the kindling of the lights on the festival of Ḥanukkah. Even over a rabbinic mitzvah one recites the benediction: "Blessed art Thou O Lord, King of the universe, who has sanctified us with His commandments and commanded us to kindle the Ḥanukkah lights." On the face of it, this is odd. How can we in honesty praise God for commanding us to kindle the Ḥanukkah lights since the whole institution of Ḥanukkah came into being after the Bible was written down? The Talmud discusses this question (tractate *Shabbat* 23a), replying that God commanded us in the Torah to obey the sages of Israel, the people who were later responsible for postbiblical institutions such as Ḥanukkah. This is another way of saying that God does not only command in the Bible but also through the experiences of the Jewish people. Since it is right and proper to commemorate God's deliverances, as on Ḥanukkah, and since God wishes us to do what is right and proper, it follows that He commands us to kindle the Ḥanukkah lights.

Adorning the Mitzvot

The Jewish tradition reveals great appreciation of beauty. It is the basis of the concept *hiddur mitzvah,* the "adornment of the mitzvah," the reason why art forms were developed for the rituals. A Sefer Torah, for example, is required to be written in a fine script and with clear ink so that it is a delight to look at. Embroidered mantles should be used to cover the scroll and the art of the gold- and silversmith called upon to produce the crowns, *rimmonim* (the word means "pomegranates," as on the coat of the High Priest in Exodus 28:33) and the pointer. Other popular examples of this kind of adornment are the skillfully-wrought mezuzah case; the box to contain the *etrog* on the festival of *Sukkot*; the *sukkah* itself; the illustrated Passover Haggadah; and the fine architecture and decorations of the synagogue. By "adorning" the mitzvot we demonstrate our regard for them as well as express our aesthetic appreciation to the greater glory of God. The Talmud (*Bava Kama* 9b) suggests that we spend an extra third of the cost of a mitzvah on its adornment. Maimonides extends the principle of the adornment of the mitzvot to acts of benevolence. If we invite the needy into our home, he remarks, we should not give them the leftovers but the choicest of our food and drink.

The Joy of the Mitzvah

The mitzvot are seen not as a heavy burden, a series of unpleasant duties we have to perform whether we like it or not, but as great opportunities to nourish the soul by catering to its need to serve God. Mitzvot, the tradition states, should not be carried out mechanically, but with energy and enthusiasm. A mitzvah should not be postponed, but performed at the earliest possible moment. If the time for performing a mitzvah has not yet arrived—the mitzvot of the festivals, for example—we should await them with joyful anticipation as one awaits an honored guest. "Be strong as a leopard, light as an eagle, fleet as a hart, and mighty as a lion, to do the will of thy Father who is in Heaven" (*Ethics of the Fathers* 5:20).

Kavvanah—Intention

It must be admitted that too much stress on the *performance* of the mitzvot can result in mere mechanical behaviorism in which certain acts are done and others avoided without much religious significance. What has saved Judaism from becoming purely legalistic and formal, devoid of inwardness, is the doctrine of *kavvanah*. This word means "direction" or "concentration" and refers to the need for having the

> *"Mitzvot should not be carried out in a lifeless, dull manner but energetically and with enthusiasm."*

> *"What has saved Judaism from becoming purely legalistic and formal is the doctrine of* kavvanah.*"*

Joy of the Mitzvot

Ḥasidism stressed the idea of joy in God's service. A Ḥasidic tale tells that Rabbi Levi Yitzhak of Berditchev stayed in a hut at the top of a mountain on the eve of Sukkot. He tossed and turned all night on his bed, unable to sleep in his longing for dawn, when he could go to the synagogue to carry out the precious *mitzvah* of taking up the *lulav* and *etrog*. As soon as it was dawn, the saint hastily put on his clothes and slid down the mountain in order to get to the synagogue as fast as possible. A similar story is told of the anti-Ḥasidic Gaon of Vilna; it is said that he wept as he lay dying. "Why do you weep?" his disciples asked him, "since you are sure to go straight to Heaven?" The Gaon replied: "That is as may be, but this I know for certain: that only in this life can one have the joy of performing *mitzvot*. In Heaven there is true reward for keeping the mitzvot, but how can this compare with the joy of actually carrying out the mitzvot?"

Only through the proper and precise structure of the violin, with all its parts in order, can the instrument produce its beautiful music. Similarly can the "restrictions" of the mitzvot be understood. Good music requires more than skill. The inner intention is essential.

correct thoughts and application of the mind before the performance of the mitzvot. This is one of the reasons why a benediction is recited before the mitzvot, as if to say: "I am fully aware of the significance of what I am about to do, that by this act I become a participant in the drama of human beings reaching out for God." A similar idea to kavvanah is that of *lishmah,* "for its own sake," that is to say, the mitzvah should be carried out without any ulterior motive. The Rabbis, being realistic, added that no one should refrain from carrying out a mitzvah because of insincere motives and intentions. The important thing is to perform the mitzvah. But the ideal is always that of kavvanah and lishmah.

Let us see how all this works in practice. An appeal is made on behalf of a worthy cause, help for the poor for example, and you are asked for a contribution. Helping is undoubtedly a mitzvah. Now you may give in an offhand way without really thinking of what you are doing. That would be carrying out the mitzvah without kavvanah. Or you may give because you want others to admire you for your generosity. That would be lacking in lishmah, since your motive would be a selfish one. Nevertheless, it is better to give without kavvanah and for the wrong reasons than not to give at all, since the poor need the money and the important thing is that they receive it. Charity funds would be grossly impoverished if contributions were accepted only from completely altruistic donors! Yet the ideal is that you have kavvanah, reflecting on how God-like it is to give, and how sublime to carry out God's will—and you should do it lishmah, to relieve the distress of the poor and to obey God's will that we should be feeling, kindly people, not hard-hearted and hard-fisted. Kavvanah keeps the mitzvot from becoming mechanical; lishmah prevents us from showing off or patting ourselves on the back when we do what is right.

Duties of the Heart

Not only is inwardness to be encouraged when carrying out any of the mitzvot, but some of the mitzvot themselves are commands not to *do* this or that but to *think and feel* in a certain way: the mitzvot, for example, of loving God, of trusting in Him, of loving our neighbors, of being compassionate and modest and true to our higher nature. The great medieval Jewish moralist, Baḥya Ibn Pakuda, called these mitzvot, in the title of his famous book, "duties of the heart," as opposed to "duties of the limbs." For while Judaism does believe that good deeds have a subtle effect on our character if carried out regularly, there is also the more direct appeal to the improvement of our character. It is not only a matter of doing certain things but also of being a certain kind of person.

Naḥmanides, for instance, in his commentary on the biblical command to be holy (Leviticus 19:2), explains that it is quite possible to be a thoroughly unworthy person without actually disobeying any of the laws. A person may never eat forbidden food and yet gorge on permitted food, may never drink forbidden beverages and yet be a drunkard, may never do anything illegal but cheat others in business. Consequently, said this great thirteenth-century Spanish teacher, the Torah commands us to "be holy," that is, to cultivate gentle, pure, and wholesome character. A prophet said it, in fact, long ago: "It hath been told thee, O man, what is good, and what the Lord doth require of thee; only to do justly, and to love mercy, and to walk humbly with thy God" (Micah 6:8). Or as the Baal Shem Tov, the founder of Ḥasidism, put it: "The true aim of the Torah is that man should himself become a Torah." That is why, besides the laws and the mitzvot in the Torah, there are so many stories about the patriarchs, Abraham, Isaac, and Jacob. It has been said that a good way to understand these stories is to see the patriarchs as symbols comparable to Uncle Sam or Abraham Lincoln for the American people. The patriarchs are examples of the kind of person the Jew should strive to be. "Give your heart to Me," the Rabbis depict God as saying, "and you will be Mine."

"It is not only a matter of doing certain things but of being a certain kind of person."

5
The Chosen People

The Choice

The idea that the Jewish people has been especially chosen by God to carry out His purposes is prominent in the Bible and in subsequent Jewish teaching. The usual Hebrew word to express this choice is *bahar*, correctly translated as "choose." But this word does not imply rejection of those not chosen. Nowhere is it suggested that other peoples have no role to play in God's plan for humanity. When, for instance, a great sculptor picks out a piece of marble on which to work, it does not mean he will not use other pieces of marble, but only that this particular piece is the most suitable for the work at hand. The other pieces may be more suitable for a different kind of work at another time.

Some Biblical Passages

Several biblical passages deal with the "chosen people" theme. After warning Israel not to go after strange gods, the idols worshiped by the surrounding nations, the Book of Deuteronomy (7:6–8) describes Moses as saying: "For thou art a holy people unto the Lord thy God: the Lord thy God hath chosen thee to be His own treasure, out of all peoples that are upon the face of the earth. The Lord did not set His love upon you, nor choose you, because ye were more in number than any people—for ye were the fewest of all peoples—but because the Lord loved you, and because He would keep the oath which He swore unto your fathers, hath the Lord brought you out with a mighty hand, and redeemed you out of the house of bondage, from the hand of Pharaoh king of Egypt."

God is here described as the Creator of all the earth in connection with His choice. He created the other peoples as well as Israel and is concerned with their welfare, but He has a special love for Israel, not because of their size—God is not impressed by size—but because their ancestors were faithful to Him. These two ideas in connection with the choice, that God is the Lord of all and that He chooses Israel because of the love their ancestors had for Him, is found again in Deuteronomy 10:14–15: "Behold, unto the Lord thy God belongeth the heaven, and the heaven of heavens, the earth, with all that therein is. Only the Lord had a delight in thy fathers to love them, and He chose their seed after them, even you, above all peoples, as it is this day." In the account of God's revelation at Sinai in the Book of Exodus it is said (Exodus 19:5–6): "Now therefore, if ye will hearken unto My voice indeed, and keep My covenant, then ye shall be Mine own treasure from among all peoples; for all the earth is Mine: and ye shall be unto Me a kingdom of priests, and a holy nation."

A Kingdom of Priests

This term, "a kingdom of priests," also suggests that the choice of Israel must not be understood as excluding others. In ancient Jewish life the priest, the *kohen,* was special only in that it was his privilege and duty to serve in the Temple and he enjoyed his status because he was a descendant of Aaron, the first priest, and not because of any merit of his own. Neither the priest nor the ordinary Israelites who were not priests would have dreamed of thinking that the priests were intrinsically better than the non-priests. It was true that, for instance, only the priests recited the priestly blessing, but it was also true that those who were blessed were not priests. There could be no priestly blessing without priests, but neither could there be one without non-priests to be blessed.

A fine interpretation of a biblical verse was given by the famous Rabbi Meir Simḥah Kagan of Dvinsk in Latvia (1843–1926). The verse speaks of Israel as God's "first-born" (Exodus 4:22). Rabbi Kagan pointed out that parents love all their children. What, then, is so special about the firstborn? The answer is that before their firstborn child comes into the world, a husband and wife are not yet parents. Once they have a child they become parents. Thus it is the firstborn who makes them parents. By the same token, God loves all His creatures. He is the Parent of all humanity. But it was among the people of Israel that God was first recognized as the Parent of humanity and this very fact imposes special obligations upon them and is the cause of their special relationship with God.

But the Choice Is an Embarrassment to Some

Some Jews are embarrassed by the whole idea of Israel's chosenness. Why should God choose a special people for a particular role? The problem was put in the little rhyme:

> How odd
> Of God
> To choose
> The Jews

to which one reply was given:

> It isn't odd
> The Jews
> Chose God.

As Israel Zangwill said, the *chosen* people is a *choosing* people. All this is fairly reasonable, yet it does not go deeply into the real problem. The oddness is not in God's choosing the Jews. If we may put it

"Nowhere is it suggested that other peoples have no role to play in God's plan for humanity."

"Why not make the whole human race the instrument for the fulfillment of His purpose?"

so, if He had to choose, what better choice could He have made? No, the oddness is in His having to choose at all. Why not make the whole human race the instrument for the fulfillment of His purpose?

Some Jewish thinkers, like Maimonides, have simply replied that we do not know. All we can say is that it is His will, much as He so created the world that strawberries grow in some lands and not in others. But perhaps we can get a little nearer to understanding this whole idea if we realize that all the great achievements of humanity have been made by particular people living in a particular way. Take the plays of Shakespeare. They could have been produced only by an Englishman writing in English and in an English environment, because no literature can be produced in the abstract. And yet, though the plays are English, millions of people who are not English have appreciated them and gained much from them because they deal in beautiful language with the hopes and fears and strivings of all human beings, not just British citizens. Great art is the result of experience and we all have our richest experiences in our own immediate circle. God's choice of the Jews is in terms of their experience of God. It was upon that experience that they based their teachings about what He demands of people. To be authentic it had to be confined, at first and also later, to a particular group with its own traditions and way of looking at things. But what came out of it all and, Judaism believes, what will come out of it, is for all humanity.

A Less Convincing Way of Looking at It

Other Jewish thinkers have interpreted the idea of the chosen people as meaning that the Jew has a special kind of soul, superior to the souls of non-Jews. Even these thinkers do not suggest that this entitles the Jew to act as if non-Jews can be used for his own ends. They mean that, on the contrary, since the Jew has a superior soul the demands made on him are the greater and the more severe. His higher soul has been created, they argue, not to use beings of inferior soul but to serve them, to bring them to God and to help them carry out His will. One who followed this line was Judah Halevi in the Middle Ages. In

Helping Others

Rabbi Nathan Zevi Finkel (1849-1927) was known as "The Old Man of Slobodka," the town near Kovno in Lithuania where he established a great Yeshiva in the spirit of the Musar movement. Rabbi Finkel loved to teach the need to revere the image of God in which every man, non-Jew as well as Jew, is created. In his teaching, the true dignity of man is perceived when he reaches out to others, when he is God-like in being a giver. The ideal is to enjoy helping others, particularly life's unfortunates. One of his favorite sayings was: "The Torah tells us to love our neighbors as ourselves. This means that just as we care for our own needs because that is how we are made, so, too, we should not need a *mitzvah* in order to love our fellow human beings. Love of others should come naturally to us; we should strive to be that kind of person."

that period all creation was divided into four categories: minerals (inanimate things, like earth, water, and stones), plants, animals, and human beings. But according to Halevi, Jews belong to a fifth category. They are, he said, as different from all other human beings as human beings are from animals, animals from plants, and plants from stones. On the face of it, this seems a very offensive way of looking at the chosen people idea. None of us likes to feel that some people are intrinsically superior to others. Nowadays we tend to call such an attitude racist, and racism is rightly looked upon with extreme disfavor. However, Judah Halevi and those who think like him go on to point out that a flower that has faded is more pathetic than water that has become stagnant; the carcass of an animal is more nauseating than a dead tree; a human corpse is more frightening than a dead animal. Precisely because of his superior soul, these thinkers argue, a rotten Jew is very rotten indeed; a bad Jew is far worse than a bad non-Jew.

Nonetheless, most of us recoil from this kind of interpretation. For one thing, there is no evidence that the Jewish soul is inherently superior. Second, non-Jews can be converted to Judaism and become full Jews even though they were born with the "ordinary" human soul (unless it be argued, which does not seem very satisfactory, that they acquire a new soul on their conversion to Judaism). Third, and this is a fatal blow to the superior soul theory, there is no such thing as a pure Jewish race. In their long history, the Jews have mingled so much with other peoples that there is no Jew alive today whose veins do not have non-Jewish blood. Far better, surely, to understand that because of a common tradition and a series of doctrines and teachings —in a word, because of the Torah—the Jews, if they are faithful to the Torah, are singled out to serve God and humanity. In the blessing recited before reading the Torah we say: "Blessed art Thou . . . who hath chosen us from all peoples and given us His Torah." The Hebrew letter *vav*, translated as "and," can also mean "by" so that the deeper meaning of the blessing is perhaps: "who hath chosen us from all peoples *by* giving us His Torah."

The "Chosen People" concept does not mean Jews are more privileged than other people. As a well-known quip says, "Thou hast chosen us from among the nations; isn't it time to choose someone else?"

"Because of the Torah, the Jews are singled out to serve God and humanity."

God Is Not Concerned Only with Jews

One thing is quite certain. The idea of the chosen people does not mean that God is concerned only with Jews. Such a perverse idea would be entirely contrary to Jewish teaching, which, after all, believes in the God who created all people in His image. Listen to this verse in the Bible (Isaiah 19:24–25). To appreciate it fully one must realize that Egypt and Assyria, great powers with their own interests, were often at war with little Israel. The prophet can still say: "In that day shall Israel be the third with Egypt and with Assyria, a blessing in the midst of the earth for that the Lord of hosts hath blessed him, saying: "Blessed be Egypt My people and Assyria the work of My hands, and Israel Mine inheritance." Whatever the date of this verse (some scholars think it was added at a later date), it has been part of the biblical teachings since antiquity, and while Israel is called God's inheritance, Egypt is called His people and Assyria called the work of His hands.

The Torah for Non-Jews

According to the Talmud, even the Torah is not only for Jews, but part of the Torah is seen as God's will for all people. That is the part known as "the seven mitzvot of the sons of Noah," because, in the biblical narrative, Noah was the father of all people born after the Flood. There is more than one version of what precisely these seven mitzvot are, but the usual formulation is:

1. To have only one God and not to worship idols;
2. To lead a moral life and not to commit adultery or incest;
3. To be a useful member of society and not to commit murder;
4. To be honest and not to steal;
5. To have respect for God and not to blaspheme;
6. To have law courts and to practice justice;
7. To be kind to animals and not to be cruel to them.

(This last is interpreted as not to eat anything torn from a living animal, evidently a not uncommon practice in talmudic times among the heathens.) In other words, while the Torah in its fullness is for Jews only (of course, non-Jews who wish to share in it can be converted to Judaism), decent behavior is demanded of non-Jews as well. The Talmud goes even further. Any non-Jew who behaves properly by keeping the seven mitzvot is known as one of the righteous of the nations of the world and will enjoy eternal bliss in the Hereafter.

A Convert to Judaism

Although the story of Valentine Potocki, the eighteenth-century Polish count who became converted to Judaism, has been told and retold, gathering legends in the process, it does seem based on fact. Potocki, through his association with Jews, became convinced of the truth of Judaism, eventually settling near Vilna as a proselyte, taking the name of "Abraham son of our father Abraham." He was imprisoned for abandoning his Christian faith. It is reported that the famed Gaon of Vilna visited him in prison in order to encourage him to remain steadfast in his new faith. Eventually, he was burnt at the stake at the foot of the fortress of Vilna, declaring his belief in the One God. This event took place on the second day of Shavuot in the year 1749. It is said that a pious Jew risked his life in order to rescue from the flames some of the ashes and a finger. These were buried in the Jewish cemetery. A tree grew over the spot, which was called the resting place of the *Ger Tzedek* ("Righteous Proselyte"). The spot was a place of pilgrimage for Jews. Legend has it that when the Vilna Gaon visited him before his martyrdom the Gaon assured him that there was no cause for grief, only for rejoicing, in that he would soon enter the world of eternal bliss.

Judaism: Particularistic or Universalistic?

We can now answer the old question: Is Judaism particularistic (concerned only with Jews), or universalistic (concerned with all humanity)? The uncomplicated answer is that Judaism is both. It is particularistic in that it stresses the importance of the Jewish people, for which it sees a special role of service in God's world. Judaism is universalistic in that it believes in the One God, Who desires good for all people, whose Torah is addressed to all people, and who recognizes the good in all people.

What of Other Religions?

What of the millions of human beings who either have no God or too many, worshiping idols of one kind or another? Are they to be rejected because they violate one of the seven mitzvot? The Rabbis would probably have said that sincere, good people who are Hindus or Buddhists or atheists or agnostics can claim to belong to the righteous of the nations, either because they have been brought up in the way they have and know no better or are really worshiping God without knowing it by the very fact of their basic goodness. Yet for all its tolerance of the beliefs of others, Judaism refuses utterly to compromise with anything but pure belief in the One God, and for Jews to worship other gods is a sin of the very worst kind.

A Question of History

It would be useless to deny that in the long history of Judaism there have sometimes appeared narrower views of the non-Jewish world. Negative sayings about non-Jews have provided ammunition for Jew-

Jewish tradition does not require all people to observe all of the Torah's obligations. The Seven Mitzvot of the Sons of Noah are the only parts of the Written Torah seen as universal ideals (left).

Only by blowing into the narrow end of the shofar can a musician create beautiful, rich sound in the wide end. This example illustrates the Jewish belief in the relationship between particularism and universalism. The Jews as a particular people have a role of service for the good of all people (right).

A Righteous Gentile

The expulsion from Spain in the fifteenth century brought to the fore again the problem of Jewish homelessness. Where were the exiles to go? Where could they rest secure in a new land? One of the rulers who offered them asylum was King Ferdinand I of Naples, a man who abundantly deserved the epithet Jews bestow on Gentiles who are moved by compassion and justice, "the righteous among the nations of the world." He not only admitted many of the exiles into Naples but did his utmost to alleviate their plight. When a pestilence broke out among the refugees, King Ferdinand told the survivors to bury their dead at night so that the general population would not know what had happened and not be enraged at the risks to which the Jews exposed them. When the epidemic did eventually become known and there was fierce agitation to get rid of the unwelcome strangers, Ferdinand refused to listen. It is even said that he threatened to resign the throne if the Jews were expelled. Among those to whom Ferdinand offered the hospitality of his realm was the great statesman and biblical commentator, Don Isaac Abarbanel, who became the king's fiscal adviser.

Garden of the Righteous, Yad Vashem, Jerusalem

haters; collections of these sayings have even been made by anti-Semites for the purpose of discrediting Judaism. But these adverse views were stated in times when Judaism was a despised faith and when Jews were suffering death and torture for holding fast to the religion of their ancestors. When in those dark days some Jewish teachers expressed themselves harshly about non-Jews, they were thinking of their tormentors and persecutors. If a rabbi, innocent of any crime, found himself in a Nazi concentration camp, where he witnessed the murder of fellow-Jews because they were Jews, he would not be human if he did not cry out against the *goyim*, meaning the Nazis. And Judaism has known better days when non-Jews offered Jews hospitality and a warm welcome. In those times, Jewish teachers virtually competed with one another in singing the praises of the righteous of the nations.

The Sanctification of the Name

Another Jewish concept regarding the relationship between Jews and non-Jews is known as *Kiddush ha-Shem*, the "sanctification of the Name." It is based on the verse: "And ye shall not profane My holy name; but I will be hallowed among the children of Israel" (Leviticus 22:32). It means that the Jewish people bears God's name. God has, as it were, a stake in their conduct, so that if they behave badly they cause non-Jews to speak ill not only of them but of their religion and their God. When non-Jews see a Jew behaving dishonestly they conclude that his religion cannot be worth much if this is what it produces. Conversely, if Jews behave well and are thoroughly decent people, non-Jews will admire the religion that produced them. Thus in a sense it is even more important for Jews to conduct themselves with complete integrity toward non-Jews than to their fellow Jews since in their relationship to non-Jews they carry the banner of Judaism.

Ways of Peace

Another principle found in rabbinic literature regarding behavior to non-Jews as well as to Jews is that of promoting harmony in society. This is called *darkhe shalom*, "ways of peace." It means that, as Aristotle says, people are social animals, whose lives are disturbed and incomplete unless they can live in harmony with those around them. That is why the Talmud tells us that the great teacher Rabban Johanan ben Zakkai, who lived 2,000 years ago in the holy land, would always say, "Shalom" to others in the street before they greeted him, including his pagan associates. The Talmud rules that just as Jews are bound by their religion to give charity to their fellow-Jews, to bury the dead, to visit the sick, to comfort the mourners, they are obliged to do the same for their non-Jewish neighbors. Jews have, in fact, a proud record of giving generously to all good causes, Jewish and non-Jewish.

Simeon ben Shetah

In the Jerusalem Talmud this story is told of an early teacher of Judaism, Simeon ben Shetah, to illustrate the principle of Kiddush ha-Shem. Simeon ben Shetah was a poor man, unable to devote as much time to the study of the Torah as he would have liked because he had to earn a living as a donkey-driver. He bought a donkey from an Arab and when he took it home he discovered a precious pearl concealed in the saddlebag. His disciples urged him to keep the pearl, saying that now his troubles would be over. He would be a rich man and able to devote himself entirely to the study of the Torah. The disciples held that the Arab was evidently unaware that he had lost the pearl, which he could well afford to lose, and that Simeon would now be able to devote himself to study, which was more important than anything the Arab could do with the pearl. Simeon ben Shetah would have nothing to do with his disciples' specious arguments. "I bought a donkey," he roundly declared, "I did not buy the pearl." And he returned the pearl to the Arab, who exclaimed: "Blessed be the God of Simeon ben Shetah." Note that the Arab praised Simeon ben Shetah's *God* and not the rabbi himself. His good deed acts as a credit for all Jews.

"In a sense it is even more important for Jews to conduct themselves with complete integrity toward their non-Jewish neighbors."

6
The Bible

The Bible: Source of Judaism

There are twenty-four books in the Hebrew Bible. They form sacred Scripture and are the source of all Jewish teaching, though they need to be interpreted and the interpretation is as much part of the Torah as the written texts. The English word, Bible (from the Greek *biblia*, "books"), is somewhat misleading because it is in the singular, suggesting that the Bible is a single book. Actually, it is a great collection of books produced over many centuries by different hands and in different places. Three stages can be traced in the development of the Bible. First, there are the original words of the prophet or author (for example, the words originally spoken by Isaiah). Second, are the words written down by the prophet's disciple and scribe (e.g., Baruch, Jeremiah's scribe). Third, over a long period of time there was a kind of sifting of the many literary works that had come down from the past until eventually the twenty-four books of our present Bible alone came to be accepted by the Jewish people as sacred literature.

Tanakh

The Hebrew name for the Bible is *Tanakh*, formed out of the initial letters of the words *Torah* (the Five Books of Moses); *Neviim* ("the Prophets"); and *Ketuvim* ("The Writings," such as Psalms, Proverbs, and Job). While the Jewish tradition considers all three divisions of Scripture to be sacred and inspired by God, the tradition distinguishes between degrees of inspiration. Thus the Torah is more "inspired" than the prophetic books, because the Torah is seen as a more direct communication from God to Moses. Similarly, the books of the Prophets are seen as more inspired than the Writings, which are said to result from the less intense form of communication known as the "holy spirit." To this day many pious Jews, in order to emphasize the differences in inspiration, will never place one of the books of the Prophets on top of a copy of the Torah, or a copy of the Psalms on top of a book of Prophets. The historical books of Joshua, Judges, Samuel, and Kings belong to the Prophets because they are believed to have been written by prophets, under this more intense type of inspiration, while the historical books of Daniel, Ezra, Nehemiah, and Chronicles belong to the Writings because they are believed to have been written under the "holy spirit." It should be noted that the Jewish tradition does not know of the division of Samuel, Kings, and Chronicles into books I and II. This, and the chapter divisions now in our Bible, were adopted by Jews from the Christians during the Middle Ages for easier reference in Jewish disputations with Christians. From time to time, attempts have been made to give up these "non-Jewish" divisions, but they seem to be too deeply-rooted.

The Twenty-Four Books

Here is a list of the twenty-four books of our present Bible in its threefold division:

Torah
1. Genesis
2. Exodus
3. Leviticus
4. Numbers
5. Deuteronomy

Neviim
6. Joshua
7. Judges
8. Samuel I and II
9. Kings I and II
10. Isaiah
11. Jeremiah
12. Ezekiel
13. The Book of the Twelve: Hosea, Joel, Amos, Obadiah, Jonah, Micah, Nahum, Habakkuk, Zephaniah, Haggai, Zechariah, and Malachi

Ketuvim
14. Psalms
15. Proverbs
16. Job
17. Song of Songs
18. Ruth
19. Lamentations
20. Ecclesiastes
21. Esther
22. Daniel
23. Ezra and Nehemiah (treated as a single book)
24. Chronicles I and II.

The Book of the Twelve, although containing the work of twelve prophets, was treated as a single book and written on a single scroll before the invention of printing (and even today by some devout Jews). The probable reason is, as the rabbis suggest, that they are very small books (Obadiah is only one chapter) and if written separately could easily be lost. The twelve together are just large enough to be written in a single scroll. In English these twelve are sometimes called "minor prophets." Apart from the fact that this term is unknown in Hebrew, the word "minor" refers to the size of the books, not to the quality of their teaching. If someone says that Micah, for instance, was only a minor prophet, not a major one, he is using the term incorrectly.

Books 17 through 21 are known as the Five Scrolls (*Ḥamesh Megillot)*, though it is Esther that is generally referred to as *the* Scroll, the *Megillah.* The Book of Esther tells the story of Purim and is read in the synagogue on that festival; the Song of Songs is read on Passover because it refers to the Exodus from Egypt and speaks also of the spring; Ruth is read on Shavuot because of the references in it to the harvest (Shavuot is a harvest festival), and because Ruth embraced the Torah, whose giving Shavuot celebrates. Ecclesiastes is read on

There are many common misconceptions about the Prophets. They were neither men on street corners predicting doom nor soothsayers looking into the future.

the festival of Sukkot, the autumn festival when the leaves begin to fall, an appropriate time for a melancholy book; and Lamentations is read on the Fast of Av.

Some scholars conjecture that in ancient times parts of the Psalms, Proverbs, and Job were read in the synagogue. It is certain that our present practice of reading each week from the Torah and from the Prophets (the *Haftarah*) is very old. Traditionally, Scripture is read in the synagogue with a chant, the musical notes being provided by signs in the printed editions. Each type of literature has its own melody, that of the Torah differing from that of the Prophets; that of Lamentations more sorrowful and tragic than that of Esther; and that of Ruth, Ecclesiastes, and the Song of Songs uniform, but different from the others.

The Prophets

There were very many more prophets in ancient Israel than those whose work is now found in the Bible. The Rabbis say that there were hundreds of thousands of true prophets, but only those were recorded in Scripture whose messages were not only for their own day but for later generations as well. Indeed, religious people always find fresh and relevant teaching in what the prophets said so long ago. When Amos castigated injustice and Hosea spoke of loving-kindness, their words were addressed to their contemporaries, but men and women in every age find guidance and inspiration in them.

The prophets should not be seen chiefly as people who could gaze into the future. Some believe even today that it is possible to detect in the books of the Prophets the foretelling of events that are happening now, such as references to "the kingdom of the north" applying to Soviet Russia. Such an approach is absurd and does scant justice to the genius of prophecy, treating it as if it were a kind of

"A mistaken view of the prophets is to see them chiefly as people who could gaze into the future."

magic. It is very hard to see how a person living over 2,000 years ago could have foreseen events long after their time, and the prophets themselves make no such claim. True, they speak of what is to happen *in a general sense,* that if, for example, the people oppress the poor they will suffer catastrophe; but that is very different from describing *in detail* what is to happen in generations still unborn. The main thrust of the prophetic teaching consists in speaking out with the utmost courage that God wants people to practice justice, show mercy, and be holy. It has rightly been said that the Hebrew prophets were not *foretellers* but *forthtellers.*

What is a prophet? How did these remarkable people become so convinced that God had communicated His will to them as to enable them to declare: "Thus saith the Lord"? We do not know and cannot know unless we are prophets ourselves, and according to the tradition, prophecy ceased in Israel after Malachi, the last prophet. What we do know is that these books express in matchless language teachings that have changed the world and which still speak to our hearts with such power that the prophetic claim of a direct communication from God seems justified. All the prophets express themselves in accordance with their own temperaments and social backgrounds. Amos, a farmer, uses metaphors taken from country life, while Isaiah, a prince, uses the language of the royal court. As the Rabbis remark, each prophet has his own style of speech. For this reason one should not think of prophecy and inspiration as a kind of divine dictation in which God simply puts words into the prophet's mouth. The message from God is given through the personality of the prophet. God does not make him a passive tool. He lets him glimpse eternal truth, and express it in his own terms.

The Problematical Books

It took some time before the books of Ezekiel, Song of Songs, and Ecclesiastes were acknowledged as being part of sacred Scripture. For a long period the matter was debated by the Rabbis. The reason for the doubts about Ezekiel is that some of the laws mentioned in the book contradict the laws laid down in the Torah, the description of the service in the Temple, for example. But attempts were made to resolve these contradictions and the book was not "hidden away" (left in storage and not adopted for public reading).

A similar debate took place on the Book of Ecclesiastes. This was held to be composed by King Solomon and was recognized as containing the wise sayings of the wise king, but it was questioned whether they were inspired words or Solomon's own. Eventually it was accepted as part of Scripture. Even though it seems to teach the vanity of all human activities, the Rabbis say it means worldly activities, not matters of Torah. The Song of Songs, this too, was considered the work of Solomon, yet it seems to be no more than a collection of secular love poems. This book was interpreted not as a dialogue between earthly lovers but between God and Israel, expressing in alle-

The Song of Songs, in its most literal meaning, is an erotic love poem. From a more traditional point of view, it is seen as an allegory of Israel's love of God—and God's love of Israel. Because of the sensual language of the text, it was the subject of debate before being included in the Bible.

Aleph א	42,377
Beth ב	38,218
Gimel ג	29,537
Daleth ד	32,530
Hei ה	47,754
Vav ו	76,922
Zayin ז	22,867
Ḥeth ח	23,447
Teth ט	11,052
Yod י	66,420
Kaph כ	37,272
Final kaph ך	10,981
Lamed ל	41,517
Mem מ	52,805
Final mem ם	24,973
Nun נ	32,977
Final nun ן	8,719
Samekh ס	13,580
Ayin ע	20,175
Pei פ	20,750
Final pei ף	1,975
Tzadi צ	16,950
Final tzadi ץ	4,872
Ḳuph ק	22,972
Resh ר	22,147
Shin ש	32,148
Thav ת	36,140
	792,077

Throughout the ages, the scribes have taken great care to make sure that the exact text of the Torah remained unchanged; they even counted every single letter!

gorical form Israel's complete loyalty to God and God's response in His love for His people. "All the writings are holy," said Rabbi Akiba, "but the Song of Songs is Holy of Holies." The books often referred to as "the Apocrypha" were never accepted as part of Scripture. Tobit, the books of the Maccabees, Ben Sira, and the other Apocryphal books were treated with respect but excluded from the sacred Bible. It was forbidden, for example, to read them in any public synagogue reading, for that would suggest that they, too, were in some way sacred.

The Text of the Bible

The present text of the Bible is known as the Masoretic Text (*Masorah*, from the root *masar*, "to deliver," means "Tradition"). It is very reliable because the greatest care has always been taken by the scribes when copying the manuscripts. This is especially true of the Torah for which there are very strict rules regarding the making of copies, so that all the copies in all the synagogues of the world today have exactly the same text, with not a single letter differing from one to another. But even the text of the other books was very faithfully copied. If you pay a visit to the Shrine of the Book in Jerusalem you will see displayed a complete copy of the Book of Isaiah. This copy was probably written about 2,000 years ago (it was found among the Qumran documents at the Dead Sea) and yet apart from minor differences it is exactly the same as our present copies of the Book of Isaiah.

Moreover, many of the later translations have been made by Christians with a Christian understanding at variance with the Jewish. For example, Dr. Harry Orlinsky, in his notes to the new Jewish translation of the Torah into English, remarks that the older translations render Genesis 1:2 as: "The spirit of God hovered over the face

The Masorites

Those responsible for the *Masorah,* the *Masorities,* lived mainly in Palestine some centuries before the year 800. We have to think of them as dedicated scholars and scribes, carefully noting every letter of the biblical text, remarking on the number of times unusual words occur, pointing out parallels, comparing manuscripts, sifting the evidence for variant readings and noting them in the margins of the text, and providing as much information as possible for the establishment of a standard text. From rabbinic times, such things were noted as how many verses a particular biblical book contains and which is the letter exactly in the middle of the Torah text. (It is the *vav* of the word *gahon* in Leviticus 11:42, which is, therefore, traditionally written as a large letter.) A typical note of the Masorites is that the eighth verse of Zephaniah, chapter three, contains all the letters of the Hebrew alphabet, including the final forms of the letters.

Bible Translations

The Bible has been translated into many other languages. The earliest was the *Septuagint;* the word means "seventy." Legend has it that it was translated into Greek by seventy scholars isolated in their individual chambers who nonetheless all hit on a uniform rendering of the text. The translation into Aramaic is known as *Targum* (which means, in fact, "translation"). There are translations into Latin, French, German, and English, and into practically all the languages under the sun. It is naturally quite impossible for even the best translation to convey fully the meaning of the original Hebrew. The difference between reading the original and a translation has been colorfully described as the difference between a groom kissing his bride on her lips and kissing her through a veil.

Moreover, many of the later translations have been made by Christians with a Christian understanding at variance with the Jewish. Dr. Harry Orlinsky, for example, in his notes to the new Jewish translation of the Torah into English, remarks that the older translations render Genesis 1:2 as: "The spirit of God hovered over the face of the water." Orlinsky maintains that only in Christian thought is the notion found of a disembodied spirit of God apart from man. In biblical passages it is said that God put His spirit into a person, a very different concept. Consequently, says Orlinsky, the correct translation of the Hebrew *ruah* is not "spirit" but "wind" (the word can mean both), and he translates the verse: "the wind of God hovered over the face of the water." For all that, while great caution must be exercised, it is better to read the Bible in translation than not to read it at all. Best of all is to read it in Hebrew.

of the water." Orlinsky maintains that it is only in Christian thought that the notion is found of a disembodied spirit of God apart from man (in biblical passages it is said that God put His spirit into a person, a very different concept). Consequently, according to Orlinsky, the correct translation of the Hebrew *ruaḥ* is not "spirit" but "wind" (the word can mean both) and he translates the verse: "the wind of God hovered over the face of the water." For all that, while great caution must be exercised, it is better to read the Bible in translation than not to read it at all. Best of all is to read it in Hebrew.

"All the copies of the Torah in all the synagogues in the world have exactly the same text, with not a single letter differing from one to another.

Authorship of the Biblical Books

The traditional view regarding the authorship of the biblical books is stated in many of the old sources but is spelled out particularly in a talmudic passage (tractate *Bava Batra* 14b–15a) which we here paraphrase. Moses, it is said, wrote "his" book (the Pentateuch) with the exception, according to some opinions, of the last eight verses which tell of Moses' death. These were added after Moses' death by his disciple Joshua. Joshua wrote the part of the book that bears his name up to the recording of his death, which was added later. The prophet Samuel wrote the book that bears his name (the account of his death being added later) as well as the Books of Judges and Ruth. David wrote the book of Psalms but he used earlier material. Jeremiah wrote the book that bears his name as well as the Books of Kings and Lamentations. King Hezekiah and his associates wrote the Books of Isaiah, Proverbs, Song of Songs, and Ecclesiastes. According to one opinion the Book of Job was written by none other than Moses. The Men of the Great Synagogue (those teachers who came at the end of the prophetic period after the return from the Babylonian exile) wrote the books of Ezekiel, the Twelve, Daniel, and Esther. Ezra wrote the book that bears his name as well as the book of Chronicles up to the record of his own life, which was added later.

In this remarkable passage it can be seen that the talmudic Rabbis did not take too literally the names at the headings of the various books. They recognized that the books had editors. For example, although the Rabbis undoubtedly believed that King Solomon was the author of Proverbs, Ecclesiastes, and Song of Songs, he did not put them in their final form. Similarly, although it was believed that Isaiah spoke the utterances that bear his name, the book was edited at a later date into its present form. It can also be seen that the Rabbis were far from the view that a prophet sees into the future and records future events. They state clearly that if a prophetic book tells of the prophet's death and of subsequent events, such material must have been added later.

Biblical Criticism

Many Jews today are aware that the so-called Bible critics (the term really means those who investigate the Bible, not those who sit in judgment on its value) offer a picture of how the Bible came to be that differs from the traditional view. There are two aspects to biblical criticism: the lower criticism, which refers to the study of the biblical text; and the higher criticism, which refers to how the books were composed and compiled. On textual criticism, it suffices here to note that the critics, while acknowledging the basic reliability of the Masoretic text, note that there are other versions, such as the Septuagint (the Greek translation of the Bible produced in Alexandria 2,000 years ago) which sometimes have differed from the Masoretic text, and which may at times be more accurate.

A community of Jews living in the wilderness near the Dead Sea created what we now call the Dead Sea Scrolls. Among the fragments were found the oldest known examples of Jewish scripture (opposite page).

"It is said that critics make the Mosaic law into a mosaic, a mere collection of stray passages with no coherent scheme."

The Dead Sea Scrolls

In the spring of 1947 a Bedouin boy found some jars in a cave near the Dead Sea. In them were scrolls, obviously very old, but in a language he could not understand. The report of the find soon became widespread, and various attempts were made by dealers in antiquities to obtain the scrolls. Eventually, more scrolls were discovered at Qumran, the Arabic name for the district, and in other areas nearby. Scholars managed to purchase some of the scrolls and the work of deciphering began. Prominent among the scholarly pioneers in this field was Professor E. L. Sukenik, father of Yigal Yadin, of the Hebrew University. The finds revolutionized biblical scholarship and historical investigation into the history of the Jewish people at the beginning of the present era. Among the fragments discovered, for example, were passages from biblical books dated hundreds of years earlier than any Hebrew manuscripts extant at the time; and there was a complete scroll of the book of the prophet Isaiah, which can now be seen proudly displayed in the Museum of the Hebrew University. It is quite remarkable that, apart from minor differences, the book is exactly the same as our text of Isaiah.

At first there was vehement debate in the scholarly world regarding the dating of the Dead Sea Scrolls. Professor Solomon Zeitlin carried on a battle for several years to show that they were medieval works deposited in the caves in Roman jars. But the scholarly consensus now is that the scrolls are indeed ancient and testify to the existence of a community of monk-like Jews living in the wilderness with their own doctrines and practices. We know from other sources that various sectarian groups flourished at the time of the destruction of the Temple, but here, for the first time, was a complete sectarian library plus other evidence, in the shape of pottery, lamps, and so forth, of their way of life. The study of these documents still proceeds. It is one of the greatest archaeological discoveries of all time.

For instance, in our text Genesis 4:8 reads: "And Cain spoke unto Abel his brother. And it came to pass, when they were in the field, that Cain rose up against Abel his brother, and slew him." There seems to be something missing here. Usually when Scripture states that someone *said* something, we are told what he *said*. The ancient version supplies the missing words, reading: "And Cain said to his brother Abel: '*Let us go out into the field*' and when they were in the field. . . ."

The higher criticism examines the biblical books in order to discover what they actually say or imply regarding authorship. On the basis of this kind of investigation, the critics hold that some, at least, of the Pentateuch was not written by Moses and that it contains sections produced at different periods. The same applies to the Book of Isaiah. The critics hold that there are at least two Isaiahs, that the second part of the book, from Chapter 40, was compiled over a hundred years after the time of Isaiah.

The majority of Orthodox Jews reject all biblical criticism, especially of the Pentateuch, as destructive of faith. Once one begins to question the traditional view, these Jews hold, where will it end?

They say that critics make the Mosaic law into a mosaic, a mere collection of stray passages with no coherent scheme. Other Jews are more open-minded about biblical criticism, arguing that the study of how the books actually came to be ought not to affect our attitude toward them as sacred Scripture. Take, for example, the Book of Psalms. The traditional view is that the whole book was compiled by King David, including Psalm 137 which begins: "By the rivers of Babylon, there we sat down, yea, we wept, when we remembered Zion." This can only mean that the tradition does hold fast to the view (although, some Rabbis were not so confident) that a prophet could see into the future in detail; David's seeing by means of the holy spirit events which did not happen until hundreds of years later.

The modern critical view is that David may well have written some, even many, of the Psalms, but that some of them, like Psalm 137, must have been added later. Thus, Psalm 137 was composed by a contemporary or near-contemporary of the events in Babylon. Although the new picture is untraditional, does it really affect our appreciation of the religious value of the Book of Psalms? It is in some ways like the question of who wrote the plays of Shakespeare. The historian of English literature does well to investigate this kind of question, but the result matters little to the reader of these plays. Whether they were composed by William Shakespeare or by Sir Francis Bacon, their value lies in what they say and in the way they say it.

The higher criticism of the Bible is now associated with the German scholar Wellhausen, its foremost exponent. Wellhausen is now to some extent "old hat," but this only means that modern scholarship has advanced beyond his theories. Nevertheless, very few scholars indeed have given up biblical criticism and the vast majority regard the Torah not as a single text conveyed all at one time to Moses, but as a series of texts or traditions combined by a later editor or editors and composed at different periods in Israel's history.

What becomes of the authority of the Torah and the mitzvot if this view is accepted? We can see how this authority need not be affected by the new knowledge if we reflect on the idea of the Oral Torah. It is not necessary to believe that God conveyed His truth *to* the Jewish people as passive recipients. Even if Wellhausen is correct, an observant Jew can still keep the mitzvot as the will of God, but that will has been conveyed *through* the historical experiences of the Jewish people in their long quest for God. Biblical criticism does not invalidate the doctrine of divine revelation but views it in more dynamic terms.

"What is demanded by biblical criticism is not an abandonment of the doctrine of divine revelation, but a new view of it."

Biblical Commentaries

Jews have studied the Bible with great diligence throughout the ages. The names of the famous Jewish biblical commentators occupy an honored place in the history of Jewish literature—Rashi, the greatest of them all, Naḥmanides, Kimḥi, Rashbam, Ibn Ezra, Gersonides, and a host of others. Besides their valiant attempts to discover the original, plain meaning of Scripture, they record how the Biblical texts have become fruitful in Jewish life and how they were applied in the Jewish tradition. Nowadays, many devout Jews avail themselves of both modern critical results and the comments of the medieval giants; the former for their new insights, the latter for information on how the Bible can be read in a Jewish way by Jews striving to lead a life based on the Torah. We do not have to choose between modern criticism and Jewish tradition. There is no reason why we cannot have both.

7

Talmud and Midrash

Some Terms and Dates

If we needed any evidence of the significance Judaism attaches to study it is amply provided in the terms used for the Jewish classics, all of them connected with roots meaning "to teach." The word Torah itself is the first example, to which we can add: Mishnah; Talmud; Gemara (in Aramaic); and Midrash. Mishnah is from the root *shanah*, "to repeat" and hence "to learn"; Talmud from the root *lamad*, "to learn," Gemara from the root *gamar*, "to complete" and hence "to study repeatedly"; and Midrash from the root *darash*, "to inquire," or to investigate Scripture in order to discover its fullest meaning.

Three dates should be remembered (they are only approximate, but are easily remembered in the round figures given): the year 200 (of the present era) for the Mishnah; the year 400 for the Palestinian Talmud; the year 500 for the Babylonian Talmud. We can state right away that the Mishnah is the work in Hebrew, edited by Rabbi Judah the Prince, that contains a digest of all the Jewish laws and practices that had come down to his day; the Palestinian Talmud or Gemara is the summary of all the discussions on the Mishnah by later teachers and edited in Palestine (the language is Western Aramaic); the Babylonian Talmud or Gemara is the similar work edited in Babylon (the language is Eastern Aramaic).

Basically the terms Talmud and Gemara are synonymous but, nowadays, the Talmud generally refers to the Mishnah and Gemara together; the two are always printed as a single work. The two Talmuds are also called the *Yerushalmi* ("Jerusalem") and the *Bavli* ("Babylonian"), though there were no scholars in Jerusalem at the time when this Talmud was compiled. To understand what happened and how the Talmud (really the two Talmuds) came to be, it is necessary to look at the history of the Jewish people in Palestine and Babylon in postbiblical times.

Tannaim and Amoraim

The editing of the Mishnah in the year 200 is the great dividing line—the teachers who lived before that time and whose teachings are recorded in the Mishnah, are known as the *Tannaim* (the word means "teachers" or "scholars"). The post mishnaic teachers in both Palestine and Babylon, who commented on the Mishnah and dis-

"The Talmud refers to the Mishnah and Gemara together; the two are printed as a single work."

56

cussed it, are known as the *Amoraim* ("interpreters"). The Tannaim lived in Palestine, as did, of course, the Palestinian Amoraim, while the Babylonian Amoraim, naturally, lived in Babylon. The two communities of Palestine and Babylon were in close contact, and travel between them was not too difficult. Consequently, although the names Palestinian and Babylonian Talmuds might suggest that their teachings belong solely to the scholars of these lands, such was not the case. The Palestinian Talmud records some opinions of the Babylonian Amoraim and the Babylonian Talmud records opinions of the Palestinian Amoraim.

All these rabbis, Tannaim, and Amoraim were in no way professional or salaried officials. One was a shoemaker, another a smith, another a rich merchant, others farmers or artisans. The authority they enjoyed was due to their vast learning. Of Rabbi Akiba it was even said that in his youth he was a determined foe of the Rabbis. His wife encouraged him to study the Torah at the feet of Rabbi Eliezer and Rabbi Joshua. When he became a famous teacher of the Torah with thousands of disciples he said to them: "My Torah and yours is really hers." Rabbi Simeon was a fierce political opponent of the Roman occupation, refusing to listen to a good word about the Roman conquerers of his homeland. He had to fly for his life before the fury of Rome. He hid in a cave for many years, where he and his son lived a hermit-like existence, totally immersed in the study of the Torah. When the danger was past, the two scholars came out of their cave but were distressed to see people ploughing and reaping. They gazed

In every Jewish community throughout history, the study of the Torah has been a central pillar of Jewish life. Here in the Jewish ghetto of Casablanca, a teacher studies with his young pupils (1949).

Only in recent generations has the occupation of rabbi become a full-time profession. In former times, rabbis had other careers and performed their rabbinic duties separately.

with displeasure on this worldly activity and, such was their holy power, the story goes, wherever they gazed the produce in the fields was destroyed. A heavenly voice then proclaimed: "Have you come out of your cave to destroy My world? Go back into your cave." In other words, it is given to few to emulate Rabbi Simeon and his son, the Babylonian teacher Abbaye later said. The majority of people have to earn their living in the normal way, and the Torah approves of this.

The two great teachers in third century Babylon, Rav and Samuel, were quite different in character and temperament, though united in their love of the Torah. Rav was a liturgical poet (some of the hymns he composed, such as the *Alenu*, attributed to him in some sources, are still recited in synagogues all over the world). He was also a great religious organizer, largely responsible for Babylon's becoming the outstanding center of Jewish religious life after a long interval of spiritual stagnation. Samuel was of a more practical cast of mind; an astronomer, physician, and jurist. Samuel once observed that he was as familiar with the paths of the heavenly bodies as he was of the streets of his native town, Nehardea. The Talmud contains many debates between these two teachers. Later generations followed Rav in matters of religious law and Samuel in civil law.

Rabbi Judah the Prince and Rav Ashi were editors, respectively, in a general sense, of the Mishnah and the Babylonian Talmud. It is said that they enjoyed "both Torah and worldly greatness," that they were not only the Torah and spiritual leaders of their day but were wealthy and influential political figures. Behind this is the fact that these two were suited by the circumstances of their time and persons to collect the material that had accumulated up to their time and to present it in intelligible form.

We have seen that the doctrine of the Oral Torah implies a constant succession of teachings handed down from generation to generation. These teachings, some said to date back to Moses, others to pretannaitic teachers such as Hillel and Shammai, began the process culminating with the Tannaim. Strictly speaking, the term Tannaim refers only to the teachers in the first two centuries of the present era. Hillel and Shammai are really pretannaitic (they lived about one hundred years before the destruction of the Temple in the year 70) but their opinions and the opinions of the rival Schools they founded (the School of Hillel and the School of Shammai) are treated extensively in the Talmud. The most famous Tannaim were Rabbi Akiba, Rabbi Joshua, Rabbi Eliezer, Rabbi Simeon, Rabbi Tarfon, Rabbi Jose, Rabban Gamaliel and Rabban Johanan ben Zakkai.

In the amoraic period there were schools in which the Torah was taught by masters to chosen disciples (in Tiberius, Caesarea, and Sepphoris in Palestine and in Sura and Pumbedita in Babylon, as well as other places in these two lands). Among the Palestinian Amoraim are R. Johanan (the "R." stands for "Rabbi"), R. Simeon ben Lakish, R. Eleazar ben Pedat, R. Joshua ben Levi, and R. Avun. Among the Babylonian Amoraim are: Rav, Samuel, R. Nahman, R. Huna, R. Hisda, Abbaye, Rava, R. Pappa, Rav Ashi, and Ravina.

The Tannaitic Midrashim

The teachings of the Tannaim are to be found in the Mishnah and in the tannaitic Midrashim (plural of Midrash). There were two methods of presenting the teachings of the Tannaim: (1) the Midrashic, in which rules of behavior are drawn out of the biblical text (hence the term Midrash, to inquire of Scripture what it really says); (2) the Mishnaic, in which the rules are formulated without reference to the text of Scripture. There are three main tannaitic midrashim: (1) the *Mekhilta* (the word means "measure") to the Book of Exodus; (2) the *Sifra* ("book"), otherwise known as *Torat Kohanim* ("Law of the Priests") to the Book of Leviticus; (3) The *Sifre* ("Books") to the books of Numbers and Deuteronomy. There is no tannaitic Midrash to the Book of Genesis, probably because these Midrashim are mainly of a legal character and there are very few laws in Genesis.

The Mishnah

Rabbi Judah the Prince arranged the tannaitic and pretannaitic material into a concise, clearly arranged work covering the whole range of Jewish life, even those rules and regulations no longer in force in his day, such as the rules of Temple worship. This great compilation is the Mishnah. He included in the Mishnah only those matters he considered of major importance. Various collections of the rest of the material were made by some of Rabbi Judah's disciples and these, too, are frequently commented on in the Gemara. These collections are known as *Baraitot* (singular *Baraita*), "the outside works," works not incorporated into the official Mishnah.

The Mishnah is arranged in six great sections, called "Orders," the Six Orders of the Mishnah. In Hebrew this is *Shishah Sedarim*, the initial letters of which form the word *Shas*, another name for the Talmud as a whole.

"The great compilation of law arranged by Rabbi Judah the Prince is known as the Mishnah."

Mishnah

To convey something of the flavor of the Mishnah we can do no better than quote the very first section (tractate *Berakhot* 1:1) dealing with the times when the evening Shema is to be recited: "From which time can one read the Shema in the evening? From the time the priests go in to eat their sacred tithes (the reference is to priests who had come into contact with some source of ritual contamination, such as a dead reptile, and who, after their immersion, were not allowed to eat their semi-sacred tithes until night had fallen), until the first watch of the night (either a third or a quarter of the night; this is debated). These are the words of Rabbi Eliezer. But the Sages say: (it can be read) until midnight. Rabban Gamaliel says: Until dawn (it can be read at any time during the whole of the night). It once happened that his sons returned from a wedding banquet (after midnight) and said to him: "We have not read the Shema." He said to them: "If the dawn has not yet risen you are still obliged to recite it."

The Six Orders of the Mishnah

1. *Zera'im* ("Seeds"), dealing with agricultural laws.
2. *Mo'ed* ("Appointed Times"), dealing with the Sabbath and the Festivals.
3. *Nashim* ("Women"), dealing with marriage laws.
4. *Nezikin* ("Damages"), dealing with law proper, such as buying and selling, the law courts, and criminal law.
5. *Kodashim* ("Sacred Things"), dealing with the sacrificial system.
6. *Tohorot* ("Purities") dealing with ritual impurity in Temple times (so that "Purities" is a euphemism).

The Palestinian Talmud

We do not know who edited the Palestinian Talmud. Nor do we know the exact date it was edited, except that it was approximately the year 400. This Talmud is the record of all the discussions on the Mishnah, chiefly by the Palestinian teachers but also by some of the Babylonian Amoraim. Its style is of such brevity that at times the observations seem cryptic. For instance, in tractate Rosh Hashanah of the Palestinian Talmud there is a statement about God Himself obeying His laws. He, too, comforts mourners, visits the sick, helps the poor, and does all the other things He demands of humans. Suddenly there appears in the discussion what seems to be a meaningless jumble of letters which make no sense until it is noticed that these words are, in Hebrew letters, a quotation from the Greek, to the effect that a human king does not have to obey the law, but, God, unlike a human king, does obey His own laws. The background reflects the conditions which obtained in Roman Palestine. There are far more references, for example, to Roman institutions than in the Babylonian Talmud and far more Greek words. There are even complete quotations from Greek proverbs.

"The Talmud is the record of all the discussions on the Mishnah."

Babylonian Talmud

The Babylonian Talmud is far more complex and elaborate than the Palestianian. In it there are lengthy discussions of the utmost subtlety that have sharpened the minds and fired the imaginations of talmudists from the fifth century, when the work was edited, down to the present day. The traditional view is that the Talmud was edited by Rav Ashi and Ravina in the fifth century, but this cannot be taken too literally since there are numerous passages which have clearly been added later. Most printed editions of the Babylonian Talmud comprise some thirty huge volumes with commentaries, and commentaries on the commentaries. Scholars have described the work as "the sea of the Talmud." It is, indeed, like a vast sea, requiring expert

"The Talmud is like a vast sea, requiring expert navigation to sail safely through its often turbulent waters."

navigation to sail safely through its often turbulent waters. In fact, the only way to study the Talmud is at the feet of a competent talmudist who also studied the work at the feet of other masters. There is an excellent translation of the whole work in English published by the Soncino Press, but it is a rare student who will succeed in mastering the Talmud without the aid of a teacher. No work of Jewish literature, not even the Bible, has been studied by Jews with greater application and devotion than the Babylonian Talmud.

The first press edition of the Talmud was printed in Venice between 1520 and 1523. The layout of the pages has barely changed in over four centuries.

Halakhah and Aggadah

The rules on the types of oil and wick that can be used for the Sabbath lamp are Halakhah, but the statement that one who keeps these rules will have children learned in the Torah is Aggadah. Also belonging to the Aggadah is the lovely saying that two angels, one good and one bad, accompany a man home on Sabbath eve. If he finds all prepared for the Sabbath, the lamps lit, the table laden with good food, his wife and family there to rejoice on the Sabbath with him, and an atmosphere of serenity and holiness pervading the home, the good angel proclaims: "May all your Sabbaths be as this," and the bad angel is compelled to answer "Amen." The rules about who takes precedence when the charity funds are to be distributed belong to Halakhah but the saying that charity is true when it is given with love is Aggadah. The Halakhah is the body of the rules; the Aggadah their soul. An aggadic saying is: "If you wish to get to know the One who spake and the world came into being, study Aggadah."

Halakhah and Aggadah

In both the Babylonian and the Palestinian Talmuds there are two kinds of material. These are: (a) *Halakhah*, "law" (from a root meaning "to go," the way in which the Jew should walk in life), consisting of debates and discussions on rules and regulations (this forms the major part of the Talmud); (b) *Aggadah* (from a root meaning "to tell"), all the nonlegal material such as history, morals, medicine, folklore, legends, biblical comments, stories of the masters, philosophy, geography, and politics. The Halakhah is the prose of the Talmud, the Aggadah its poetry. For instance, in tractate Shabbat, the detailed treatment of the laws regarding work on the Sabbath, what is permissible and what forbidden, constitutes the Halakhah, while the admonitions to keep the Sabbath and the stories about pious folk who observed the Sabbath constitute the Aggadah.

Aggadic Midrashim

The tannaitic Midrashim are almost entirely halakhic and an attempt to extract from the legal passages of the Bible further implications for the practice of the law. But in the amoraic period, especially in Palestine, a more fanciful, aggadic type of Midrash was produced. This, too, was centered on Scripture but the exegesis is much freer and even more farfetched. It is the aim of these Midrashim to provide comfort and consolation to the people rather than accurate biblical commentary. For example, one of these Midrashim tells that when a rabbi, preaching in the synagogue, saw that the congregation was nodding he suddenly remarked that a woman in Egypt gave birth to 600,000 children, which certainly caused the congregation to sit up and take notice. He then explained that he was thinking of the mother of Moses (who led 600,000 people out of Egypt). There are scores of these aggadic Midrashim, dating from different periods. The best-known, the series on the Pentateuch and the Five Megillot, are called *Midrash Rabbah* ("the Great Midrash").

This does not mean that these Midrashim are just smooth words of consolation. They contain a treasury of rabbinic teachings on every aspect of life, summoning the people to a life of the highest moral and religious standards. For instance, the numerous Midrashic statements about the character of Abraham are not intended primarily as biblical exegesis. Their intent is to hold up the example of Abraham, his magnanimity, his search for God, his generosity, and his faithfulness, as a model, so that he becomes the prototype of the ideal Jew. Or when the Midrashim suggest that King David was really a superior rabbi who rendered decisions in Jewish law, they are really saying that learning and obedience to the Torah are more praiseworthy than military conquest even in a king.

"The first qualification of a Gaon was to know the whole of the Talmud thoroughly by heart."

The Savoraim and the Geonim

Immediately following the amoraic period was that of the *Savoraim* ("expounders," from *sevara*, "theory"). They added many touches to the Babylonian Talmud, such as stating the actual ruling where the Talmud leaves the matter open and fixing the framework of many of the debates. We do not know exactly how much of the Talmud itself is the result of the work of the Savoraim, but modern scholars are inclined to think it is far more than used to be attributed to them. After the conquest of Babylon by the Muslims, to the late tenth century, there were two great schools in Babylon, one at Sura and the other at Pumbedita. The heads of these schools were called the *Geonim* (singular, *Gaon*, "Excellency"). It was said that the first qualification of a Gaon was to know the whole of the Talmud thoroughly by heart. The Geonim studied the Babylonian Talmud so assiduously in their schools *(Yeshivot)* that the Babylonian Talmud became authoritative in Jewish life.

There are three reasons why the Babylonian rather than the Palestinian Talmud became *the* Talmud and the final authority. First, the Babylonian Talmud is far more comprehensive than the Palestinian. Second, it was later, and the general tendency is to follow the later authority on the grounds that the earlier authority must have been taken into account. Third, and most important, the Geonim were the direct successors of the Babylonian Amoraim, continuing their work and referring to the Babylonian Talmud as *our* Talmud.

The Talmud as the Final Word

"All the masters of the law appealed to the Talmud as having the decisive voice in every controversial matter."

During the period of the Geonim, the Karaite movement arose. The Karaites (*Karaim*, from *kara*, "to read," that is, the Bible) came to deny the whole of the Oral Torah, considering that the laws of the Bible alone are binding, not the rabbinic interpretations found in the talmudic literature. The Geonim and their followers treated the Talmud as a sacred work, second only to the Bible itself; indeed, in a sense, as more significant since it provided the final authority for Jewish observances. So great was the reverence for the Talmud that in the Middle Ages the maxim was coined: "The Talmud is the final word accepted by the whole Jewish people. From it nothing must be diminished and to it nothing must be added." After the fall of the Karaite movement, the authority of the Talmud was never challenged until the rise of the Reform movement in the nineteenth century. All the masters of the law, the compilers of the great Codes and rabbis everywhere, turned to the Talmud for the decisive voice in every controversial matter.

The Rabbis of Blessed Memory

"Maimonides rejected belief in astrology as nonsense even though it was a belief shared by all the talmudic rabbis."

As a result, the individual Tannaim and Amoraim whose teachings are found in the Talmud came to be treated as spiritual superbeings who were infallible because they had been guided by the holy spirit. Indeed, the individuality and personal temperaments of the hundreds of rabbis in the Talmud were overlooked almost entirely. They were lumped together, as it were, and referred to as Ḥazal, standing for Ḥakhamenu Zikhronam Liverakhah, "Our Sages of Blessed Memory." It came to be considered sheer heresy to question any opinions of Ḥazal.

Nevertheless, at times voices were raised even in the rabbinic camp against an excessive veneration of the talmudic rabbis. One of the late Geonim, Samuel ben Hophni, for example, felt free to disregard some of the aggadic passages in the Talmud (though never the halakhic) such as the aggadic understanding of the story of the Witch of Endor (I Samuel chapter 28), that the witch really brought Samuel up from the dead. Many Geonim, too, refused to allow the people to use the cures for diseases found in the Talmud, arguing that the Rabbis had only the medical knowledge of their day and did not speak with the voice of God, as they did in matters of Halakhah. Maimonides rejected belief in astrology as nonsense, even though it was shared by all the talmudic rabbis. He disregarded also the talmudic statements that imply a belief in the existence of demons. In sixteenth-century Italy the first real Jewish historian, Azariah de Rossi, in his book *Meor Eynayim*, went so far as to deny that the talmudic rabbis were always accurate in matters of history. The Talmud says, for instance, that Titus was killed by a gnat that entered his brain through his nostrils and grew into a huge bird which pecked away at the brain, whereas de Rossi knew from the Latin sources that Titus died a natural death. Not all rabbinic scholars agreed with people like de Rossi. Some of them wished to ban his book and even sought to have it burned. Yet today in many Orthodox circles it is not considered heretical to treat the rabbis as fallible human beings except that the halakhic authority of the Talmud is preserved unimpaired.

Cures in the Talmud

"This is the cure for lumbago. Take a pot of fish brine and rub it in sixty times round one hip and sixty times round the other. This is the cure for stone in the bladder. Take three drops of tar and three drops of leek juice and three drops of clear wine and pour the mixture on the place."
(Babylonian Talmud, tractate *Gittin* 69b).

"Our Rabbis taught: Asparagus-beverage is beneficial for the heart, good for the eyes and how much more so for the digestion; so if one makes a habit of drinking this beverage it is good for the whole of his body; but if he becomes intoxicated therewith, it is harmful for his whole body."
(Babylonian Talmud, tractate *Berakhot* 51a).

These are but two examples among many rabbinic cures found in the Talmud. Now the Talmud became the authoritative work for Judaism, second only to the Bible, and many Jews came to believe that the talmudic rabbis were infallible guides not only in religion and morals but also in general matters. It was tempting for these believers to rely on such cures. Very courageously, some of the Geonim, the post-talmudic teachers, came out against any reliance on cures found in the Talmud. The talmudic rabbis were not medical experts. They simply wished to share the medical knowledge they had acquired from their gentile neighbors. Consequently, the Geonim declared, no one must use any of the cures mentioned in the Talmud without first consulting his own doctor. Another example: the talmudic rabbis believed that regular bloodletting is beneficial to health, but no one nowadays, not even the most Orthodox, resorts to this, just as we do not argue that because the Rabbis had no telephones we should not use them.

The Study of the Talmud

In some Jewish communities the study of the Torah meant the study of the Talmud, to the virtual exclusion of every other topic! There were scholars whose knowledge of the Bible was derived only from biblical quotations in the Talmud. Even in those communities where a wider range of Torah study was encouraged, the chief subject studied was the Talmud, especially in its difficult halakhic portions. Only the good Talmud student was respected as a scholar, he alone was given the title reserved for the learned person—*talmud ḥakham* ("disciple of the wise") and *lamdan* ("learned"). And this study can become so exciting and so intellectually stimulating that the student who has "caught the bug" will hardly ever give it up, devoting all leisure time to "learning." In Eastern Europe before the Second World War, it was not unusual for the father of a girl to send a proficient talmudist to see if a prospective bridegroom knew the Talmud. Only if the young man's knowledge was up to expectations would the father consent to the match.

In modern times Jewish scholars have used the Talmud as a rich mine of information regarding Jewish life over a period of about 1,000 years. The author of one of the best talmudic dictionaries, Marcus Jastrow, rightly notes in his introduction: "The subjects of this literature (the Talmud) are as unlimited as are the interests of the human mind. Religion and ethics, exegesis and homiletics, jurisprudence and ceremonial laws, ritual and liturgy, philosophy and science, medicine and magic, astronomy and astrology, history and geography, commerce and trade, politics and social problems, all are represented there, and reflect the mental condition of the Jewish world in its seclusion from the outside world, as well as in its contact with the same whether in agreement or opposition."

The study of the Talmud has engaged the minds of the most intelligent Jews for 1,500 years. The sheer joy of debate and argument, of solving difficult problems, of keen logic and legal subtleties, is far from the whole story. Talmud study has always been seen as a mighty attempt to discover the will of God in every situation. Even if many of the cases discussed in the Talmud will never arise in real life, the mind engaged in them is seeking to discover the very will of God. The Ḥasidic leader, Rabbi Shneur Zalman of Lyady, went even further. In the talmudic debates, he writes, when A argues thus and B argues otherwise, all who study these debates on the Torah are, in reality, united with the will of God, and since the will of God is identical with God, the mind of the student is, as it were, at one with the Mind of God. There is no higher human pursuit than this, to have this wondrous intimacy with the Creator. Even if this idea is too mystical for some tastes, something of the sort is behind the complete devotion to Talmud studies that is typical of the talmud hakham, the student who is never "wise" but always a disciple because the "sea of the Talmud" has no visible limits.

"Only the good Talmud student was respected and given the title reserved for the learned person."

8 Rabbinic Literature

The Posttalmudic Rabbis

As we have seen, the activity of the talmudic rabbis in discussing, debating, learning, teaching, and applying the teachings of the Torah were continued by the Geonim and their schools. This activity took place in many other centers after the Geonic period, among them North Africa, Spain, Italy, France, and Germany and, from the sixteenth century, Palestine, Poland, and Lithuania. Distinguished rabbis recorded in writing the results of their researches. The works they produced are known as the rabbinic literature, to distinguish it from the talmudic literature. The rabbinic literature is of many kinds, but chiefly it consists of Commentaries, Codes, and Responsa.

Commentaries

We have seen that the Talmud is a very difficult work to understand. Apart from the complicated subject matter, there are many expressions which are hard to fathom because they are either idiomatic or are in foreign languages—Greek, Latin, and Persian, as well as in Aramaic. Again, there are numerous references to animals, plants, baking processes, kitchen utensils, costume, caravans, trading, markets, battles, art, and music, all of which require some knowledge of social conditions in talmudic times. For this reason the Talmud would have been a closed book if not for the great commentators who, partly by the keenness of their intellect and partly because they had authentic traditions regarding the meaning of the texts, were able to throw light on many obscure passages.

Maimonides wrote a commentary to the whole of the Mishnah in Arabic, the language used by cultured Jews in his day. To each paragraph of the Mishnah he supplies a brief elucidation of the points at issue and boldly differs, on occasion, from the interpretation of the Mishnah given in the Gemara. Maimonides *does* accept, however, the rulings based on the Gemara's interpretation rather than on his own. Evidently he believed that theoretical freedom of interpretation is allowed, but not where it results in practical changes in the law. The same principle guided some of the medieval commentators to the Bible.

Maimonides prefaces his commentary to the Mishnah with a lengthy introduction in which he describes the way the tradition was

> *"Rabbinic literature is of many kinds, but chiefly it consists of Commentaries, Codes, and Responsa."*

Maimonides.

handed down until it reached the talmudic rabbis, the methods of the Rabbis, and their general philosophy of learning. Furthermore, to a number of sections he provides philosophical statements—for example, on the section of the Mishnah which reads: "All Israel have a share in the World to Come," Maimonides records his famous statement of the thirteen principles of the Jewish faith. Again, in his commentary to the section of the Mishnah known as *Ethics of the Fathers*, he has a profound excursus, in eight chapters, dealing with Jewish ethical attitudes, particularly in relation to Greek attitudes.

Maimonides' work was translated into Hebrew and is still extensively used, but the most popular commentary to the Mishnah is the clear, concise, Hebrew work of Obadiah Bertinoro of Italy in the fifteenth century. Bertinoro summarizes the discussions of the Gemara and is very readable. A more detailed commentary to the Mishnah is that of Yom Tov Lipmann Heller of Prague (1579–1654) known as *Tosefot Yom Tov*. The third standard commentary to the Mishnah is that of Israel Lipschutz (1782–1860) known as *Tiferet Yisrael*. Although very traditional, it discusses modern problems. In a comment on the mishnaic statement about the dignity of humanity, he refers to famous non-Jews who have made contributions to civilization, and in another comment offers advice to would-be public speakers. He was the first traditional rabbi to accept scientific evidence, such as fossils, that the world is older than the tradition states, and tries ingeniously to square tradition with modern thought. All three commentaries—of Bertinoro, Heller, and Lipschutz—are printed together in the better editions of the Mishnah. (Although the Mishnah is always included in the Talmud, it is also printed separately as a work on its own with the standard commentaries).

On the Talmud, the indispensible commentary is that of Rashi (R. Solomon ben Isaac, in eleventh-century France). Rashi provides brief comments to every difficult passage and even to individual words. He has an uncanny ability to anticipate the questions every serious student will raise and simply supplies the answer. Anyone who has studied the Talmud together with Rashi knows how frequently it happens that the text seems puzzling until a glance at Rashi makes it all clear. At times a question that presents itself is not dealt with till later in the talmudic passage. When that happens,

> *"The Talmud would have been a closed book were it not for the efforts of the great commentators. . . ."*

> *"Anyone who has studied the Talmud together with Rashi knows how puzzling the text can seem until Rashi makes it all clear."*

Synagogue Architecture

There is no reference anywhere in the traditional sources as to the synagogue's being required to have any special size or form. Authorities conclude, therefore, that the synagogue can be square or oblong or octagonal, with a dome or a flat roof, or, indeed, in any architectural style the architect wishes if the congregation agrees. The two provisions are: (1) It should not be so ostentatious as to suggest that the congregation is more interested in externals than with prayer and inwardness; (2) It must in no way resemble a church, for example, by having a steeple or bells. Some hold that ideally a synagogue should have twelve windows corresponding to the twelve tribes of Israel, each having its own "gateway to Heaven."

Rashi says in so many words to the student: "Do not worry. You are quite right to think of this difficulty, but if you carry on you will find it discussed later in the Gemara."

Rashi had three learned daughters but no sons. His sons-in-law and grandsons (the most famous grandson was Jacob ben Meir, known as Rabbenu Tam) introduced the method of study known as the *Tosafot* ("additions" or "supplements"). In the schools founded by these men in France, Germany, and England, passages in the Talmud were contrasted with one another, arguments were analyzed, difficulties were raised, and attempts made to solve them, all with a brilliance bordering on genius. The various collections of the tosafists reintroduced into Talmud studies something of the original thrust and parry, argument and counterargument so typical of the talmudic rabbis themselves. In practically every edition of the Talmud, Rashi is printed on one side of the text and the tosafot on the other, so that the study of the Talmud came to mean examining these two commentaries as well as the text, and was called *Gefat*, meaning Gemara, Perush ("Commentary," that is, Rashi), *Tosafot*.

A need arose to codify the law, organizing the many details of Jewish tradition into a practical format.

Codes

The Talmud is more a record of discussions and debates about the law than a code of law. True, the Talmud often concludes a discussion or debate with a statement that the law is such-and-such, but often the actual decision is left in abeyance, to say nothing of the difficulties in determining the ruling when discussion is so involved that it escapes ordinary student entirely!

But observant Jews who wish to live by the Torah law have to know with certainty what the law actually is. To take a simple example, there are cases recorded in the Talmud in which one Rabbi sides with one contestant and the other with his opponent. Now the student of the Talmud may be quite content to study the involved arguments for their own sake and is not called upon to render any practical decision. But a judge must know in whose favor to decide. Consequently, the need was soon felt for detailed codes of law with clear-cut decisions.

The latest and greatest of these codes is the *Shulḥan Arukh* ("Arranged Table") of Rabbi Joseph Caro (1488–1575). It was preceded by three earlier codes: (1) The earliest of these was compiled by Rabbi Isaac Alfasi (1013–1103) of Fez in Morocco (hence the name *Alfasi*, "from Fez," or, as he is frequently called "The *Rif*" from "Rabbi Yitzhak Fasi"). The Rif's compilation is really a kind of abbreviation of the Talmud in which the discussions are omitted and the conclusion stated with a view to practical guidance. (2) The second, Maimonides' code, is called *Mishneh Torah* ("Second to the Torah") or *Yad ha-Ḥazakah* ("The Strong Hand"). It is in faultless Hebrew and

Joseph Caro

Rabbi Joseph Caro, author of the *Shulḥan Arukh,* one of the greatest legal luminaries of all time, was a mystic with his own hidden life. For forty years he kept a mystical diary in which he recorded communications he believed came to him through an angelic mentor, called the *Maggid.* Here is a jotting from the book *Maggid Mesharim* ("Speaker of Upright Words"), the part of Caro's diary that has been published. In it the Maggid rebukes Caro, urging him to lead a more saintly life. It has been suggested that a powerful legal mind like Caro's desperately needed relief from legalism, which was provided by his mystical experiences.

"First of all you must take care never to allow your thoughts to dwell on anything other than the Mishnah, the Torah and the precepts. If any other thought enters your heart, cast it away. 2. Take care to have no other thought in mind during prayer, only the words of the prayers, not even thoughts about the Torah and the precepts. 3. Take care never to speak an unnecessary word, whether by day or by night. 4. Take care never to speak anything that leads to laughter and if you hear such, never laugh. This includes the admonition never to scoff at all. 5. Never lose your temper over merely material things. 6. Take care to eat no meat for forty days. On the Sabbath you can eat a little meat. Do not eat horseradish. 7. Drink no wine during these days except for one drink at the end of the meal. 8. Be gentle in your replies to all people. 9. Never be proud. Be exceedingly low in spirit. . . . 16. When you are at meals and experience a special longing for some food or drink, desist from it. If you do this, it will be as if you offered a sacrifice at each meal and your table will be a veritable altar upon which you slaughter the evil inclination. 17. Do not drink the wine at meals in one gulp and take care how you measure it out. Be not afraid that this may affect your eyesight. On the contrary, both your eyesight and your strength will increase. 18. Have little further to do with the pleasures of eating and drinking. Do not make a habit of eating a particular food that you enjoy especially. Substitute for it, rather, another type of food from which you do not derive such enjoyment."

covers fourteen huge volumes, embracing even the laws of the sacrificial system which had been in abeyance for 1,000 years. (3) The third is the Tur, "Row" (the full title is *Arba'ah Turim*, "The Four Rows"), compiled in Spain by the German scholar Jacob ben Asher (died 1340). This Code takes into account the varying opinions among the lawyers and tries to take a position in favor of one in each case.

Rabbi Joseph Caro was moved to compile his *Shulḥan Arukh* because, as he remarks in his introduction, despite the three earlier codes, there were still numerous differences in practice in different Jewish communities. If one went from one community to another he might find what seemed to be a different religion or, as Caro put it, the Torah had become many *torot*! To remedy the situation Caro spent many years on his gigantic commentary to the *Tur* called *Bet Yosef* ("House of Joseph"). He surveyed practically everything written on the law and by keen analytical reasoning sought to arrive at decisions acceptable to all. In his *Shulḥan Arukh* Caro cut out the arguments and reasons of the *Bet Yosef* and simply recorded the law. Following the arrangement of the *Tur*, Caro divided his *Shulḥan Arukh* into four Parts: (1) *Oraḥ Ḥayyim* ("Way of Life"), dealing with the daily life of the Jew, prayer, the synagogue, benedictions, Sabbaths, and Festivals; (2) *Yoreh De'ah* ("Teaching Knowledge"), dealing with religious law for the experts, such as the rules of *kashrut* (which food is kosher and which not), the acceptance of converts to Judaism, the writing of a Sefer Torah, the prohibition against taking interest, burial of the dead; (3) *Even ha-Ezer* ("Stone of Help"), dealing with laws of marriage and divorce; (4) *Ḥoshen Mishpat* ("Breastplate of Judgment"), dealing with civil and criminal law in all their ramifications.

"The latest and greatest of the codes is the Shulḥan Arukh, *written by Rabbi Joseph Caro."*

From the Shulḥan Arukh

The Law of a Thief Restoring the Stolen Article without the Knowledge of Its Owner.

"If a man steals an object from his neighbor's house and later returns it to its place without the owner knowing that he has returned it, then, if the owner knows that it has been stolen from him, the thief is not exempt, even when he has returned it, and he is responsible for it until the owner becomes aware that it has been returned, as, for example, when the owner counts his objects and finds them all there. Nevertheless, the thief is relieved from responsibility once the owner counts them, even if the owner was not aware of it when the thief returned it. Consequently, if a thief stole some money and then added the money he had stolen in a sum he gave to the owner for some other purpose and the owner put all the money into his money bag, then, if the owner knows how much money he has, the thief has made proper restitution, since a man constantly counts his money and will become aware that the stolen money has been returned to him. But if the thief cast the money into an empty money bag, he has not satisfied the requirements of the law and is still responsible for that which he had stolen until he informs the owner that he has returned the money to such-and-such a money bag. But if the owner is unaware that something had been stolen from him, the thief has satisfied the requirements of the law as soon as he returns that which he had stolen, even if the owner had not counted his objects." (*Ḥoshen Mishpat* 355)

The *Shulḥan Arukh* could not serve its function as a code for all Jewry because of the division among Jews into Sephardim (Jews who came originally from Spain) and Ashkenazim (those who came originally from Germany). Caro was a Sephardi and in matters about which Sephardim and Ahkenazim differed he recorded in the *Shulḥan Arukh* the Sephardi practice. For example, Caro records the Sephardi habit of eating rice on Passover, but Ashkenazi communities strictly forbade it. In order to make the *Shulḥan Arukh* acceptable to Ashkenazi Jews, R. Moses Isserles, a contemporary of Caro in the Polish town of Cracow, added notes to the *Shulḥan Arukh* which he called the *Mappah* ("Tablecloth"). The "Arranged Table" was now provided with a cloth so that all could partake in comfort, the Sephardim following the text of the work, the Ashkenazim the notes of *Rema*, as Isserles is called (*R. Moses Isserles*).

There is no doubt that one of the main reasons for the acceptance of the *Shulḥan Arukh* as the authoritative code for Orthodox Jewry is that it was the first great code compiled after the invention of printing, thus assuring the widest possible circulation. Still, many rulings of the *Shulḥan Arukh* were challenged by later rabbinic scholars and numerous commentaries were written around it. Just as the editing of the Mishnah became the divide between the Tannaim and the Amoraim, the *Shulḥan Arukh* became the divide between the earlier, pre-*Shulḥan Arukh* authorities, the *Rishonim* ("early ones") and the *Aḥaronim* ("later ones") who came after it. Generally speaking, greater weight is attached to the opinions of the Rishonim so that one of the Aḥaronim would not normally render a decision which contradicted a ruling of a Rishon unless he could discover another Rishon to agree with him. The process of discussion and codification thus continued after the *Shulḥan Arukh* down to the present day. Later codes were also published, the most popular being the "Abridged *Shulḥan Arukh*," *Kitzur Shulḥan Arukh*, by the Hungarian Rabbi Solomon Ganzfried in the last century.

Response

Conditions of human life change all the time, presenting new challenges and new needs. Even the most widely accepted and most accurate of the codes had to be supplemented by decisions on matters not referred to at all in the codes, but which could be inferred from rulings in the codes. In the geonic period, for example, with the rise of Islam, the status in Jewish law of a Jewish convert to Islam had to be discussed, and for this there could be no direct guidance in the Talmud, the ultimate authority. Was such a convert still recognized as a Jew, so that his Jewish wife could not marry someone else without a divorce? When he died, were the mourning rites to be observed by his family? Teachers unable to decide on such questions submitted them to the Geonim for their opinion, and thus was born the Responsa literature, known as *Sheelot u-Teshuvot*, "Questions and Answers."

From then on, questions have been addressed to recognized experts in the law and in Jewish doctrine. No one appointed them

experts. It was simply a matter of consensus. Rabbis acknowledged one or two of their number as particularly competent to state the actual law and these were addressed. Collections were later being made of all their replies so that today we have hundreds of responsa collections extending over the centuries and providing, incidentally, information regarding the daily life of Jewish communities all over the world. It is important to appreciate that great respondents did not claim to have a kind of "hot line" to God. Their decisions were based on their knowledge of the sources and their ability to reason from them. Often their decisions were contradicted by other prominent scholars so that the responsa literature is full of heated debates. The famous codes took notice of the responsa in formulating the law so that the processes of codification and responsa went hand in hand.

To convey something of the flavor of this fascinating literature here are a few well-known responsa. Rabbi Meir of Rothenburg (died 1923) in Germany was asked whether a cripple can lead the prayers in the synagogue. He replied in the affirmative on the grounds that God desires the broken heart. Solomon Ibn Adret (1235–1310) of Barcelona, known as the *Rashba*, was asked whether a person claiming to be a prophet should be viewed with suspicion; how the patriarch Jacob could have married two sisters, since the Torah forbids this; whether it is permissible to have the figure of a lion above the ark in the synagogue or if this infringes the second commandment; whether it is permitted for a young man to study philosophy; and thousands of other questions, to which he replied in detail. R. Jair Ḥayyim Bacharach (1638–1702) of Germany was asked whether gambling is permitted; whether printed books enjoy the sanctity of sacred literature; whether abortions are ever permitted; and what is a good program of studies for a boy just passed Bar Mitzvah age. R. Ezekiel Landau of Prague (1713–1793) was asked whether it is permitted to dissect a corpse in order to discover the disease to which the person had succumbed; whether there are rules regarding synagogue architecture; whether it is permitted to go hunting for sport; whether a priest who married a Hindu woman in a Hindu temple is disqualified from reciting the priestly blessing even after he has returned to the Jewish faith.

In the responsa by rabbis of this century we find questions modern technology gives rise to: whether, for instance, it is permitted to have a microphone in the synagogue; whether kidney transplants are allowed; whether the same dishwasher may be used for both meat and milk dishes; whether one has to recite the thanksgiving blessing for traveling overseas if one travels in an airplane; which day or part of the day is to be observed as the Sabbath if one crosses the dateline; whether it is permitted to own shares in a company that does business on the Sabbath; whether gelatin manufactured from the dried bones of a nonkosher animal may be eaten on the grounds that its chemical composition has undergone a complete change; whether it is permitted to travel on the subway on the Sabbath; whether taking out an insurance policy betokens a lack of trust in God; even, when a Jewish astronaut should recite his morning, afternoon, and evening prayers as he spins around the earth!

Is riding the subway permitted on Shabbat? The Responsa literature answers questions not specifically detailed in the Torah.

"The great respondents did not claim to have a kind of 'hot line' to God."

Some Other Types of Rabbinic Literature

"Judaism affirms that to engage the mind in the study of God's word is the highest religious obligation."

Some rabbis had other interests and wrote valuable works of a rabbinic nature but in different areas of study. A number of methodologies of the Talmud were produced which describe the types of argument used in the Talmud and codes; the literary style of the Talmud; the principles by which the talmudic rabbis investigated Scripture; and the manner in which the Talmud was put together. Some rabbis produced historical works that identify by time and

Gambling

All the authorities agree that it is wrong for a person to live solely by his earnings from gambling, for then he makes no useful contribution to the well-being of society. The debate is whether it is permitted to have an occasional game of cards for money, or to place a bet on a horse, or to buy a lottery ticket. Some frown even on this, not because the winner is getting something for nothing but because, unlike in other financial agreements, the loser agrees to pay only in the event of a loss, while believing that the bet will not lose. Thus the loser parts with the money very reluctantly, and for the winner to pocket it is a form of theft. Other authorities treat a gambling contract like any other, and therefore see no harm in an occasional bet.

Some even argue that from the references in scripture to the casting of lots, it might appear that one of the ways in which God provides is through the luck of the draw. The consensus among the authorities is that there is no harm in an occasional gamble, but it must be only occasional. When it becomes an addiction, it is time to call a halt. Overindulgence even in legitimate pursuits is frowned upon in Jewish teaching.

Responsa Discussions on Modern Inventions

1. A *mezuzah* must be hand-written. A printed mezuzah is invalid. May one use as a mezuzah a photograph of a hand-written mezuzah? It can be argued that this is inferior even to a printed mezuzah because, while the act of printing might conceivably be treated as "writing," here there is no act of writing at all. Or it can be argued that this is superior to printing since the photograph of a hand-written mezuzah might be said to be a reproduction of it. Since there were no photographs in talmudic times, there are no direct precedents and rabbis must decide the matter by considering the principles behind the laws of writing a mezuzah. One of the principles seems to be that dedicated human effort in *writing* is required since the sources always speak of a *written* mezuzah. It would follow, then, that a photograph of a mezuzah is invalid.

2. May electric light be used for the Ḥanukkah lights? Perhaps the law demands, as in the talmudic sources, a lamp with a wick, or, at least a candle, where there is combustion, but in an electric filament there is no combustion. Most rabbis permit the use of electric lights for Ḥanukkah. Their argument is that the purpose of the Ḥanukkah lights, as we are told in the Talmud, has nothing to do with the combustion of the oil and wick but is in order to celebrate the miracle by means of light. This aim can be achieved by electric light as well. Indeed, from one point of view, electric Ḥanukkah lights are better than oil or candles since these may go out whereas there is little danger of that with electric lights.

place the great scholars of the past. The best-known are *Seder ha-Dorot* ("Order of the Generations") by Jehiel Heilprin (1660–1746) of Lithuania, a remarkable account of the lives of all the Jewish teachers based on an astonishing mastery of talmudic and other sources, so that every detail is covered; and *Shem ha-Gedolim* ("Names of the Great") by Ḥayyim Joseph David Azulai (1724–1806) of Jerusalem, in which a special section is devoted to books by rabbinic authors. Encyclopedias were compiled on the whole of rabbinic literature, such as the pioneering work in many volumes of the Italian scholar and doctor Isaac Lampronti (1679–1756), called *Paḥad Yitzḥak* ("Dread of Isaac"); and the immense work, also in many volumes, of Ḥayyim Hezekiah Medini (1832–1904), Rabbi of Karasubazar in the Crimea, entitled *Sedey Ḥemed* ("Fields of Delight"). Another genre is sermonic material, relied on for inspiration by generations of rabbinic preachers, such as the work of the seventeenth-century Italian rabbi, Azariah Figo, entitled *Binah le-Ittim* ("Understanding the Times," an apt title for a book of sermons); of the sixteenth-century Polish preacher, Ephraim Luntschitz, entitled *Keli Yakar* ("Precious Vessel"); and of the giant among talmudists, Jonathan Eybeschuetz (died 1764) of Altona, Hamburg, and Wandsbek, entitled *Yaarat Devash* ("Forest of Honey").

Intellectualism

Although emotions are not entirely absent from the rabbinic literature—some of these works are not above showing displays of temper

with those who disagree with their findings and, after all, these rabbis were profoundly religious—the note sounded is of the mind. The literature is full of mental associations, brilliant flights of thought, intense scrutiny of texts, deep knowledge of myriads of passages in the sources, and acute reasoning powers. The study of this literature is daunting because the style is generally an amalgam of rabbinic Hebrew and talmudic Aramaic replete with literary allusions which only the expert can decipher. And very little of it has been translated into English; it is, indeed, doubtful whether a translation is possible. But it is all a tribute to Judaism's respect for the things of the mind and its affirmation that study of God's word is the highest religious obligation.

9

Jewish Philosophy

The Need for Jewish Philosophy

While there is the profoundest thought regarding God and humanity in the Bible and Talmud, there is no philosophy, if by philosophy we mean the *systematic* treatment of ideas and the consideration of abstract questions. For instance, Bible and Talmud have much to say about the practice of justice, but not the kind of treatment typical, say, of Plato, in which a definition of justice in the abstract is systematically attempted. The Jews of ancient times were interested in behaving justly, not in trying to pin down justice in abstract definition. Philosophical reasoning came into Jewish life when the need arose to face the challenge of Greek thinking, which was philosophical in its approach. Jews trained in schools influenced by the Greeks found themselves thinking in a systematic way, and once that happened they naturally began to consider Judaism itself in philosophical terms. That is why Jewish philosophy took root only in Greek-speaking communities such as Alexandria 2,000 years ago or in Arabic lands in the Middle Ages, in which Greek thought was known through Arabic translations and where there were many Arabic philosophers, who tried to use philosophy in the understanding of their religion, Islam.

"Philosophical reasoning came into Jewish life when the need was felt to face the challenge of Greek thinking."

Philo

The most notable Jewish philosopher of ancient times was Philo of Alexandria, who died around the year 50 of the present era. Although a devout Jew, Philo had been trained in Greek thinking from his infancy. It is even doubted whether he knew much Hebrew. Hard though it is to imagine, it appears that even the Sefer Torah in Alexandria was written not in Hebrew but in Greek translation—that of the Septuagint, which was produced by Alexandrian Jews. For this reason Philo's work was unknown to Jews for a very long period. He was never referred to in Jewish literature until his ideas were noted by the Italian Jewish historian Azariah de Rossi in the sixteenth century.

The central problem faced by Philo was how to understand the Torah, in which he had complete belief, in the light of Greek thought. The Bible seems at times to speak of God in very simple terms—that He has a hand, or an eye, and can lose His temper—and also to speak of trivial matters, far removed from the sophisticated type of thinking to which Philo was accustomed. Philo's response was twofold. Biblical descriptions of God in human form, Philo insisted, must be taken metaphorically, not literally. If the Bible says that God is angry, it is not saying that God is temperamental or like a human being in any way. It is only a way of saying that certain actions are not in accord with what God desires of humanity, that if people behave badly they are out of tune with God.

As for the apparently trivial matters in Scripture—the stories about Abraham, Isaac, and Jacob, for example—these actually happened according to Philo, but they were recorded in the Torah only to suggest deep ideas. This is Philo's *allegorical* interpretation of Scripture: The Torah has a plain meaning—the events really did happen, and for ordinary folk this plain meaning is the only one possible—but it also has a deeper meaning, telling us truths about human existence for every age. Thus, says Philo, when the Torah tells us that Abraham sent away his maidservant Hagar and remained with his wife Sarah (Genesis 21:8–14) it means that the good person, represented by Abraham, has to "send away," that is, to gain control over, physical desires, represented by Hagar, and heed the voice of reason and conscience, represented by Sarah. This way of interpreting Scripture was adopted by some of the philosophers in the Middle Ages, too, which led the opponents of philosophy to accuse them of denying that the patriarchs were historical figures.

"Philo holds that the Torah has not only a plain meaning but also a deep meaning through which we are told truths about human existence applicable to every age."

How Scholars Differ

This statement on how God's foreknowledge can be reconciled with human free will illustrates how the medieval Jewish thinkers differ.

THE PROBLEM:
Since God knows beforehand how we will conduct ourselves, how can we be free to do otherwise?

ATTEMPTED SOLUTIONS:
1. *Maimonides*: Both are true, but in a way that we cannot hope to grasp, since in talking about God's knowledge we are talking about God Himself, and this is beyond the scope of the human mind to grasp.

2. *Gersonides* (1288–1344): God does not know *everything* beforehand. He knows only that which can be known, and He therefore knows all the possible choices open to us. But the choice we finally make, being in the future, is by definition unknowable, since it has not as yet come into existence.

3. *Crescas* (died around 1412): God does know everything, including how we will choose, and therefore it follows that while we have the appearance of freedom, we are not really free.

4. *Ḥayyim Ibn Attar* (eighteenth century): In His desire to endow us with free will, God voluntarily assumes ignorance of our future choices so that His foreknowledge should not determine our choice. This is not a limit on His knowledge and power, since it is voluntarily assumed by Him.

5. *A Number of Kabbalists*: God is beyond time and sees past, present, and future all at once. It is not correct, therefore, to say that He knows our choices *beforehand*. He knows how we choose at the time we do choose.

Saadiah

Saadiah Gaon (882–942) wrote his philosophical work entitled *Beliefs and Opinions* in Arabic in order to defend Judaism against its attackers. To Saadiah, Judaism is based on reason although it is a revealed religion (that is, not made up by humans but given by God), because everything in it, if rightly understood, is in full accord with reason. He argues that people doubt the truth of Judaism only because they are too lazy to think things through. Saadiah believes that the whole universe was created for the sake of humanity. We alone among creatures in the universe have reasoning powers to enable us to lead good lives, and we have the freedom to choose. According to Saadiah, the mystery of why the righteous suffer and the wicked prosper is solved when we realize that the good are punished for their sins only in this world, but will enjoy eternal happiness in the Hereafter; while the wicked will be doomed in the Hereafter but have to be rewarded in this world for whatever good they have done.

So convinced was Saadiah of the ability of human reasoning to arrive at the truth that he feels obliged to account for the need for revelation. If people can attain the truth by reason, why did God have to give the Torah? Saadiah replies that to discover the truth by our own unaided reason, although possible, would be a long and arduous task, and only for the few philosophers. If there were no revealed Torah the majority of people would always live in error. Consequently, God gave the Torah with its detailed rules and regulations, and it is the task of the philosopher to use reasoning to discover its deep truths.

A fundamental question for all philosophers concerns the nature of Creation.

Judah Halevi

If a philosophical work can ever be called lovable, the adjective can certainly be applied to Judah Halevi's *Kuzari*. Judah Halevi (eleventh to twelfth century) lived in Toledo, Spain at a time when philosophical studies were extremely popular. His great book is in the form of a dialogue between the king of the Khazars (hence the name *Kuzari*) and a Jewish sage. The king has a dream in which he is told repeatedly that his intentions are good, but not his deeds. This leads him to seek out the Jewish sage, after first consulting a philosopher, a Christian, and a Muslim, none of whom satisfy his longings.

Interestingly enough, Judah Halevi has the philosopher tell the king that God is not concerned at all with people's deeds. According to philosophy, God is so far above the universe that it is absurd to think of Him as being concerned with what transpires on earth. As a devout Jew, Halevi cannot accept this position. His Jewish sage explains to the king that Judaism is based on the idea that God does care what people do with their lives. Instead of beginning with God's creation of the world, as do the Christian and the Muslim, the Jewish sage begins his account of Judaism with the Exodus from Egypt, as if to say, there is a caring God who sides with the oppressed against

"Saadiah argues that people doubt the truth of Judaism because they are too lazy to think things through."

Cordoba, Spain. Birthplace of Maimonides.

"Halevi believes that God is not only concerned with Jews but with all people."

their oppressors, as He did at the Exodus, and who, moreover, has a special role for the Jewish people.

As a philosopher himself, Halevi holds fast to the universalistic idea: God is concerned not only with Jews but with all people, but he understands the choice of Israel to be for the benefit of all humanity. Halevi views Israel as "the heart of the nations." When the heart is sick the whole body suffers; when the heart is healthy it affects the whole body. That is why Judah Halevi is the most "Jewish" of the medieval philosophers. He was also a poet and sang about his love for the Holy Land to which, legend has it, he eventually traveled, and lived and died there. In one of his poems, replying to a philosophical Jew who did not see much point in the particular role of either the Jews or the Holy Land, Halevi urges the man not to be enticed by Greek wisdom "which has only flowers but produces no fruit," that is, it may appear very attractive but fails to nourish the soul hungry for the nearness of God.

Maimonides, the greatest of the Jewish philosophers, wrote his *Guide for the Perplexed* at the end of the twelfth century. The work was written in Arabic but was translated into Hebrew during the author's lifetime. The "perplexed" of the title are the philosophically-minded Jews who are puzzled by the apparent conflict between Judaism and philosophical thought. Maimonides accepts a good deal of the ideas of the ancient Greek thinker Aristotle but does not accept blindly all that Aristotle says. For instance, Maimonides agrees with the Greek thinker that God cannot really be described in human terms. He understands the "attributes" of God mentioned in the Bible (that God is wise and one and so forth) in a *negative* sense. In other words, the Bible is not telling us what God *is*—this we can never know—but what He is *not*. Thus, when it is said that God is wise it means that no folly can be attributed to Him and when it is said that God is one, it means that there are not numerous gods, as the pagans suppose. Many of the descriptions of God in the Bible refer to His *acts*, not to His nature. The constant references to God's being "good," for example, apply to His acts which, if performed by a human being, would reflect a good and kindly nature.

But when it comes to the doctrine of creation, Maimonides argues against Aristotle and in favor of the Jewish view. Aristotle holds that the world is eternal. It has always existed together with God. The Bible seems to teach the opposite. In a very interesting aside, Maimonides remarks that if he had been convinced by Aristotle's arguments he would have reinterpreted the Bible so as to conform with the Aristotelian view. Since, however, he is able to refute Aristotle's arguments, he sees no reason not to accept the biblical and Jewish view that God brought the world into being "out of nothing."

Maimonides is influenced by Greek thinking in his views regarding the nature of the good life. For the Greeks, harmony was important in all things and the harmonious life is one in which extremes are avoided. This is the doctrine of the golden mean, that is, that the middle way is the one the good person should choose. Maimonides advocates the golden mean but interprets the ideal in the light of Jewish as well as Greek thinking. For Maimonides, the ideal is for people to avoid extremes. For instance, people should not be miserly but neither should they be extravagant. They should not be gluttons, but neither should they deny themselves all enjoyment. They should not wear costly garments, nor should they go about in rags. Only in two matters should people go to extremes: They should be exceedingly humble, and should never lose their tempers. This attempt of Maimonides' to reconcile Jewish and Greek ethics was severely attacked in the nineteenth century by Samuel David Luzzatto, who argued that Judaism does advocate extremes of kindness and generosity, praising Abraham for being excessively hospitable and sympathetic to the troubles of others.

"For Maimonides the ideal is for people to avoid extremes."

Maimonists and Anti-Maimonists

After Maimonides' death in the year 1204, the Jewish world was divided in fierce debate between the followers of the great sage, the Maimonists, who believed in the value of philosophical studies for Judaism, and the anti-Maimonists, who believed that these studies should be given up entirely as harmful to faith. The latter argued that the philosophers tended to water down everything, to concentrate on abstract ideas rather than on concrete Jewish observance, to substitute the God of philosophers, who is indifferent to humanity, for the living God of Abraham, Isaac, and Jacob. What did the Greeks know of God? asked the opponents of philosophy. How dare we prefer their ideas to the tremendous religious teachings contained in the works of the rabbis? Immature minds were in especial danger if they studied philosophy because they could be dazzled by its brilliance without the confidence gained by experiencing Jewish life. Solomon Ibn Adret, the great Talmudist, issued a ban in the synagogue of Barcelona against studying philosophy before the age of twenty.

The Maimonists replied that it was the unphilosophical who were endangering Judaism. Judaism is a religion full of the ripest wisdom, but in order to appreciate this one must be philosophically

The Legend of the Khazar

It is an historical fact that there once was a Khazar Empire and that the King of the Khazars, in the eighth century, together with his people, really did embrace Judaism. The Khazar people were of Turkish stock. Powerful warriors, they extended their empire from the Black Sea to the Caspian, from the Caucasus to the Volga. There is no record of the Khazar King engaging in discussions with a philosopher, a Christian, a Muslim and a rabbi, before he decided to embrace Judaism. This is a device used by Judah Halevi in his book, *The Kuzari,* for dramatic purposes. The real reason for the conversion is obscure. Eventually some of the converted Khazars did marry into the Jewish people, so that contemporary Jews may well have some Khazar blood in their veins.

educated. The naive student will interpret the Bible in a crude, unsophisticated way, reducing it to a petty level. Once having tasted the fruits of philosophy, they argued, it is impossible to examine Judaism in anything but a philosophical spirit. Even if Joshua himself came down from Heaven to tell us not to study philosophy, they declared, we could not heed him because this is our way and an inseparable part of our being!

This controversy had no conclusion, although with the rise of the Kabbalah many more scholars tended to view philosophical studies with suspicion as a rival to mysticism. To some extent the great debate continues down to the present day. Some Jewish thinkers still frown on philosophical speculation in religion as detrimental to faith, while others consider themselves to be Maimonides' disciples, though obviously, his problems are not the same as those we face.

Moses Mendelssohn

Moses Mendelssohn (1729–1786) was the first modern Jewish philosopher. The medieval philosophers had been concerned with such problems as reconciling Greek and Jewish thought, but by the eighteenth century these issues no longer carried the same weight or interest. Fresh intellectual winds were blowing throughout Europe and many Jewish intellectuals were beginning to see themselves as part of European society. The central philosophical problem in this period was that of Jewish *particularism*. Perhaps for the first time in Jewish history some Jews were questioning why they should continue to be Jewish instead of throwing in their lot entirely with their Christian neighbors. Reason, so widely hailed in the eighteenth century, was not a "Jewish" thing but belonged to all people.

Mendelssohn distinguished between the aspect of Judaism that was, indeed, universal and the aspect that was peculiar to Jews. Judaism, he argued, is not a revealed *religion* but a system of revealed *laws*. Mendelssohn was pointing out that the basic religious truths—the existence of God and the immortality of the soul—are given to all people by God in that all reasonable people can attain them if they try to be honest with themselves and to make sense of life. Judaism, which means God's particular revelation, was intended to impart not religious beliefs but a special way of life by which to express the religious emotions common to everyone.

Mendelssohn's ideas have been much studied. They are pioneering in that they set the pattern for the whole question of how the Jew was to live in Western society while retaining Jewish loyalty. But there are many difficulties in Mendelssohn's position, not least of which is that he sometimes seems to be saying at one and the same time that Judaism is both unique and not unique. A critic of Mendelssohn's once, perhaps unfairly, accused him of holding that Judaism is the only true religion because it is the only religion that does not claim to be the only true religion!

"Perhaps for the first time in Jewish history some Jews were questioning why they should continue to be Jewish."

"Krochmal states that the Jews always have something to live for, since the idea of God can never be exhausted."

Krochmal

The most profound of the modern Jewish philosophers is Nachman Krochmal (1785–1840), the Galician author of *Moreh Nevukhey ha-Zeman* ("The Guide for the Perplexed of Our Time"). The title, chosen by the historian Zunz after Krochmal's death, when the book was published, is obviously based on that of Maimonides' work. except that Krochmal was addressing himself to the perplexed of his day, whose chief problem was, why be Jewish? Krochmal was trying to see Judaism in historical terms, that is to say, to see how it developed in the past so as to be able to forecast how it will develop in the future and how to assist in that development. That is the major difference between Krochmal and the medieval Jewish philosophers. They had little notion of historical development. In the Middle Ages it was generally held that ideas had a kind of life of their own, uninfluenced by the circumstances in which people found themselves. Krochmal noted that Judaism has grown and developed, so that while one must recognize the essential spirit of the Jewish faith, one must also acknowledge that this spirit has expressed itself in different ways throughout Jewish history.

Krochmal's philosophy of Judaism is based on the notion that every people goes through three stages in its history. First, there is the period of growth, when that people is seized by an idea to which it devotes its existence, the pursuit of truth and of beauty by the Greeks, for instance. Second, there is the period of ascendency, when the idea has taken hold of the people and is realized in their national life. But once this happens, the particular idea becomes well-known and acceptable to others, just as all peoples learned from the Greeks, and then there is no further reason for the continued existence of that people as a special people. They have nothing further to live for and the third period sets in, that of decline. But, argues Krochmal, the sole exception to this historical law is the Jewish people. This is because the Jewish people has lived for that single idea—God—which encompasses all others. The Jews always have something to live for since the idea of God can never be exhausted and there is always more for which to strive. Jews, too, have had their ups and downs, periods of decline as well as periods of growth and ascendency, but, after each decline, a new period of growth followed. Krochmal evidently saw his own age as a new period of growth. That is how Krochmal explains the mystery of Jewish survival, and his ideas have been very influential in all subsequent Jewish thought.

Twentieth-Century Jewish Thought

At the center of Jewish thought, in the philosophical sense, in this century is the problem presented for Jewish belief by modern science. This is not merely the question of the apparent contradiction between the biblical account of creation and scientific theories regarding the

Mordecai Kaplan believed that God is not a Being but a Process. According to this viewpoint, when we pray, we speak to the highest within ourselves, urging our better natures to come to the fore.

> "Rabbi Kook went so far as to say that evolution should be warmly accepted as fully in accord with Jewish optimism."

age of the earth. It is not too difficult for modern Jews to do what the earlier Jewish philosophers did, interpret the Bible in such a way as to square its account with the new knowledge. Rabbi A. I. Kook went so far as to say that evolution should be warmly accepted as fully in accord with Jewish optimism, all of creation rising to ever-greater heights and nearer to God. No, the more difficult problem is that science seems to postulate a kind of mechanistic picture, everything following from its cause by necessity. This does not at first glance leave much room for a belief in God, prayer, miracles, and human freedom. If everything belongs in a deterministic scheme where do these beliefs fit it?

Mordecai Kaplan replies that what is called for is a thorough-going reinterpretation of the God idea itself. According to Kaplan, God should not be seen as a Being so much as a Process, that is, the universe is so constituted that goodness will eventually win out. Thus, when we offer prayers to God we are not really asking a Supreme Being to change the course of nature on our behalf, but we are trying rather to bring our needs into conformity with this "winning out" process. In a sense we are praying to the highest within ourselves, urging our better natures to come to the fore.

Against this, thinkers like Abraham Joshua Heschel point out that science is not a philosophy of life but a method for investigating the world. Science has nothing to say about human happiness and fulfillment, about the soul reacting in worship and in wonder to the marvelous world in which we find ourselves, and to the goodness in people that has been implanted by the Creator. We are not really living now in the age of science but in the postscientific age when people are seeking desperately for meaning to their lives, which Judaism can still provide.

A somewhat different way of reacting to the situation is that of the religious existentialists, Martin Buber and Franz Rosenzweig. Existentialists see little point in talking about such huge topics as God and the nature of the universe. What people can and should do, they say, is to meet God, to address Him in prayer and come close to Him in worship without pretending to know how the mystery of life can be solved. Buber has developed his *I-Thou* philosophy in which the individual meets God as one person meets a companion in fellowship, person to person. The medieval thinkers had difficulties with the idea of prayer but tended to speak a good deal about God. Buber, on the contrary, believes that there are many difficulties in speaking *about* God but little difficulty and much spiritual satisfaction in speaking *to* Him.

Martin Buber believed that there are many difficulties in speaking *about* God but little difficulty and much spiritual satisfaction in speaking *to* Him.

Rosenzweig has been the guide for many an assimilated Jew who wished to return to a full Jewish life, as did Rosenzweig himself.

To Rosenzweig, many of us are somewhere near the periphery of the circle, trying to find our way back to the center. We should choose those institutions and observances of Judaism which "speak" to us, which we can immediately appreciate as relevant to our quest for a more significant religious outlook, and the rest will come gradually as we are ready for it.

Franz Rosenzweig felt that many of us are somewhere near the periphery of the circle of Jewish life, trying to find our way back to the center. We should choose those institutions and observances of Judaism which "speak" to us.

Franz Rosenzweig (1886–1929)

Rosenzweig belonged to an assimilated Jewish family having only extremely tenuous connections with the ancestral faith. At one period in his short life Rosenzweig, ignorant at that time of the spiritual riches of Judaism, had considered converting to Christianity, as a cousin of his had done. But as an honest thinker he could not take this final step without first knowing more about the religion he intended to give up. When he began to study Jewish thought, and once he became acquainted with observant Jews and the wholeness and integrity of their lives, he saw that in Judaism he could find all his soul was seeking. Because of his personal quest, Rosenzweig's thought is dominated by this idea of modern Jews finding a way gradually to their spiritual home. Thus he stresses the idea that commitment to the mitzvot has to be won step by step. The mitzvot should be seen less as divine orders laid down beforehand than as means of leading the Jew to God.

It is this idea of a quest for authentic Judaism that has been particularly stressed by a number of Jewish thinkers in our day. We are not as confident as the medieval philosophers were that we can discover all the answers to our religious probings. But we have gained confidence that by trying to live Jewishly we are on the right road and that by embarking on the quest we have to a great extent already found that which we are seeking.

10

Jewish Mysticism

What Is Jewish Mysticism?

Ever since ancient times it has been believed that some Jewish teachers could achieve such a very close relationship to God that they could in a certain sense "see" Him. Needless to say, this vision of God did not mean with the physical eye, but with the eye of the spirit. The attempt to have direct experience of God is what we mean by the term "mysticism." The Talmud, for example, contains a number of accounts regarding what happened when the sages studied "*Maaseh Bereshit*" and "*Maaseh Merkavah.*" *Maaseh Bereshit* ("Account of Creation") refers to the mystical examination of the first chapter of Genesis; *Maaseh Merkavah* ("Account of the Chariot") refers to the mystical examination of the first chapter of the book of Ezekiel, in which is described the prophet's vision of God riding on His chariot. These are legends, but behind them is the fact that such mystical studies were engaged in, though only by a few chosen sages and their disciples.

Again, in the Talmud, there is the famous story of the four sages who entered "the Orchard" (tractate *Hagigah* 14b). From the description this would appear to mean that the four sages sent their souls heavenward so as to gaze on the halls "up there." The story shows that as a result of the intense mystical experience, one of the sages died, one became insane, one became a heretic, and only Rabbi Akiba came away in safety. This is one of the many warnings that too much mysticism is fraught with spiritual and even physical danger. It must also be noted that for a period of about 1,000 years—the first thousand years of the present era—there were people known as the "riders of the chariot" who tried by various techniques, such as fasting and prayer and placing the head between the knees, to "travel" through the heavenly halls "in the depths of their souls," as they expressed it. There is a vast literature produced by these mystics over the ages, known as the *hekhalot* ("Palaces") literature—*hekhal*, "palace," referring to one of the heavenly halls through which the mystic's soul journeys.

Kabbalah

While mystical ideas go back to ancient times in Judaism, it was in the twelfth century that there arose a system of mystical speculation, drawing on these ideas and developing further ones, which is generally identified with Jewish mysticism. This is the Kabbalah. The word *Kabbalah* is derived from a root meaning "to receive," that is, these teachings are considered, by its devotees, a tradition received from master to disciple by word of mouth, reaching back to the earliest times, back to Moses on Sinai, in fact, and, in many versions, even back to Adam, the first person. The notion here is that only a few particularly pious and wise people are worthy of receiving this secret knowledge. At first very little of it was written down, but eventually a huge kabbalistic literature was produced, dealing in the main with the nature of God in His relation to the world. It is impossible to survey this comprehensive literature, but we will refer to the three main stages in the growth of the Kabbalah. The three great names connected with it are the *Zohar*, Moses Cordovero, and Isaac Luria.

The Zohar

The Zohar ("Illumination") has been called "the Bible of the Kabbalists." It is a book (or, better, a collection of books) mainly in the form of a running commentary to the Five Books of Moses, verse by verse. It is written in Aramaic, not in Hebrew, and a very difficult Aramaic at that, but one which imparts to the work a strong mystical flavor by the very unfamiliarity of the high-sounding language, with crashing tones and a heavy rhythm. The verses of Scripture are interpreted in the Zohar as referring to the mysteries about the "upper world," a typical expression for the spiritual universe on high. Almost as mysterious as the book itself is the question of who wrote it. We know for

"The attempt to have direct experience of God is what we mean by the term mysticism."

An examination of the Creation legend in the Torah is basic to Jewish mystical study. (Brueghel, "The Garden of Eden")

certain that the Zohar saw the light of day just a little before the year 1300 in Spain. The man responsible for "revealing" the book was the Spanish kabbalist, Moses de Leon. The book itself speaks of revelations made in the circle of the second-century Palestinian teacher, Rabbi Simeon bar Yoḥai who is said in the Talmud to have lived in a cave as a hermit for thirteen years. Because of this, the kabbalists believe that Rabbi Simeon bar Yoḥai wrote the Zohar, which was hidden until it was miraculously discovered by Naḥmanides in Palestine and then somehow came into the possession of Moses de Leon.

Modern scholarship, however, is virtually unanimous that Moses de Leon was the real author of the book, because it contains many statements that could not possibly have been made as early as the second century. For example, there is an interpretation of the word for synagogue, *esnoga*, in which the word is said to be composed of *esh* and *nogah*, "fire" and "light." The truth is that esnoga is a Portuguese word little different from the word synagogue. Again, a number of sages mentioned in the Zohar lived long after the time of Rabbi Simeon bar Yoḥai. But to hold that Moses de Leon is the real

> *"The Zohar believes that the Torah has a deeper meaning that has to do with the very nature of God."*

Safed

After the expulsion from Spain, the town of Safed in the north of Palestine became the major center for the study and practice of the Kabbalah. The mystical circle in Safed was composed of remarkable people of learning and piety. Documents are extant in which these sages resolved to form a sacred fellowship to encourage one another in their mystical exercises. They took it upon themselves to lead severely ascetic lives, never to drink wine except on the Sabbaths and Festivals, never to be arrogant or fly into a rage, to give alms regularly, to study the Torah unceasingly. They would visit the graves of the saints of old around Safed and pray there for mystical illumination. On Sabbath eve they would dress all in white and go out into the fields to meet the Sabbath Bride. One of their number, Rabbi Solomon Alkabetz, composed the hymn, now sung in synagogues everywhere as Sabbath comes in, *Lekhah Dodi*, "Come, my beloved, to meet the Bride."

From the Zohar

1. "A rose is pink, representing symbolically the admixture of the divine sternness and judgment (red) and the divine mercy and love (white)."

2. "There is a stage of contemplation of the divine at which one can only ask the question: "What is it?" without expecting an answer. There is an even higher stage at which even the question is impermissible."

3. "If the Torah were only a collection of pleasant narratives we could invent even better stories ourselves, and there are better stories in the archives of the kings. But the stories of the Torah are only the garment which covers the laws, the body of the Torah, and the mystical ideas form the very soul of the Torah."

4. "Elijah began to praise God, saying: 'Lord of the universe! Thou art One but not numbered. Thou art Higher than the highest. Thou art the Mystery above all mysteries. No thought can grasp Thee at all.' "

5. "There is no place empty of God."

author of the Zohar does not necessarily mean that he was guilty of fraud in passing off his own writings as those of an ancient teacher. The Zohar may have been what is called a pseudepigraphic work, that is to say, a book attributed to an ancient author purely for dramatic effect, not in order to fool people.

We have seen that the philosophers tended to interpret the Torah allegorically; they accepted the patriarchs as real, historical people, but representing certain philosophical ideas. The Zohar, too, believes that the Torah has a deeper or secret meaning, but that this has to do with the nature of God. To give a well-known example from the Zohar, Abraham, who was so kind and generous, represents God's mercy; Isaac, His sternness; and Jacob, the harmony between mercy and judgment. When the Torah tells us of Abraham's readiness to sacrifice his son Isaac (Genesis 22:1–19), after which Isaac marries and has his son Jacob, the story's deeper meaning is that God's mercy, on high, has to become united with His sternness, resulting in the harmonizing principle by which God governs His universe.

Cordovero

The man who created a kabbalistic system out of the teachings of the Zohar and of the earlier kabbalists, was Rabbi Moses Cordovero (1522–1570), a leading figure among the mystics of Safed (after the expulsion from Spain, Safed in northern Palestine became the center for the study and practice of the Kabbalah). At the age of twenty-seven, Cordovero compiled his gigantic work, entitled *Pardes Rimmonim* ("Orchard of Pomegranates") in which he describes in the fullest detail the doctrines of the Kabbalah, step by step. The work is beautifully written and, unlike the Zohar itself, can be read without too much difficulty by anyone familiar with rabbinic Hebrew.

Cordovero also wrote a short ethical work on the imitation of God, entitled *Tomer Devorah* ("Palm Tree of Deborah"). It can be seen that the kabbalists were fond of flowery titles for their books because they wished to hint at a spiritual universe beyond our own which can be spoken of only in terms of wonder and glory. The *Tomer Devorah* instructs the kabbalist how to behave so that in all actions he will imitate one of God's aspects. For example, when the kabbalist loves all creatures, two things happen. First, God's actions are copied. Second—and here is the distinctive approach of the Kabbalah—those actions move God because, according to the Kabbalah, humanity is at the end of a great chain of being, with God, as it were, at the other end, so that by shaking or moving the chain in a given direction, a person causes the whole chain to sway in that direction. In other words, people have a very important place in this system of thought, for God has given humanity the power to influence Him. Thus human goodness upon earth brings about a flow of divine love and mercy throughout the universe. This is what the Zohar means when it states: "The impulse from above depends on the impulse from below."

Kabbalists speak of a "great chain of being," with humanity at one end and God at the other. One simple act of goodness—a swaying of the chain—can cause a flow of divine love and mercy throughout the universe. Thus, the impulse from above depends on the impulse from below.

"According to Luria, man has the tremendous task of assisting God by carrying out certain sacred acts which affect the 'upper worlds.'"

Luria

The greatest name in the history of the Kabbalah is that of Rabbi Isaac Luria (1534–1572). Luria was brought up in Egypt where, after his marriage at an early age, he spent about six years in solitude, except for the Sabbaths, in a hut on a small island on the river Nile, meditating on the Zohar and the Kabbalah. The result of his meditations was a new kabbalistic system, though it should be said that Luria and his disciples believed that it was not really new but in fact the true interpretation of the Zohar. The kabbalists believed further that Elijah the prophet appeared frequently to Luria to teach him the mysteries of the Kabbalah. Toward the end of his short life (he succumbed to the plague at the age of 38), Luria lived in Safed, where he was an admirer of Cordovero but held that his own teaching was more profound and closer to the "secrets." Luria wrote scarcely anything himself, but his doctrines are to be found in the huge works of his disciple Ḥayyim Vital. The chief of these is known as the *Etz ha-Ḥayyim* ("The Tree of Life").

Luria's system is far too complex to be stated in a paragraph or two. All we can do here is to note that it is an extremely elaborate, detailed picture of the manner in which God's powers form various exceedingly complex combinations (each of which is given its name), so that every human thought and action affects some entity on high. Humanity's tremendous task is to assist God, as it were, by carrying out certain sacred acts that move the worlds on high to carry out their functions. Especially during prayer the Lurianic mystic is expected to have in mind not only the plain meaning of the words but also the

Every human thought and action affects some entity on high.

divine mysteries, represented in each word or even, sometimes, each letter.

According to the Lurianic kabbalists, there are "holy sparks" inherent in all things, and by holy living the kabbalist reclaims these "sparks" from the domain of the *kelippot* ("shells"), the evil, demonic forces which seek to overcome the good and the holy. The whole of human history is seen as a battle between the forces of good and evil. Whenever the Jew reclaims a "holy spark," the greater is the power of the good. Conversely, whenever an evil deed is carried out, a flaw (*pegam*) is produced on high, impeding the flow of the divine love and mercy. Every deed and thought produces either pegam or its opposite, a *tikkun* ("rectification"). When all the "holy sparks" will have been reclaimed for the holy, the tikkun will be complete, evil vanquished, and the Messiah will come to redeem the whole world.

En Sof

The central theme in every version of the Kabbalah is that of emanation. Emanation means that God allows something of Himself to be sent out, to flow, from Himself, and eventually through this mysterious process the finite world is produced. The original emanations, from which all the others emerge in turn, are ten in number and are called the *Ten Sefirot*. These are *God in manifestation*, that is to say, God as He becomes evident in the universe. "God outside of Himself," we might say (though according to the kabbalists nothing can ever be completely separate from His power, or it could not exist at all). Of God as He is in Himself—*En Sof* ("Without Limit") as He is called— nothing at all can be said or even thought. How can a tiny, finite human mind hope to grasp, even in the faintest detail, the true nature of God?

The kabbalists go beyond the philosophers who also had difficulties with the idea that people can know God's nature. According to the kabbalists, we are not permitted to think of En Sof, of God as He is in Himself, at all! Strictly speaking, we are not even permitted to speak of En Sof as En Sof, since this also is forbidden territory. All the references to God in the Bible, say the kabbalists, are to God not as He is in Himself, but as He is revealed or manifested in the Sefirot. This must not be taken to mean, of course, that the kabbalists believe in two gods. They were strict monotheists. They are saying that there are two aspects of God: (1) the hidden, En Sof; and (2) the manifest, the Ten Sefirot. An illustration given by Cordovero to describe the relationship between En Sof and the Ten Sefirot is that of a colorless liquid poured out into ten bottles of different hues. While the liquid is in the bottles it assumes the color of the bottle into which it is poured, but when put back into the original container, it becomes colorless again. Another illustration is the sunlight shining into a room through a stained-glass window. The ray is single and undivided and yet, to the onlooker in the room, it appears multicolored because of the glass through which it shines.

The Kabbalists call God *En Sof,* **meaning "Without Limit." The finite mind cannot grasp the true nature of God.**

"Emanation is the mysterious process through which God allows something of Himself to flow into our own finite world."

The Ten Sefirot

What are these Ten Sefirot? The word *Sefirot* means "Numbers," but in the kabbalistic usage it refers to ten powers or potencies in God—or rather, emanating from Him—from En Sof. Some kabbalists think of these powers as being part of God's essence; others think of them as God's instruments. Cordovero argues that both views are correct: the Sefirot as they emerge in their separateness are only God's instruments, but they also have an inner aspect, their soul, which belongs to the essence of En Sof. Perhaps we can best understand the Sefirot by thinking of them as representing various aspects of God. To the kabbalists, God is not simple and easy to understand. The complex system of the Sefirot is their attempt to grasp, or at least to explore, the great challenge of thinking about God.

The Ten Sefirot and their individual names have been depicted in many a kabbalistic work, sometimes with involved series of lines from one to the other to show their interdependence. Here is a simple pattern of the Sefirot and their names in Hebrew and English:

	KETER (Crown)	
BINAH (Understanding)		ḤOKHMAH (Wisdom)
GEVURAH (Power)		ḤESED (Lovingkindness)
	TIFERET (Beauty)	
HOD (Splendor)		NETZAḤ (Victory)
	YESOD (Foundation)	
	MALKHUT (Sovereignty)	

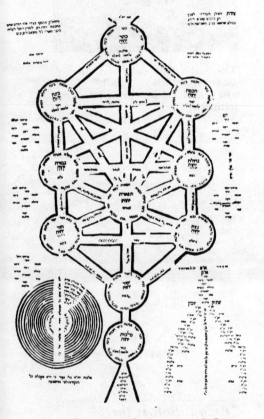

A diagram of the Ten Sefirot, known as the tree of life, the basis of Jewish mystical thought.

Keter is like the crown, above the head; it is the "highest" of the Sefirot representing God's will. *Hokhmah* is the "point," the first flash of an idea, in this instance the idea, as it were, of the whole of creation in the divine Mind. *Binah* is a kind of spelling out of all the details of creation in the divine Mind. *Ḥesed* is God's love for His creatures, which in turn has to be controlled by His *Gevurah*, the force of judgment that prevents so much love flowing that all finite creatures would be dissolved in longing for God and would be loved out of existence, as it were! *Tiferet* is the harmonizing principle, which establishes both love and power in the balance needed for the world to exist. *Netzaḥ* and *Hod* are the two "supports" of the realm of Sefirot, and *Yesod* the means by which divine light flows from the other Sefirot into *Malkhut*, the Source of all God's sovereignty below the realm of Sefirot. The kabbalists believe that all this is reflected in human life on earth. Thus the Sefirot on the left side stress God's sternness, while those on the right side stress His mercy. Many kabbalists always button their coats right on left in the belief that even trivial acts reflect the Sefirot and that placing left on right would bestir, both personally and on high, the power instead of the mercy. Similarly, the kabbalist will not cross his fingers, since the ten fingers represent the Ten Sefirot which, to function properly, must remain separate though in unison.

Thinking about the Kabbalah

It might be asked, how is all this kabbalistic speculation relevant to us today? Unless we believe that all the kabbalistic teachings were divinely communicated to the kabbalists, and few of us do, the most helpful approach is to see the Kabbalah as a richly symbolic way of expressing profound ideas about the relationship between God and man. For instance, the kabbalists were following in the best Jewish traditions when they saw human beings as playing a powerful role in the universe. We may not put it quite as the kabbalists do, that people actually sway the divine providence, but isn't there a point to the idea that human deeds matter to God? Surely there is power in the kabbalistic doctrine that the impulse from above stems from the impulse from below, that whenever a good deed is performed, God responds to our reaching out for Him and a little more spiritual light emerges in the cosmos as a whole.

The kabbalistic distinction between En Sof and the Sefirot helps us see that while we can never hope to understand God's true nature, we can observe His glory in the marvelous universe He has brought into being and in the goodness of which human beings are capable. Furthermore, if symbols have meaning, it is possible to see something like the Sefirot Gevurah at work whenever there is justice, and something like the Sefirah Ḥesed wherever there is love, and something like the Sefirah Tiferet wherever beauty and harmony are manifest.

"There is power in the kabbalistic idea that the impulse from above stems from the impulse in man below."

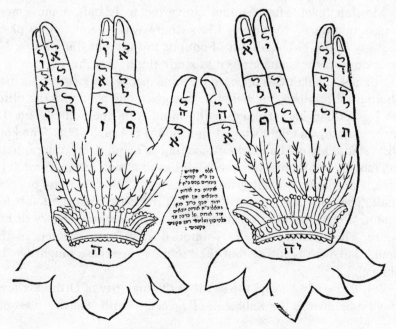

A Kabbalistic diagram published in 1610.

The prophetic vision of Ezekiel has been contemplated by Jewish mystics since ancient times.

The Practical Kabbalah

The Kabbalah is largely a matter of profound, intellectual speculation on the nature of Deity, as we have briefly noted. But since the kabbalists believe that human deeds can influence the worlds on high by reenacting the processes of Sefirot, it follows that certain prescribed acts can bring about results beneficial to the world. The attempt to accomplish this is called practical Kabbalah and is really a kind of magic. Certain divine names, for example, can be written out in the form of amulets in the belief that they will ward off danger and they bring happiness. The opponents of the Kabbalah dub this superstition and magic. The kabbalists themselves tend to draw a distinction between this kind of white magic and black magic, which uses demonic forces to harm people. Nevertheless, practical Kabbalah is somewhat frowned upon even by the kabbalists, not because they doubt the kabbalist's powers but because it is unworthy to use God's sacred names except by a famous saint for the good of humanity, and even then it is considered fraught with danger. You have no doubt heard the legend of the *golem*, the lump of clay into which the Maharal of Prague breathed life by means of divine names. Something like the Frankenstein monster, it was created, however, to protect the Jews of Prague from death and torture.

Opposition to the Kabbalah

Some of the greatest teachers of Judaism were indifferent to the Kabbalah and some were hostile to it. It was perfectly possible for a person to be acknowledged as a great scholar without ever having been introduced into the mysteries of the Kabbalah. After the excesses in the seventeenth century, when Shabbetai Żevi was hailed as the Messiah (even after he had converted to Islam!), a movement strongly influenced by Luria's ideas, there was a tendency to place the study of the Kabbalah out of bounds for any but the mature. No one under forty was encouraged to study the Kabbalah.

The Kabbalah was opposed by some teachers because it seemed to border on *dualism*, the belief in two gods, one good and the other evil. En Sof can be detached in the mind from the Sefirot, and the Sefirot themselves might suggest that God is not really One. The kabbalists staunchly defended their teaching as being strictly monotheistic. They argued that in the Kabbalah lies the "soul of the Torah," its true and authentic meaning, bringing new life into otherwise obscure rituals. The opponents refused to accept the claim that the Kabbalah contains a true tradition reaching back to the earliest history of humanity. They admit that the Talmud does refer to "secrets of the Torah," but who is to say that the "secrets" are those taught by the Kabbalah?

It is probably correct to say that the majority of Orthodox Jews today do believe in the Kabbalah as revealed truth. Yet this does not

"Practical Kabbalah, the attempt to directly influence God, is really a kind of magic."

mean that they will necessarily study the Kabbalah. They might argue, as many do, that there is enough studying of the "revealed" things of the Torah to last a lifetime. In our day, with the revival of interest in mysticism and the occult, there is a renewed interest in the Kabbalah on the part of many non-Orthodox Jews and there is a spate of allegedly kabbalistic works in English. Very little of this material is sound, much of it being what we might term "pop" Kabbalah, on a par with popularizations of yoga, transcendental meditation, Zen, and astrology.

"No one under the age of forty was encouraged to study the Kabbalah."

11
The Sabbath

The Importance of the Sabbath

We read in the Book of Exodus (31:16–17): "Wherefore the children of Israel shall keep the Sabbath, to observe the Sabbath throughout their generations, for a perpetual covenant. It is a sign between Me and the children of Israel forever; for in six days the Lord made heaven and earth, and on the seventh day He ceased from work and rested."

Here we find all the basic ideas associated with the Sabbath: it is part of the covenant God has made with Israel; it is one of the "signs," one of the chief means of Jewish identification; and it is a reminder that God is the Creator of the universe. One of the important Jewish teachers of this century, known as the Ḥafetz Ḥayyim, developed the idea of the "sign" in this way: If there is a family business with a sign outside the door of the shop with the name of the family, then even if the shop is closed for a time the customers know that it will open again for business. Once the sign has been removed, however, people know that the shop has closed for good. No matter how remote a Jew has otherwise become from Jewish life, there is still hope if he keeps the Sabbath, for it indicates that the sign of the family firm has not been pulled down!

The third-century Palestinian teacher, R. Simeon ben Lakish, said (tractate *Betzah* 16a) that on the Sabbath every Jew acquires an additional soul (*neshamah yeterah*). Rashi explains this to mean that somehow on the Sabbath the Jew acquires a greater capacity for enjoyment, and can eat and drink more than usual without harmful aftereffects. But other commentators explain it more poetically to mean that a person's soul, one's spiritual nature, becomes enlarged on the Sabbath. There is time to think, time to study the Torah, time to communicate with the family, time to delight in the religion, all of which brings a person into closer contact with the eternal spiritual values.

God Rested

In the verse from Exodus and in the creation narrative at the beginning of the Book of Genesis, the significance of the Sabbath is said to be derived from the fact that on this day God rested from His labors. As the rabbis point out, "rested" must not be taken too literally, since God required no effort when He brought the world into being. God "rested" means that He ceased from His creative activity. There is a marvelous additional comment that even on the Sabbath itself, God created something! By "resting" He brought into the world the con-

A march on New York's Lower East Side, ca. 1957.

BUSINESS WORRIES? REST ON THE SABBATH & G-D WILL DO THE REST

96

cept of rest and refreshment from work. Rest is a creation and is also creative. No creative person—whether a writer, a painter, a musician, a scientist, or a philosopher—can work adequately all the time. He needs periodic rests to be able to think about the work and to survey it in tranquility.

Philo understands the concept that God created and rested as meaning that on each Sabbath, humanity imitates and repeats the pattern set by the Creator. People are called upon to rest after the week's labors, just as God rested on the seventh day after His creative acts. But on the whole, in the talmudic literature the Sabbath is not seen as an imitation of God. The Torah is not saying, you must rest on the Sabbath in order to be God-like. Rather, it says, acknowledge God as the Creator of the universe by resting from your weekday endeavors, leaving the running of the universe solely to God. In other words, during the rest of the week, God has made humanity His partner in creation (a remarkable rabbinic idea, that God allows people to cooperate with Him in keeping the world in existence and in making it a better place), but on the Sabbath people surrender their powers to God so as to acknowledge Him as the sole Creator.

Also, there is danger we may think too much of our powers, and use them for destructive instead of constructive purposes. All the more reason then, to have a periodic reminder that human powers are God-given and we must render an account to God for how we use them.

God has made humanity His partner in creation during the week (also, lower left and right).

An Example

The illustration has been given of a thoroughfare open to the public for its use but closed occasionally by its owners. They close it to demonstrate that even when the public does use it, they do so not because they have a right to it, but by permission of the owners.

The Shulḥan Arukh rules that young men who enjoy running and doing exercises are permitted to engage in them on Shabbat.

"No matter how remote a Jew has become from Jewish life there is still hope if that Jew keeps the Sabbath."

Seen in this way, the Sabbath is a profound and constant testimony to God's sovereignty over His world. It need not disturb us, therefore, that the Torah speaks of God creating the world in six days when we now know that the world took millions of years to evolve. Most religious people nowadays understand the passage about the six days not as literal, but as a poetic way of stressing what is significant, that it is God and God alone Who brought the world into being.

Work

There are hardly any indications in the Torah itself as to what constitutes the "work" (Hebrew: *melakhah*) that is forbidden on the Sabbath. The talmudic rabbis fill in the gap. They tell us that, according to their reading of the narrative, the people who were erecting the Tabernacle in the wilderness were ordered by Moses to stop all their "work" on the Sabbath (Exodus 35:1–3). Important though the building of the Tabernacle was, the Sabbath was even more important. It follows, declare the Rabbis, that every activity required for the erection of the Tabernacle constitutes "work" and is forbidden on the Sabbath.

On the basis of this, the Rabbis speak of thirty-nine main categories of work—those that were for the purpose of erecting the Tabernacle, and many others resembling them and derived from them. The Mishnah (*Shabbat* 7:2) lists thirty-nine main categories of work: "Sowing, ploughing, reaping, binding sheaves, threshing, winnowing, cleansing crops, grinding, sifting, kneading, baking, shearing wool, washing or beating or dyeing it, spinning, weaving, making two loops, weaving two threads, separating two threads, tying a knot, loosening a knot, sewing two stitches, tearing in order to sew two stitches, hunting a gazelle, slaughtering or flaying or salting it or curing its skin,

The Mishnah lists thirty-nine main categories of work. Among the activities forbidden on the Sabbath are the writing of two letters (near left) and the sewing of two stitches (far left).

scraping it or cutting it up, writing two letters, erasing in order to write two letters, building, pulling down, putting out a fire, lighting a fire, striking with a hammer, and taking anything from one domain into another." This forms the basis of all the involved discussions of forbidden work.

Two things must be noted: First, that these were types of work engaged in at the time the Mishnah was recorded. When, in different kinds of communities, other types of activities were engaged in, it had to be determined whether such activities fell into any of the forbidden categories. For example, with the invention of electricity the question arose as to whether switching on an electric light or driving an automobile came under the category of "lighting fire." (Orthodox Jews, today, hold that these do come under that category and are therefore forbidden on the Sabbath. Many Conservative rabbis permit them on the grounds that they differ in important respects from the mishnaic categories).

The second point is that work as such is not forbidden, but *creative* work. This makes sense if the main aim of the Sabbath is to acknowledge God as the Creator. For example, there is no technical infringement of the law (though it might not exactly fit in with the positive concept of Sabbath rest) if one spends some of the Sabbath day jogging, because it is not creative as are, say, sowing and ploughing. In fact, the *Shulḥan Arukh* rules that young men who enjoy running and doing exercises are permitted to engage in them on the Sabbath. Similarly, there is no objection to playing games on the Sabbath if they are not played for money and no forbidden "work" is involved. To handle money on the Sabbath does not fall under the category of "work" but is forbidden by rabbinic law under the heading of *muktzah*, "that which is set aside," that is, as a weekday pursuit unsuitable for the Sabbath.

"We acknowledge God as the Creator of the universe by resting from our weekday endeavors on the Sabbath."

"It is not work as such that is forbidden but creative work."

Oneg Shabbat

Thus far we have written about what might be termed the negative side of the Sabbath, the prohibition of work. But the prophet declares: "And call the Sabbath a delight" (Isaiah 58:13). On this is based what might be termed the positive concept of *oneg shabbat* ("Sabbath delight"). The Sabbath is to be a day of spiritual and physical delight, of peace and tranquility. In obedience to this concept, the Jewish tradition requires that we eat three meals on the Sabbath, sing the special joyous family songs, *zemirot*; that we wear our best Sabbath clothes on this day; that we spend some time in prayer in the synagogue and in study of the Torah; that we do not converse about weekday activities; that we try to experience, in the words of the Rabbis, a foretaste of Paradise. Furthermore, the home should be adequately illuminated on the Sabbath, light being both a symbol of the Sabbath delight and conducive to a pleasant atmosphere. It was only during the Middle Ages that it was suggested that in addition to the ordinary illumination, at least two special Sabbath candles should be lit before the Sabbath arrives.

On the Sabbath there should be no anxieties or cares, if they can possibly be avoided. That is why the weekday prayers for success of various kinds are not recited on the Sabbath: they call attention to our needs. Very interesting, however, is the ruling that, although it is forbidden to weep on the Sabbath, if weeping affords relief from a heavy emotional burden, the weeping itself constitutes oneg shabbat and is permitted. There is the kindred concept of "honoring the Sabbath." Some of the Rabbis, even though they had servants, would themselves make some of the preparations for the Sabbath, such as putting the finishing touches to the delicacies to be eaten on the day. Others would save a choice dish or food especially for the Sabbath. Students of the very difficult halakhic literature would turn to easier and lighter reading on the Sabbath. In modern times, many people meet together for an oneg shabbat of song and discussion.

Kiddush

Judaism attaches a good deal of importance to the family and to the family's worshiping together in the home. It is the custom before the Sabbath meal on Friday evening for parents to bless their children, saying to a son: "God make thee as Ephraim and Manasseh" (the two sons of Joseph, see Genesis 48:20) and to a daughter: "God make thee as Sarah, Rebekah, Rachel, and Leah." In this way, the family bond is strengthened; children appreciate all that their parents mean to them and parents give thanks for the gift of children; and the present generation of Jews is linked with the former generations, reaching back to the heroes and heroines of the Bible. In many homes, *Shalom Aleichem*, a song greeting the angels, is sung (this is based on the lovely idea that when the Sabbath is observed, the very angels of Heaven abide in the home). The husband then recites the verses from the

"The Jewish tradition requires that we eat three meals on the Sabbath, attended by special, joyous family songs."

"The Sabbath is holy whether or not we acknowledge it as such."

On the Sabbath one should put aside anxieties and cares.

Book of Proverbs (31:10–31) in praise of his wife: "A woman of valour, who can find . . ."

Then the *Kiddush* is recited. The word Kiddush means "sanctification" and refers to the benediction in which Sabbath is declared holy. The idea here is that although the Sabbath is holy whether or not we acknowledge it as such, yet there is much point in our declaration that the day is holy for us, that we are ready joyfully to keep the Sabbath. The Kiddush is recited over a cup of wine. Judaism does not encourage drunkenness but it recognizes that wine can be festive if taken in moderation. That is why on every joyous occasion, such as a wedding, when benedictions are recited, the blessing over wine is said before the others. Two loaves of white bread (*ḥallot*) over which the blessing for bread, the Grace before Meals, is recited, are on the table. The two loaves are said to be a reminder of the manna in the wilderness which did not fall on the Sabbath, but which fell from Heaven in a double portion the day before the Sabbath (Exodus 16:4–36). The two loaves are covered with a cloth, just as the manna was covered with dew. Here again is a link with the Jewish past, as well as the lesson that God provides, and that He can provide for our needs without our working on the Sabbath.

Sabbath Quotes

"The Sabbath sweetens the world."
—Cordovero

"When a person praises God for creating the world and resting from creating on the Sabbath, that person becomes a partner with God in the work of creation."
—The Talmud

"If Israel would keep two Sabbaths as they should be kept, the redemption would come at once."
—The Talmud

"The perfect Sabbath rest is the attuning of the heart to the comprehension of God."
—Maimonides

During the Havdalah service, all five senses are exercised.

The Kiddush itself begins with the verses from the Creation narrative (Genesis 1:31–2:3) telling how God rested on the Sabbath and how He blessed and sanctified this day. The first letters of the first four words of this section are *yod, hey, vav, hey,* which form the letters of the Tetragrammaton, the special four-letter symbol for God. It is followed by the benediction thanking God for giving us the Sabbath "in love and favor." In this benediction, too, the Sabbath is said to be both "a memorial of the creation" and "in remembrance of the departure from Egypt." Thus, on the Sabbath we are reminded both of God as the Creator of the universe and as the Redeemer of our people from Egyptian bondage (slaves toiling under the lash of the Egyptian taskmasters were unable to rest on any day of the week).

Havdalah

One of Judaism's most beautiful ceremonies is the *Havdalah* ("division"), marking the distinction between the Sabbath and the weekdays. It is important to appreciate that for Judaism the ordinary days of the week, in which we earn our living, also have their great value. Work, too, is a precious gift from God. But the Sabbath has a special distinction, so that as the Sabbath departs we recite the Havdalah. In addition to the special Havdalah benediction—in which God is praised for distinguishing between the sacred and the secular, light and darkness, Israel and the other nations, the seventh day and the other six days—two special benedictions are recited, one over sweet-smelling spices and one over a lighted candle.

The blessing over the spices is a symbol that the new week should be fragrant in deeds. There is also the idea, referred to earlier, that on the Sabbath the Jew has an additional soul that departs when the Sabbath is over. To compensate for its departure, the spices are inhaled, refreshing the soul. Of all the physical senses the sense of smell is said to be the nearest to the soul because it is the most refined and the least tangible. The blessing over the candle's flame is to thank God for the gift of fire. Strictly speaking, we should thank God for this all the time, but we do so at the beginning of the new week and immediately after the Sabbath, during which fires have not been lit. A Greek legend tells of Prometheus, who was condemned by the pagan gods because he had taught people the art of making fire. The Jewish legend, on the contrary, tells how Adam, seeing that the sun had gone down on the first day of his life, was terribly disturbed until God taught him how to light a fire that would illumine his darkness and warm him in the cold of night.

Another interesting idea has been read into the Havdalah ceremony. In this ceremony all five senses are brought into play: the sense of sight on seeing the light; the sense of smell on inhaling the spices; the sense of taste in drinking the wine; the sense of hearing in hearing the benedictions; and the sense of touch when, as is the custom, a person extends his fingers towards the light. Thus, we acknowledge our indebtedness to God for the life of the senses and resolve to use them to good purpose.

Sabbath vs. Sukkah

A Ḥasidic master once declared that the mitzvah of the sukkah is in one sense superior to all other mitzvot. "When I perform any other mitzvah the mitzvah is, as it were, outside me. But when I sit in the sukkah I have the mitzvah all around me and am embraced by it." Another Ḥasidic master declared that the Sabbath is superior even to the sukkah. "On Sukkot I am embraced by the mitzvah only when I am in the sukkah. But on the Sabbath I am embraced by the mitzvah wherever I am, wherever I go, and all through the day."

Rabbi Simeon ben Lakish said: "On the eve of the Sabbath, God gives us an extra soul and He takes it away from us when the Sabbath is over."
—The Talmud

Sabbath Table Hymn

Rest and rejoicing and light for the Jews!
Sabbath day, Sabbath, O day of delights!
All those who keep it so proudly declare
The world was created in six days and nights.

Sabbath Dishes

The Roman Emperor asked Rabbi Joshua: "Why is it that the Sabbath dishes are so tasty?" Rabbi Joshua replied: "We have a certain spice called *Sabbath*." The Emperor asked Rabbi Joshua to give him some of that spice for use in the kitchens of his palace. But Rabbi Joshua said it had an effect only for those who keep the Sabbath.
—The Talmud

In welcoming the Sabbath, we open ourselves to peace and tranquility, quietude and safety.

The Gift That is the Sabbath

In Jewish thought, the Sabbath is held to be the supreme example of how the spiritual side of things can be assisted by the physical. Judah Halevi states that God delights more in our enjoyment of physical pleasures in a spirit of devotion on the Sabbath than in fasting and self-torment for God's sake. The medieval thinker and preacher Isaac Arama taught that the Sabbath represents the three basic concepts of Judaism: that God created the world; that God revealed the Torah (because the Torah is studied on the Sabbath); and that the good person is rewarded with eternal spiritual bliss (because the Sabbath is a foretaste of Paradise). Nowhere is the ideal of Sabbath observance stated so comprehensively and powerfully in a short paragraph as in the Sabbath afternoon prayer. Here the Sabbath is described as: "a rest granted in generous love, a true and faithful rest, a rest in peace and tranquility, in quietude and safety, a perfect rest wherein Thou delightest. Let Thy children perceive and know that this their rest is from Thee, and by their rest may they hallow Thy name."

The Festivals

All the festivals of the Jewish year celebrate some great event in the Jewish past. Originally, it would seem, most of these festivals were connected with the harvest in one way or another and there are many traces of this in the Bible. All ancient peoples had their seasonal festivities when they prayed for good crops and a rich yield of corn and cattle. In Judaism, however, each of the festivals was eventually also connected with a particular historical event, the implication being that God protects His people in the present as He protected them in the past. The Jewish mystics say that on each festival the light that shone at the event it commemorates shines again to illumine the soul. This is a way of saying that, for example, when we celebrate Passover and recall God's redemption of our ancestors from Egyptian bondage, we once again take to heart the message of freedom. In the Bible, the festivals are occasions for rejoicing, *simḥah*, "joy." It is interesting that we do not find the term simḥah used of the Sabbath, but only the term *oneg*, "delight." It appears that on the Sabbath the rejoicing is quieter and more spiritual, whereas on the festival there is more mirth and merrymaking. Each festival sounds its own individual note. As Franz Rosenzweig puts it, the Jewish calendar is like a golden ring set with the precious jewels that are the festivals, with no two alike.

Passover

Passover (*Pesaḥ*) celebrates the deliverance from Egypt, God's bringing out the people of Israel from bondage, where they were miserable slaves, to make them into a holy people. No leavened bread (*ḥametz*) is eaten during the eight days of the festival (seven days in Israel), but unleavened bread (*matzah*) is eaten on the first night, at the Seder. The reason given in the Passover Haggadah is: "Because there was no time for the dough of our fathers to become leavened before the supreme King of Kings, the Holy One, blessed be He, revealed Himself unto them and redeemed them, as it is said: 'And they baked unleavened cakes of the dough which they brought forth out of Egypt, for it was not leavened, because they were thrust out of Egypt, and could not tarry, neither had they prepared for themselves any victual'" (Exodus 12:39).

The difficulty with this explanation is that the people were told

"The Jewish mystics say that on each festival the light which shone at the event it commemorates shines once again to illumine the soul."

A thirteenth-century Jewish calendar.

105

Extra Festival Day

Jews outside Israel keep an extra day of the festivals (two days at the beginning and end of Passover and Sukkot and two days of Shavuot). In ancient times, *Rosh Ḥodesh* ("new moon," the beginning of the month, from which the festivals in that month were counted) might fall on the thirtieth day or the thirty-first day of the previous month, depending on when the new moon was actually observed. Before a fixed calendar was arrived at by calculation, Rosh Ḥodesh was declared by the authorities only when witnesses had actually *seen* the new moon. Consequently, it was necessary to inform people when Rosh Ḥodesh had been declared in Jerusalem, the seat of the High Court, so that they would know on which day to celebrate the festival.

For the people in the land of Israel there was no problem, since none of them lived very far from Jerusalem and they could be informed in time. The communities of the Diaspora, however, lived so far away that it was not possible to inform them in time which day had been declared Rosh Ḥodesh. In order to make sure, the Diaspora communities always kept the holidays two days. Once the calendar had been fixed, there was no longer any doubt. Everyone now knew the exact date of the festivals. Nevertheless, the Palestinian authorities, we are told by the Talmud, urged the Diaspora authorities to hold fast to the custom of their ancestors by keeping the two days, and this has been the practice ever since. Reform congregations do not observe the second day, and more recently a number of Conservative congregations have abolished it in order to keep pace with the custom in Israel. The Orthodox argument is that a practice hallowed by 2,000 years of observance should be maintained. The festival of Rosh Hashanah, which falls on Rosh Ḥodesh *Tishri* itself, is observed for two days even in Israel.

The prophet Elijah is a guest at every Passover Seder table. Special wine cups, like this nineteenth-century kiddush cup, possibly from Bohemia, await the honored visitor.

to eat matzot while they were still in Egypt (see Exodus 12:8). When the famous medieval scholar and traveler, Abraham Ibn Ezra, was in England he noticed that the prisoners in the dungeons were given unleavened bread, not unlike matzah, to eat, because it was cheap and coarse. This led him to surmise that when the Israelites were prisoners in Egypt, they were given matzah to eat and then when they were being freed they still had to eat matzah because the dough was baked hurriedly. Consequently, matzah is the symbol both of freedom and of slavery. We rejoice on Passover that we are no longer slaves, while we rejoice in the freedom that is now ours. As Professor Isaiah Berlin once suggested in a different connection, there are two kinds of freedom—freedom *from* and freedom *to*—the first is the mere removal of coercion, the second is our choice to do as we wish. Of course, Judaism teaches that what we really wish is to follow God's commandments.

The details of the Seder and the reading of the Haggadah are well-known. What should be noted is the astonishing way in which great concepts are expressed, not by spectacular staging (after all, one could have had a huge dramatic presentation of the Exodus) but by small things such as the eating of the bitter herbs, the telling of the simple stories, the drinking of the four cups of wine, the opening of the door to show that we are unafraid. The truth is that little things can make the deepest impression because the big things are so external, so noisy, and so obvious that they remain surface experiences.

Shavuot

The "Feast of Weeks" is so called because it comes after seven weeks have been counted from the second day of Passover. This two-day festival (one day in Israel) was originally solely a harvest festival; in rabbinic times it was interpreted as the holiday commemorating the greatest event in Jewish history, the giving of the Torah. There are no special Shavuot ceremonies and rituals as there are on the other festivals. We can express many Jewish ideas symbolically but it is impossible to have a particular symbol for the Torah as a whole. Strictly speaking, we should not need a reminder of the Torah at special times, but should be aware of it all the time. Nevertheless, in the Middle Ages it became customary to eat dairy dishes on Shavuot. One reason given is that the Torah can be compared to milk, which nourishes and which cannot be kept in golden vessels because it will become sour. The person who is like a "golden vessel," proud and puffed-up with self-importance, will never be able to know very much about Judaism. It is a recent custom to decorate the synagogue on Shavuot with plants and flowers, a symbol of the fragrance and life-giving properties of the Torah. The Midrash states that although Sinai is a barren mountain, when the Torah was given it brought forth every kind of aromatic plant. In the sixteenth century, the custom arose of spending the entire night of Shavuot studying the Torah, and many communities still do this.

"We rejoice on Passover that we are no longer slaves, and we rejoice at the same time in the positive freedom that is now ours."

A Midrash

"Although Israel voluntarily accepted the Torah when it was offered to them, saying, 'We will do and we will obey,' God still suspended the mountain over them and threatened to bury them there and then unless they accepted the Torah. Why did God compel them to accept what they had already assumed willingly? It was because of the law in the Torah that if a man forces a woman to have relations with him, he must marry her and never send her away. God forced Israel to accept His Torah because He wished so to be bound to them that He could never send them away from Him."

A Midrash

According to the Midrash the two tablets of stone on which the Ten Commandments were written were six handbreadths in length. Moses held two of these in his hand, God held the two at the opposite end and there were two handbreadths in the middle. When it is said that there was a glorious shine on Moses' face, it was from these two handbreadths in the middle. This has been interpreted as follows: The two handbreadths grasped by God represent that part of the Torah that is so near to Him and so distant from human life in this world that none can hope to apprehend it. The two handbreadths grasped firmly by Moses represent those aspects of the Torah that are for all. Every student who applies himself can learn to know some of the Torah. The two handbreadths in the middle represent those aspects of the Torah that are neither too profound for anyone to understand nor so accessible that anyone can grasp them. To comprehend them requires great effort and dedication, but those who make the effort are rewarded by glorious illumination.

Sukkot

The two central ceremonies performed on the eight days of Sukkot (seven days in Israel) are eating and drinking in the *sukkah*, and lifting up the four species of plant, the *lulav* (palm branch), the *etrog* (citron), the myrtle, and the willow. The command to "dwell in booths" is stated in the Book of Leviticus (23:42–43), "Ye shall dwell in booths *(sukkot)* seven days; all that are home-born in Israel shall dwell in booths; that your generations may know that I made the children of Israel to dwell in booths, when I brought them out of the land of Egypt: I am the Lord your God." "Booths" *(sukkot)*, after which the festival is named, are simple, open structures. According to tradition, they must have at least three walls and must be covered with things that grow in the soil. The sukkah should be decorated with hangings, pictures, and the like, on the principle of adorning the mitzvot. The reason for the sukkah is stated in the above verse: Israel dwelt in similar booths during their forty years in the wilderness until they reached the Promised Land. Another idea that has been read into the observance of the sukkah is that leaving one's comfortable home for the frail dwelling is a reminder of how transient material things are—they do not last forever, nor do we live forever here on earth. True happiness (Sukkot is described as "the time of our rejoicing") is found in the eternal values symbolized by the sukkah open to the skies of Heaven.

Maimonides understands the taking of the four plants simply as a means of thanking God for His bounty, for they represent the fruitfulness of the Holy Land. But since the time of the Midrash, various colorful interpretations have been given to the rite. One is that the lulav has fruit (the dates) but no fragrance; the etrog has both taste and fragrance; the willow has neither taste nor fragrance; and the myrtle has fragrance but no taste. "Fragrance" symbolizes the sweet

"One idea read into the observance of the sukkah is that leaving one's home to be in the frail dwelling reminds us of how transient material things are."

"You shall dwell in booths *(sukkot)* seven days." (Lev. 23:42)

On Rosh Hashanah Jews symbolically cleanse their souls by walking to a nearby river or stream, emptying their pockets of crumbs, and praying for Divine forgiveness.

scent of good deeds, while "taste" represents the good sense of the Torah. Some people have both learning and good deeds; others have only one; and others have none. All four must be accepted because it takes all sorts to make a world and all Israel, good or bad or mediocre, must be united. Another interpretation is that the lulav is like a human backbone, the etrog is like the heart (heart-shaped), the willow is shaped like a mouth, and the myrtle like an eye. The good Jew must have backbone, unbending in loyalty to Judaism; a good eye, looking upon others with kindness and generosity; a good mouth, speaking well of others and engaging in prayer and study; and above all, a good heart.

The last two days of this festival are *Shemini Atzeret* ("Eighth Day of Assembly"), during which prayers for rain are recited; and *Simḥat Torah* ("Rejoicing of the Torah"), when the annual cycle of Torah reading is completed and begins over again. In Israel these two holidays are both celebrated on the eighth day.

Rosh Hashanah

Rosh Hashanah ("Beginning of the Year") is the two-day Jewish New Year festival. Traditionally, although it is a *Yom Tov*, a festival, it is a solemn occasion because on it we make our New Year resolutions to lead better lives in the year ahead. From Rosh Hashanah to Yom Kippur there are ten days inclusive, known as the Ten Days of Penitence. It is typical of Judaism that the first ten days of the New Year should be spent especially in examining our lives and seeing what we have made of them, resolving to undo, so far as we can, any harm we have done, and joyfully accepting new responsibilities as well as a renewal of old ones.

"The first ten days of the New Year are spent in examining our lives and seeing what we have made of them."

The Dreidel

Since the late Middle Ages it has been customary for children on Ḥanukkah to play with a *dreidel* (in modern Hebrew, *sevivon*). This is a spinning-top with a different letter on each of its four sides. The letters are: *nun, gimmel, hay, shin,* the initial letters of *nes gadol hayah sham* ("a great miracle was performed there"). In Yiddish these letters stand for various moves in the game. For example, if the top stops spinning on the letter *nun,* it means *nem* ("take" —take the kitty) or if it stops at *gimmel* it means *gibt* ("give"—put some more into the kitty). It is thus a game of chance played for money or for some other valuables and as such was barely tolerated by the more staid Rabbis. The more mystically-minded read all kinds of mystical ideas into the dreidel. For instance, the spinning of the top suggests that the fortunes of the Jewish people revolve and Jews have had to seek a home in many different places. But the top is directed by the spinner, just as the fortunes of man are directed by God, who is in full control of His universe. If the mystics had spoken English, they might have said: "If man has faith in God, he will come out on 'top' "!

The central rite of Rosh Hashanah is the sounding of the shofar. Maimonides' famous explanation of this rite is that the shofar has a piercing sound calculated to wake people up. Its notes call to us: "Wake up from your sleep! Life is serious and yet supremely worthwhile, so do not waste your life in nonsensical pursuits, but make the most of it, as befits man created in God's image." Various other meanings have been read into the rite, among them the remarkable idea that trumpets are sounded when a king is crowned and Rosh Hashanah is the coronation day of the King of Kings. Still another interpretation relates to the four notes sounded, the *tekiah, shevarim, teruah, tekiah.* Now the first and last are long drawn-out tones, while the shevarim consists of three broken notes and the teruah nine very short blasts; these last two are said to be rather like weeping. Thus on Rosh Hashanah we begin with confidence in God, represented by the unbroken note of tekiah. Then we dwell in weeping on the lack of wholeness and integrity in life represented by the shevarim and teruah. But in the end we regain confidence and become firm in our resolve to do better in the year ahead, and this new resolve is represented by the final tekiah.

Yom Kippur

"Yom Kippur is a day of confession of sin, but it is also a day of pardon of sin and hence a day of joy."

For the majority of Jews, Yom Kippur is the most sacred day in the Jewish year. It might seem odd to call a day of fasting a "festival" but in the Jewish tradition it is not only a day of confession of sin, but also a day of pardon and hence a time of joy. In a way, Yom Kippur is a happy day of reconciliation between God and people, and people and their fellows. The custom is to drape the ark in white and many of the worshipers wear white, the symbol of purity.

Why do we fast on Yom Kippur? First, to express our remorse at having sinned. Judaism does not believe in self-denial, but it is right and proper that on this day of atonement we should express our sorrow for having sinned, not only by confessing our sins but through a concrete act. Second, in a day during which no food or drink passes our lips and which is spent in prayer, we have a better sense of the spiritual, which is why the Rabbis say that on this day Israel is like the angels on high. Third, by going hungry and thirsty on one day, we learn how bitter hunger is and will try to banish hunger and poverty. We are moved by our minor discomfort on this day to do something about, and to feel sympathy for, the suffering that millions of people have to endure all their lives.

Ḥanukkah

Ḥanukkah is a minor festival (although it has become a very popular one) which celebrates the victory of the Macabees in the second century of the common era over Antiochus's attempt to destroy the Jewish religion. According to the Talmud, the Ḥanukkah candles are kindled as a reminder of the miracle of the one-day supply of oil in the menorah that burned for eight nights until fresh oil could be obtained. Many Jews still believe that a miracle did occur in those far-off days, with God intervening directly to change the course of nature. Other Jews prefer to understand the miracle of the oil as a symbol of the light of the Torah, which has continued to shine unabated throughout Israel's history and is the greatest miracle of all.

We are told in the Talmud that the School of Shammai held that on the first night, eight lights should be kindled, on the second night seven, and so on until only one is kindled on the eighth night. Evidently, this School held that it is better to give the fullest expression to our appreciation of the miracle on the first night, when its power first hits us, and then to become progressively less excited as we become accustomed to it. But the School of Hillel ruled—and this is the opinion today—that one has to work up to appreciation of the miracle. Therefore, on the first night one candle is kindled and one is added each night until on the eighth night the whole candelabra is ablaze with light.

Purim

Purim is another minor festival, celebrating the events related in the Book of Esther when the Jewish people were saved from Haman's plot to destroy them all. The Book of Esther is read in the synagogue and, though one of five Megillot ("scrolls"), is often called the Megillah, "the scroll." Objections have been raised occasionally, especially in modern times among some Jews, to the celebration of Purim, because there are doubts whether these events really did happen and because it is vindictive to celebrate the downfall of our enemies.

But many have defended the historicity of the narrative, and others argue that in any event there have been innumerable Hamans in Jewish history, and it is Jewish deliverance throughout the ages

"The miracle of the oil is a symbol of the light of the Torah."

Ḥanukkah is often known as the Festival of Lights.

A Scroll of Esther, Russia, ca. 1830.

that is being celebrated. By a pun on the words Purim and Yom Kippurim, the Jewish mystics go so far as to compare Purim with Yom Kippur because on both the fate and destiny of Israel is changed from bad to good. Actually, it is remarkable how little malice is shown to Israel's enemies in the Megillah. Haman is really a figure of fun. All the stress is placed on God's miraculous sparing of His people. Something of this is expressed in the curious rabbinic injunction to drink

Purim Customs

Purim is the one festival when pious Jews "let their hair down." In many communities it was the practice to appoint a special Purim Rav, a "rabbi" for the day, whose job was to entertain his "congregation" by frivolously manipulating religious texts. For instance, one piece of "Purim Torah" asks: "What is Noah doing in the Megillah?" (The Hebrew word *noaḥ*, meaning "at ease," can be read as Noah). The answer: "Haman needed a gallows fifty cubits high, as we are told in the Megillah, upon which to hang Mordecai. Now Noah's ark was fifty cubits wide so Haman asked Noah to give him a plank of the ark. Naturally Noah would not give the plank to Haman. So Haman pulled at one end, Noah at the other, until finally Haman pulled Noah into the Megillah." In many communities, too, people dressed up in costumes and held Purim carnivals. The Purim *gregger*, a kind of rattle, was (and in many places still is) rattled in the synagogue by the children in obedience to the command to blot out the name of Amalek, from whom Haman was descended. Some Rabbis were unhappy about these forms of merriment, but they were too deeply rooted in custom to be eradicated. Some see a psychological value to Purim frivolity: relief, on one day of the year, from worry and care.

so heavily on Purim that we do not know whether we are blessing Mordecai or cursing Haman! Jewry has generally preferred to concentrate on blessing its benefactors rather than on cursing the anti-Semites. It has also been argued that it is not unhealthy on one day in the year to rid ourselves of our aggressive instincts in a harmless way.

Purim traditionally is a day of friendship, when presents are sent from house to house. It would not be a Jewish festival if it did not demand that we remember the poor and needy. Following the example in the Book of Esther, gifts of food and drink (*seloah manot*, "sending presents") are sent to friends and alms distributed to the poor (*mattanot la-evyonim*, "gifts to the poor"). This is a typically Jewish approach. Jewish joy is always held to be incomplete if it is self-centered. One has to share with others and to think especially of those in need. As the Book of Esther puts it: "the days wherein the Jews had rest from their enemies, and the month which was turned unto them from sorrow to gladness, and from mourning into a good day; that they should make them days of feasting and gladness, and of sending portions one to another, and gifts to the poor" (Esther 9:22).

"There have been innumerable Hamans in Jewish history, and it is Jewish deliverance throughout the ages that is being celebrated."

Work on the Festivals

On the basis of the verse, "no manner of work shall be done in them, save that which every man must eat, that only may be done by you" (Exodus 12:16), the Rabbis state that on Rosh Hashanah, Passover, Shavuot, and Sukkot (that is, on the festive days, not on Ḥol ha-Mo'ed, the intermediate days of Passover and Sukkot) the only work that may be done is work for our benefit on the festival itself. (The words "that which every man must eat" are interpreted liberally to include not only cooking and baking but lighting a fire for warmth and other activities that cater to the needs of the festival. For instance, smoking is permitted.) These festivals are not like the Sabbath, on which there has to be a complete cessation from work. Yom Kippur is like the Sabbath in this respect, but all manner of work may be done on the minor festivals of Ḥanukkah and Purim.

Jews from Bukhara, Russia, celebrating Passover in Israel.

The Days of Mourning

There are days of mourning in the Jewish calendar that commemorate calamities in Jewish history. The most important of the fast days is the Ninth of Av, *Tish'ah B'Av*, the day on which both the first and second Temples were destroyed. On this day, Jews mourn the tragedies of the past and the near-present. Most Jews today have in mind the Nazi Holocaust, during which six million Jews were killed. The three weeks from the seventeenth of *Tammuz* to the ninth of *Av* are traditionally days of mourning, though not of fasting. Weddings, for instance, do not take place during this period. On the ninth of Av the Book of Lamentations is read in the synagogue. Even now that the State of Israel has been established, most religious Jews still see a

"Judaism has something optimistic to say even about the Ninth of Av."

point in observing Tish'ah B'Av, though perhaps not with the same intensity as previously.

It is good that we mourn for the terrible happenings of the past because, by reminding ourselves and the world of what evil people can do to the innocent, we help build a world in which such dreadful deeds do not occur. And Judaism has something optimistic to say even about the ninth of Av. It is on this day, according to an ancient tradition, that the Messiah will be born and this day, despite the suffering and tragedy it commemorates, is called a "festival" because Judaism believes that out of the darkness light will eventually come.

13
The Synagogue

How It All Began

When did synagogues first emerge in Jewish life? We cannot know for certain but some scholars hold that there were meeting places for prayer and for study as early as the Babylonian exile 2,500 years ago. On the other hand, there are only a few definite references to a synagogue in the literature from the period of the second Temple. It is probable that synagogues became prominent after the destruction of the second Temple in the year 70, as the synagogue took the place of the Temple that was no more.

Professor Solomon Zeitlin has made the interesting conjecture that the *Bet ha-Knesset* (literally "House of Assembly," which is also the meaning of our word synagogue, from the Greek) was originally a place like the town hall in which the elected members of the community conducted their affairs. (Do not forget that the modern Israeli parliament is called the Knesset.) It is suggested that these meetings opened and perhaps closed with prayers and that from this evolved the institution of the synagogue. On the biblical evidence it seems highly probable that public prayer came much later than private prayers—the vast majority of the prayers in the Bible are those offered by individuals in private. Other names for the synagogue are *Bet ha-Tefillah*, "House of Prayer," and *Bet ha-Midrash*, "House of Study."

Praying Together

The talmudic rabbis ruled that some of the most sacred prayers and hymns, such as the *Kaddish*, the *Kedushah* ("Holy, holy, holy is the Lord of Hosts") and the repetition of the *Amidah*, as well as the reading of the Torah from the scroll with the benedictions, require a *minyan* ("number," "quorum") of ten adult males (Conservative rabbis have recently extended this to include women). The Rabbis considered community prayer so important that they remark: "A man's prayers are heard by God only when he prays as part of a congregation." In another talmudic passage it is said that when ten are present the *Shekhinah*, the Divine Presence, does not wait for them to arrive, but is there beforehand to welcome them to the synagogue. This helps us to understand the insistence that prayer be recited in the midst of a congregation. We are all influenced by our surroundings and by other human beings. When we pray alone, the prayer is still of great value but there is a special spirit and concentration when we are part of a congregation who reinforce one another.

There is a special spirit and concentration when we pray as a congregation. The individual prays *for* the community—*with* the community. (The Great Synagogue, Tel Aviv.)

Ancient Synagogues

As a result of archaeological digs, the ruins of ancient synagogues have been uncovered in many places in the Middle East. It is fascinating to compare them with later synagogues, including our own. The shape of practically all these ancient synagogues was rectangular, with the entrance facing Jerusalem, which, if the practice of facing Jerusalem in prayer was in vogue then, must have meant that the worshipers faced the entrance. More startling is the fact that there is no place for the ark in these synagogues, which supports the view that the ark was not fixed in the synagogue wall, as it is today, but was a portable chest. The Mishnah tells us that on public fast days the ark was taken out into the town square. In some ancient synagogues, notably at Dura-Europas, there are the remains of paintings, including those of biblical personalities. A striking omission is the special women's compartment or gallery. On the basis of this, and of talmudic references, the Israeli scholar Dr. Samuel Safrai has argued that in the early synagogues there was no segregation of the sexes. Some ancient synagogues, judging by the archaeological evidence, must have been huge. The Talmud, too, tells us of a synagogue in Alexandria which was so vast that the people at a distance could not hear the end of a benediction so as to respond with "Amen" and had to be signaled by a man waving a flag. In some of the ancient synagogues, too, there are plaques indicating donors who contributed to the building fund.

Some synagogues are small, others large; some are simple, others grand. But all aim for dignity and an atmosphere of holiness.

In the language of the talmudic passage, the Divine Presence can come later if we pray on our own, but when we pray with a congregation the Divine Presence anticipates us, something happens to electrify the atmosphere. This can be seen even in secular activities. There is all the difference in the world, for example, between reading a play from a book in our own homes, and witnessing its performance in a crowded theater. There is nothing phony, as some imagine, when our deeper emotions are stirred by sharing an experience with others since that is how human nature functions. Furthermore, public prayers are less selfish than private ones. When we pray together in a congregation, we ask God's aid not only for ourselves but for the whole community. In practically every standard Jewish prayer, the plural "we" is used rather than the singular "I." "Grant us long life, health and strength" is nobler than "Grant me."

That is why the synagogue building is important. In viewing synagogue attendance as a religious duty, we are trying to capture the spirit of true prayer, and both the congregation and the architecture of the synagogue help. The synagogue is therefore known in the Jewish tradition as *mikdash me'at*, "a Temple in miniature." The Rabbis say that it is meritorious to run (that is, to proceed eagerly and in haste) to the synagogue, and equally meritorious to leave it slowly and reluctantly.

Which Synagogue?

Contrary to the now popular view that it is the Jewish ideal to worship in small groups, the Rabbis advise the building of large edifices with numerous congregants. They quoted the verse, "In the multitude of people is the king's glory" (Proverbs 14:28); the more people there are, the greater the honor paid to the King of Kings (tractate *Megillah* 27b). It is true that groups like the Ḥasidim preferred to worship in little conventicles (*shtiebelach*) but that was either because they could not afford anything bigger or because they disagreed with the members of the communal synagogue.

Jewish tradition does teach that it is important to pray together with like-minded folk because prayer requires a tranquil atmosphere free from distractions and a place in which harmony and peace reign. Although "synagogue-sampling" is not the worst of faults, and we all need an occasional change, the traditional ideal is a fixed place for worship, as the Rabbis put it; to have our own synagogue, where we offer our prayers regularly. It is in the fixed nature of our attendance that our constancy and reliability is established.

Synagogue Architecture

The fact is that there are hardly any rules on how a synagogue should be built. The few rules can be summarized briefly: there should be an ark in the east wall of the synagogue to contain the *Sifrey Torah*; there should be a *bimah* ("platform") from which the Torah is read; and the synagogue should have windows. Otherwise everything is left to the good taste of the congregation and the architect, which explains why synagogue architecture is so varied. The famous eighteenth-century authority, Rabbi Ezekiel Landau of Prague, was asked whether a synagogue has to be oblong or whether it may be octagonal or any other shape. In his reply he proved from the sources that it can have any shape, though he added that on grounds of propriety, the building should not be too ostentatious or flamboyant.

The Ark

Ideally, a synagogue should be so constructed that the ark is fixed in its east wall. This is based on the idea that the worshipers should face Jerusalem when they pray. But if for some reason the ark has been built into a different wall, the congregation should face the ark, even though they will not face east.

The Talmud refers to the ark as the *tevah*. This word means a box or a chest, so it would seem that in talmudic days the Sefer Torah was kept in a portable container. This can also be seen from the description in the Mishnah of the special prayers on fast days when the rains had failed to come. Since they would take the tevah out into the market place, obviously it was portable. But it has long been the universal custom to build the ark into the synagogue wall as a permanent structure. The Hebrew word for the ark is *aron*, the word used for the golden box in which the two tablets of stone were kept in the Tabernacle erected in the wilderness (Exodus 25:10–16). Because the

"When we pray on our own the prayer is still of great value, but it is much harder to get into the correct mood than when we are members of a congregation."

"It is important to pray together with like-minded folk because prayer requires a tranquil atmosphere."

narrative of the Tabernacle refers to a curtain (*parokhet*) which hung in front of the ark (Exodus 26:31–33), a curtain is hung in front of the ark today (or inside the ark doors). In many synagogues, two tablets representing the Ten Commandments are placed above the ark.

The Lost Ark

The ark in the Tabernacle in the wilderness, and later in Solomon's Temple, contained the two tablets of stone on which were engraved the Ten Commandments. It stood in the Holy of Holies. The ark was made of wood but was overlaid with gold within and without—a hint, say the Rabbis, that the student of the Torah must be as honest and pure in his heart as in his external appearance. The ark was covered with a thin golden piece upon which, in the Tabernacle, there were two winged figures, the *cherubim*. (In Solomon's Temple, the cherubim stood apart from the ark. A Midrash has it that these figures had the faces of children: only when children are trained in the way of the Torah can Judaism survive. There were two staves in the rings of the ark which were never to be removed; another midrashic lesson is derived from this: that the supporters of the Torah, the patrons of Jewish learning, are indispensible to the life of the Torah. The Jewish ideal has always been that willing and generous people will support scholars, enabling them to devote themselves to learning. There was no ark in the Second Temple, its place being taken by a large stone. According to one tradition, this stone is still there, on the site of the Holy of Holies, often identified with part of the Dome of the Rock in Jerusalem. No one knows what happened to the ark. According to one tradition it was buried in a spot on the Temple mount when the Temple was destroyed. Another tradition says it was carried off into Babylon and is there, somewhere, to this day. Still another version has it that the ark is buried in a cave near the River Jordan. A beautiful Midrash describes the ark lifting up those who carried it. The lesson here is that the Torah is not a burden. When we put our shoulders beneath it to bear it aloft, it carries us to greater heights.

The Eternal Light

"The Hebrew word for ark is aron, *the word used for the golden box in which the two tablets of stone were kept in the Tabernacle."*

Above the ark there burns an eternal light. In Hebrew this is called *ner tamid*, referring to the verse about the menorah in the Tabernacle: "to cause a lamp to burn continually" (Exodus 27:20–21). But, in fact, by "continually" the verse means each night. The menorah did not burn during the day. Scholars have noted that there are no references at all to an eternal light in the synagogue before the eighteenth century, so it seems to be a comparatively modern innovation. Yet it is now to be found in all synagogues and symbolizes both God's guiding light and protection, and the light of the Torah, which the Jewish people must always keep burning brightly.

The Bimah

The *bimah* is the elevated platform from which the Torah is read. (In olden days the reader did not lead the prayers from the bimah, but from a low stand in front of the ark to signify humility in God's presence.) Maimonides states that the bimah should be in the middle of the synagogue. At the beginning of the last century, some Reform synagogues placed the bimah at the ark end of the synagogue. This departure from tradition was severely criticized by the Orthodox on the grounds that it copied Christian churches where the altar is at the east end. However, Rabbi Joseph Caro, the author of the *Shulḥan Arukh*, stated as long ago as the sixteenth century that the only reason for the bimah to be in the center of the synagogue is so that everyone can hear the reading of the Torah. Consequently, he rules, in smaller synagogues, where one can hear very well wherever the bimah is situated, it can be placed at one end of the synagogue, which may even be preferable aesthetically. Sermons used to be preached from the bimah, but nowadays there is sometimes a special pulpit for preaching.

While some synagogues have a special section for women, others have done away with all such divisions and even have women rabbis.

Other Features of the Synagogue

The Talmud advises that prayer be recited in a house that has windows. This has been interpreted symbolically as meaning that the prayers should not be narrowly confined to the house but should move outwards, as it were, in concern for others and their needs. There is a later tradition that advises that a synagogue have twelve windows, one for each of the twelve tribes of Israel. This has been understood to mean that there is more than one way to God, each tribe having its own window to Heaven. Orthodox synagogues are built either with a special gallery for women or with a *meḥitzah*, "division," between men and women. The archaeological evidence from ancient ruins of synagogues does not suggest that anything like this existed in ancient synagogues. Nevertheless, it has been the traditional practice to have a separate compartment for women, known as the *ezrat nashim*, "the court of the women," after the court of that name in Temple times. Conservative and Reform synagogues see no point in having this division today, when in other areas of life the sexes mingle freely.

The Synagogue as a Center

Nowadays the synagogue is far more than a place where people meet for prayer, though this is still its chief function. Jews identify with the Jewish religion through the synagogue, and in most synagogues there are a host of activities, social, educational, and philanthropic, in which members come into closer contact with their fellow-Jews. In former times, too, there were *kehillot*, Jewish communities with their own governing bodies, and most larger synagogues today try to further the *kehillah* idea.

"The synagogue is far more than a place in which people meet for prayer."

Prayer

Prayer in general is of two kinds: the prayer of petition, in which we ask certain things of God, and the prayer of praise, in which we praise God and worship Him. Many find great difficulties with the whole idea of asking God to grant our requests. Does He need to be told or reminded of our needs? Surely if it were His will to grant us what we ask, He would do so without our asking, and if it is not His will, what is the point in asking? When we pray, are we not asking God to change His mind? This whole question is very involved, but the standard reply is on the following lines: God should not be seen as arbitrarily granting favors because we coax Him. Rather, it is His will that we turn to Him and thus direct our needs to His will. For instance, if we pray for wealth, we must ask ourselves whether we want it solely for our own selfish satisfaction or to use for the betterment of others, too. Similarly, when we ask God for knowledge, if we are sincere we will see the absurdity of such a request to God if we do not try to acquire knowledge. Seen in this light, our prayers are really exercises in self-scrutiny and attempts to be honest with ourselves in the presence of God. And then, indeed, we become different people, so that God can grant our request, not because He has changed but because we have. If it were not His will to grant the request before, the prayer and its implications may have changed us into the kind of person whose request can be granted.

There is a different objection to prayers of praise. Does God need to be told how wonderful He is? We do not think too highly of people who so lack self-confidence that they must always be reassured by praise. Here, again, the simple answer is that it is not God who requires our worship but we who need to worship. The human being is constituted with an urge to worship the highest. What is our sense of awe at the universe if not a call to proclaim that it is all so wondrous? Further, by praising God for being compassionate or holy or just, we are declaring that these qualities are at the heart of the universe; that if we want to achieve the best of which we are capable and be at one with God, we must try to be compassionate, holy, and just.

Melody

Prayer is a reaching out to God and, therefore, far more than a series of theological statements. It is hope, longing, suffering, love, entreaty, a leap into the unknown, a soaring of the spirit, all of which require the aid of music for their expression. Words alone are insufficient. The power of music to move the heart is well-known. That is why there are traditional melodies for the prayers in the synagogue. There is a special melody for each part of the service as more festive melodies for the festival prayers and more solemn chants for Rosh Hashanah and Yom Kippur prayers. In addition, ḥazzanim (cantors) have composed their own melodies, many of which have become standard in synagogues in the West. The Sephardic and other Eastern communities have their own melodies. The Zohar says that there are gates in Heaven that open only to song or to tears.

In Reform and Conservative synagogues, instrumental music, especially of the organ, sometimes accompanies the service. Orthodoxy objects, however, to the organ, even though an organ-like instrument appears to have been used in the Temple. The opposition is based chiefly on two grounds: that it is forbidden by rabbinic law to play a musical instrument on the Sabbath and on festivals, and that, the organ is so identified with Christian worship that its use in the synagogue would be copying another religion. It should be noted that on the same grounds, some Orthodox rabbis objected to a formal choir in the synagogue, although today there is hardly any opposition to synagogue choirs if the voices are male. (Orthodoxy does generally object to female voices in the choir on the grounds that it is distracting for men to hear a woman sing during prayer.)

The Rabbi and the Sermon

Traditionally the rabbi was connected with a town, not a synagogue, and his role was to render decisions in Jewish law. He rarely preached sermons. That function was carried out, at least in Eastern Europe, by the *Maggid*, the officially appointed town preacher or one who visited several towns during the year to preach in the synagogues, rarely during the morning service but for hours on end in the afternoon. Moreover, the sermon was in part a lengthy exposition of biblical and rabbinic texts.

The modern rabbi, although fulfilling the ancient role of teacher of the Torah (and, frequently, deciding questions of Jewish law) carries out other functions, too. The rabbi is a pastor who visits

"The rabbi is a pastor who visits congregants, an adviser, and a psychologist of sorts."

"Prayer is hope, longing, melancholy, a leap into the unknown."

congregants; an adviser; a psychologist of sorts; perhaps a fund-raiser; and, especially, a preacher in the contemporary idiom, that is, in the language the people speak and related to the world with which they are familiar. In addition, the sermon has become an integral part of the service. If we go back far enough, all this is not necessarily untraditional. There is a good deal of evidence that in rabbinic times, for example, the Rabbis were often preachers who taught during the services. The various midrashic collections are, in part, notes or digests of the sermons they gave.

The modern Jewish sermon has a number of aims. It seeks to instruct the people in the teachings of Judaism; to inspire them to lead more intense Jewish lives; to exhort them to behave well in their dealings with their fellows; to appeal for funds when needed for worthy causes; and to discuss topical questions in the light of Judaism. Many modern rabbis, however, tend to emphasize teaching, so that on many Sabbaths the sermon is an exposition of verses of the current *sidra*, the portion of the week.

The Cantor

The cantor leads the congregation in prayer. The Hebrew name for the cantor is ḥazzan. This word comes from a root meaning "to see," that is, to see the needs of the community and attend to them. In the early literature, the ḥazzan was not the cantor but the overseer of the community, a kind of secretary or administrative official. The earlier name for the cantor was *sheliaḥ tzibbur*, "deputy of the congregation," the one who speaks to God on behalf of the congregation, for which purpose he has been "sent" (sheliaḥ is from the root *shalaḥ*, "to send"). The *Shulḥan Arukh*, relying on earlier sources, states the qualifications of the sheliaḥ tzibbur: he must have a pleasant voice; should be an adult, preferably with a family; should have an impeccable reputation; and should be acceptable to the congregation.

The Daily Services

There are three daily services: *Shaḥarit* ("morning"); *Minḥah* ("afternoon"); and *Ma'ariv* ("night"). The origin of these is hard to determine but there is clear evidence that all three had been long established by the second century. In fact, according to one opinion, it was the patriarchs, Abraham, Isaac, and Jacob, who first introduced these services (Abraham, Shaḥarit; Isaac, Minḥah; Jacob, Ma'ariv), though, of course, this is really an aggadic way of saying that we follow our remote ancestors whose prayers at these times of day are recorded in the Bible.

The other opinion (both are mentioned in the Talmud) is that the three daily services correspond to the three occasions in the day when the sacrifices were offered in the Temple (the daily offerings in the morning and afternoon, and the burning of the sacrificial fat on the altar at night). In all probability, this opinion expresses the idea that after the Temple was destroyed, the daily services took the place of the sacrifices, though we are certainly not justified in concluding from this that there were no synagogues in Temple times. There were but, according to this opinion, the services were less fixed and formal than they are now. The Talmud records a debate between Rabban Gamaliel and Rabbi Joshua, the former holding that the Ma'ariv service is as obligatory as the other two, whereas the latter holds that this service is optional. It is desirable that it be recited, he says, but not obligatory. (This may be because in those days, when the streets were not adequately lit, it was difficult for people to go to the synagogue at night.) The ruling given in the Talmud is that the Ma'ariv service is optional. However, later codifiers state that nowadays Jews everywhere have taken it upon themselves to recite the Ma'ariv prayer so that it has become an obligation by consensus of the community. It is as if Jews had taken a kind of solemn vow that they and their descendants would not treat this service as inferior to the other two.

The Reading of the Torah

On Sabbaths and festivals the Sefer Torah is taken from the ark and the Torah is read. Originally there was no special reader, and each person called to the reading recited a portion. But later on, when many people were unable to read the Hebrew from the scroll, which has no vowels, and would be embarrassed if called to read, a special reader was appointed, which is still the practice everywhere. Traditionally, on the Sabbath seven portions are read; on Yom Kippur six, on the other festivals five; for the new month four; and on Mondays and Thursdays three. Again, traditionally the Torah is divided into *sidrot,* "portions," each of which is read in turn so that in a year the whole Torah is read.

In rabbinic times in Palestine (though not in Babylon), the weekly portions were much smaller, divided in such a way that it took three years to complete the reading. This is called the triennial (three-year) cycle. Various attempts to reintroduce it have not been accepted by Orthodox Jews. Reform and Conservative Jews do frequently adopt a variation of the triennial cycle or, in any event, read only a portion of the weekly sidra.

It is considered a great honor and privilege to be called up to read the Torah, so that people compete for the right to be called up, and regulations had to be made as to who was entitled to the honor. These are: a person who has *Yahrzeit,* commemorating the death of a father or mother; a person who has lost a near relative and has completed the period of mourning; a bridegroom on the Sabbath before his wedding; a boy who is *Bar Mitzvah;* the father of a Bar Mitzvah; a man whose wife has given birth to a child.

It should be noted that although traditionally only men were called to the Torah, today in Reform congregations and in some Conservative synagogues, women are granted this privilege, too.

Our sages taught that it is meritorious to run to the synagogue and that it is equally meritorious to leave the synagogue reluctantly.

14

Tallit, Tefillin and Mezuzah

"The fringes serve as a constant reminder of God and His laws, rather like our practice of tying a knot in our handkerchiefs."

Some Jews wear a small *tallit*, known as *arba kanfot*, under their daily clothing, in accordance with the biblical command "Have them make fringes on the corners of their garments."

The Tallit

According to the law as stated in the Book of Numbers (15:37–41), the Children of Israel were commanded to have "fringes" *(tzitzit)* in the corners of their garments. The passage does not state how many corners a garment must have to require that tzitzit be affixed to it, but in the Book of Deuteronomy (22:12) we read: "Thou shalt make thee twisted cords upon the four corners of thy covering, wherewith thou coverest thyself," so evidently the garment requires tzitzit only if it is four-cornered. The medieval commentators explain this command as a constant reminder of God and His laws, rather like the practice of tying a knot in our handkerchiefs to remind us of something we are in danger of forgetting.

So far as we can tell, in ancient times men did wear garments with four corners to which the tzitzit were attached. The name for the most popular of these four-cornered garments in rabbinic times was the *tallit*. It was not a sacred garment, but simply a cloak or robe. In fact, some scholars have suggested that the word tallit is a Hebraized version of the Latin word *stola*, a cloak, from which the word "stole" is derived. Students of the Talmud often begin with tractate *Bava Metzia*, in the first mishnah, which discusses a case where "two men hold a tallit," each claiming it is his. The meaning there, as elsewhere, is a simple robe.

Thus, originally the tallit was in no way a ceremonial object

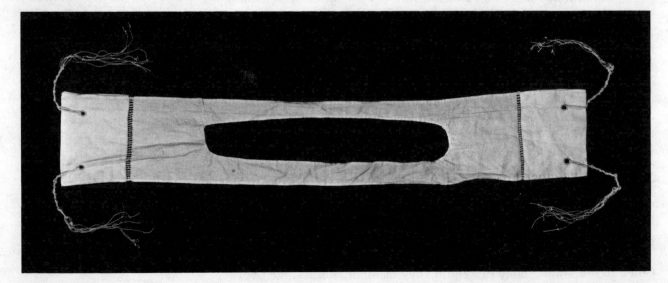

and the mitzvah consisted simply in attaching the tzitzit. But when Jews moved to Western lands they gave up wearing four-cornered garments, and since the mitzvah of tzitzit requires a four-cornered garment, there was no longer any need for tzitzit. Some medieval rabbis, however, seeing that the mitzvah would vanish from Jewish life, suggested that, for prayer at least, Jews wear a tallit on which there is an obligation to have tzitzit, so that the mitzvah would not be forgotten. That is how the ordinary tallit became the "prayer shawl."

The Thread of Blue

There is a traditional way of fixing the tzitzit to the tallit, one long thread being wound around the others to produce eight strands together with knots. But the Numbers passage says: ". . . and that they put with the fringe of each corner a thread of blue" (Numbers 15:38). A rabbinic interpretation is that the blue thread is a reminder of the blue of the skies and hence causes us to lift our eyes Heavenward. The traditional view is that this special blue, known as *tekhelet*, is a dye obtained from a certain marine animal called *hillazon*, and since we can no longer identify this animal, the tekhelet is no longer found in the tzitzit.

"The blue thread is a reminder of the blue of the skies."

Rabbi Mordecai Kaplan recently made the interesting suggestion that the real reason Jews gave up wearing the tekhelet is that it was not "blue" but "purple," the famous dye used by Roman nobility —"wearing the purple." The Jews in Palestine under Roman rule did not dare to wear purple threads lest it suggest that they were in rebellion against Rome, arrogating to themselves the special dye reserved for the Emperor. Be that as it may, the tekhelet is no longer worn, but it has become customary to have a number of blue or black stripes on the tallit itself as a reminder of the tekhelet. In the last century, the Ḥasidic Rabbi Gershon Henoch Leiner of Radzyn spent some time in Naples where he claimed to have rediscovered the marine animal called the hillazon. Being of a strongly independent mind he set up a small factory in his native town where he manufactured what he claimed to be the tekhelet. The other rabbis of his day refused to heed him but his followers did believe him, and to this day you may occasionally spot someone wearing the blue thread in the tzitzit. If you do, he may be a follower of the Radzyner Rebbe.

In some prayer books the following kabbalistic meditation before putting on the tallit is printed: "I am here wrapping myself around with a tallit to which tzitzit are attached, in order to carry out the command of my Creator, as it is written in the Torah: They shall make them a fringe upon the corners of their garments throughout their generations. And just as I cover myself with the tallit in this world, so may my soul deserve to be clothed with a beautiful spiritual robe in the World to Come, in the Garden of Eden. Amen."

In most congregations the tallit is worn around the shoulders as a kind of shawl. But many pious Jews prefer to wear a longer tallit

---

Tzitzit Knots

There are five knots in the *tzitzit*, corresponding to the Five Books of Moses. There are four sets of twirls, the first of seven, the second of eight, the third of eleven and the fourth of thirteen. This yields a total of thirty-nine twirls. The letters of the words "The Lord is One" also total thirty-nine (the Tetragrammaton = 26; *chad*, "one" = 13).

"In prayer one should be enveloped entirely with the object of the mitzvah, lost to the world with one's heart open to God."

that can be wrapped around the body, because originally the tzitzit had to be attached to a "garment" or "robe." You may also have seen Jews praying with their tallit over the head, the idea being that in prayer one should be enveloped entirely with the object of the mitzvah, lost to the world with one's heart open only to God. Nevertheless, in the Jewish tradition, the tallit and the tzitzit are not sacred in themselves (like tefillin or a mezuzah) but are only aids to the performance of a mitzvah. It is not therefore considered offensive to keep other objects in the tallit beg with the tallit.

Tefillin

In four passages in the Torah there is an injunction to have "these words" bound upon the arm and upon the head (Exodus 13:9, 16; Deuteronomy 6:8; 11:18). The traditional explanation takes the injunction literally, and has these four sections of the Torah written on parchment and tied to the arm and to the head. These are the *tefillin*.

Here is a brief description of how tefillin are manufactured. The four sections (the third of which is the Shema) are written on one piece of parchment and placed in a small box. This is the "hand tefillin." The same four sections are written on four pieces of parchment, which are placed in a container that is divided into four small compartments. These are the "head tefillin." Straps attached to the tefillin are wound around the arm and the head. The chief idea behind the tefillin is that of "carrying God's name" as a reminder of His deliverances in the past. The hand tefillin are worn on the left hand. The usual explanation is that, being near the heart, the hand tefillin are a reminder to direct the heart to God. In a rabbinic saying, God declares: "If you give your heart to Me you become Mine." However, there is the further idea that the hand tefillin must be worn on the "weaker" hand (perhaps to suggest that it is the weaker part of our nature that needs to be strengthened by the word of God). Therefore, a right-handed person wears the tefillin on the left arm, but a left-handed person wears them on the right arm.

The Significance of the Tefillin

The word tefillin seems, at first glance, to be connected with the word *tefillah*, "prayer." If this were so it would suggest that, like the tallit, the tefillin are aids to prayer. But this can hardly be correct since in

The ancient tradition of *tefillin* has been passed from generation to generation since biblical times.

How Tefillin Are Worn

The *tefillin* are placed first on the hand (i.e., on the upper part of the arm and the strap is wound seven times around the arm and then around the fingers). The tefillin for the head are then placed on the middle of the head just above the forehead. Rashi and his grandson, Rabbenu Tam, in the Middle Ages, differed as to the arrangements of the sections in the tefillin. For this reason the Ḥasidim and some other pious Jews wear two pairs of tefillin, those of Rashi and those of Rabbenu Tam. There is a story that a man was asked why he did not wear tefillin. He answered: "I understand that there is a debate on the matter between Rashi and Rabbenu Tam—and you won't catch me getting mixed up in an argument!"

A rabbinic Aggadah states that God showed Moses the knot of the tefillin (i.e., of the tefillin worn by God, as it were, in praise of Israel). Obviously this is a poetic way of saying that God's providence extends over all, but the binding knot is provided by Israel keeping God's laws.

talmudic times it was the practice to wear the tefillin all day, not only for prayer. (Nowadays we wear them only during the weekday morning prayers because, it is held, we could not concentrate enough on their meaning to justify wearing them the whole day.) Some scholars, therefore, hold that it is just a coincidence that the words tefillin and tefillah resemble one another, and that the word tefillin either means "attachments" or "marks of distinction."

In some prayer books there is another kabbalistic meditation before the wearing of the tefillin, beautifully summarizing the significance of the tefillin. This reads: "I am here intent upon the act of putting on the tefillin, in fulfillment of the command of my Creator, who has commanded us to lay the tefillin . . . Within these tefillin are the four sections . . . that declare the absolute unity of God, and that remind us of the miracles and wonders which He wrought for us when He brought us out of Egypt, even He who hath power over the highest and the lowest to deal with them according to His will. He hath commanded us to lay the tefillin upon the hand as a memorial of His outstretched arm; opposite the heart, to indicate the duty of subjecting the longings and designs of our heart to His service, blessed be He; and upon the head over against the brain, thereby teaching that the mind, whose seat is in the brain, together with all the senses and faculties, is to be subjected to His service, blessed be He. May the effect of the commandment thus observed be to extend to me long life with sacred influences and holy thoughts, free from every approach, even in imagination, to sin and iniquity. May the evil inclination not mislead or entice us, but may we be led to serve the Lord as it is in our hearts to do. Amen."

Rashi and Rabbenu Tam

A fascinating episode in the history of tefillin is the debate between the great French commentator Rashi and his grandson, Rabbenu Tam in the eleventh century. The correct interpretation of a talmudic passage determined in which order the Torah portions are to be placed in the container. Rashi holds that they have to be placed in the order in which they occur in the Torah, but Rabbenu Tam disagreed (despite his respect for his grandfather, he felt that the truth as he saw it took precedence), and held that the Shema should be placed on the outside. Consequently, some pious Jews, just to make sure, wear two pairs of tefillin, those which follow Rashi and those which follow Rabbenu Tam! Sephardic Jews who do this wear both at the same time, but Ashkenazic Jews who do it wear the tefillin of Rashi first, and at the end of the service put on the tefillin of Rabbenu Tam. This is done only by extremely pious Jews (otherwise it would be showing off). The rule today is that Rashi is followed.

A very interesting discovery among the Dead Sea caves at Qumran was a number of tefillin, some in the order understood by Rashi, others the order as understood by Rabbenu Tam! This shows

Inscribe them on the doorposts of your house and upon your gate. [Deut. 6:9 and 11:20]

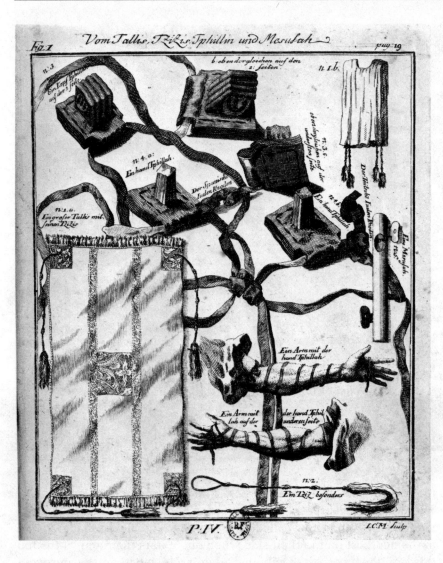

An eighteenth century engraving indicates one of the traditional methods of putting *tefillin* on one's arm.

that long before Rashi, there were two schools of thought in the matter, and that the debate between Rashi and his grandson goes back to ancient times. There is a delightful legend that Rashi, wearing his tefillin, held his little grandson, later to become the famous Rabbenu Tam, on his knee, whereupon the child innocently pulled the tefillin off Rashi's head. This was supposed to foreshadow that some day the grandson would hold a different opinion on the tefillin than his grandfather.

Mezuzah

In two portions of the Torah—Deuteronomy 6:4–9 (the Shema) and 11:13–21—it is said that "these words" shall be written on the door-posts (*mezuzot*) of thy house. Again, the tradition understands this literally—that these two portions must be written by hand on a piece of parchment, placed in a case, and affixed to the doorpost of every

room used for residential purposes (not storerooms or bathrooms). The word for "doorpost," *mezuzah,* became identified with the parchment itself, with is now called the mezuzah. The mezuzah is fastened to the doorpost on the right side when one enters the room, at the top third of the doorpost. Opinions differ as to whether the mezuzah should be in a vertical or a horizontal position. In typical Jewish compromise, and to satisfy both opinions, it is the custom to fix the mezuzah slanting inward, with the top on the section of the doorpost nearest to the room, so that it can be said to be both vertical and horizontal. On the principle of adorning the commandments, beautiful mezuzah cases are made. Some of those produced now in the United States and in the State of Israel are wonderful examples of the artist's craft.

The Significance of the Mezuzah

"The mezuzah, like the tzitzit and the tefillin, is a constant sign of our obligations to God."

Like the tzitzit and the tefillin, the mezuzah is a constant reminder of our obligations to God. Affixed to the doorpost, it also marks the house as a Jewish home dedicated to Jewish living. But even in ancient times some Jews saw the mezuzah in a superstitious way, as a kind of amulet to protect the house from demons. In the Middle Ages some people wrote on the mezuzah, in addition to the two Torah portions, various magical names and devices; and some wrote the text so that each line was shorter than the preceding one, so the writing tapered to a point, a not uncommon way of writing magical formulas. The great Maimonides was incensed at this perversion of a mitzvah. He writes of such practices: "It is not enough that these fools have set a mitzvah aside but have converted a great mitzvah—the unification of God, blessed be He, and His love and worship—into an amulet for their own benefit, imagining, in their stupidity, that this has an effect in terms of worldly vanities." Maimonides would presumably have disapproved of the practice of fixing a mezuzah to an automobile to protect it against accidents or of wearing a mezuzah as a charm.

Surrounded by Mitzvot

There are those who like to think of religion in what they imagine are purely spiritual terms and are particularly embarrassed by tzitzit, tefillin, and mezuzah which, in their opinion, are too concrete, too physical. As Jewish tradition sees it, however, human beings do require concrete, material symbols if they are to be in close touch with the spiritual universe. No religion is without its symbols, because abstract religious truths are easily overlooked without them. Judaism does not apologize for using the material world, wool or silk for the tallit and tzitzit, parchment and leather for the tefillin and the mezuzah, because the material is put into the service of the spiritual. There is no denying that these mitzvot are treated by some in a superstitious way. But all the great Jewish sages have urged us to see them as mitzvot, divine commands, a means of bringing us closer to God. They are pointers to eternal truth, religion in action in a positive way.

We can let Maimonides have the last word. At the end of the section of his code dealing with mezuzah, Maimonides writes: "Since it is a permanent obligation binding upon all, a man should take great care with regard to the mezuzah. Whenever he enters or leaves he is confronted with the unification of God, blessed be He, and he should remember His love, awakening from his sleep and concern with worldly vanities so as to acknowledge that nothing lasts for ever apart from the knowledge of the Rock of the world. On the spot he will then recover his mind's stability to walk in the paths of uprightness. The sages of old declared: 'Whoever has tefillin on his head and arm, tzitzit attached to his garment and a mezuzah fixed to his door, it is the strongest presumption that he will not sin, because he has so many reminders. And these (the mitzvot of tzitzit, tefillin, and mezuzah) are the angels which save man from sin, as it is said: 'The angel of the Lord encampeth round about them that fear Him, and delivereth them' (Psalm 34:8)." Note how careful Maimonides is to avoid any suggestion that these mitzvot have magic power in themselves. They are "reminders" and the means by which people may be surrounded by the angels (again, Maimonides does not interpret angels as beings, but as the spiritual forces inherent in the mitzvot themselves) that protect us from sin and guide us toward the truth.

The word *Shaddai*, a name for God meaning "Almighty," appears on every *mezuzah* parchment.

"As the Jewish tradition sees it, human beings require concrete, material symbols to be in touch with the spiritual universe."

15
The Dietary Laws

"*By eating some foods and refraining from others we elevate the act of eating so that it can become a vehicle for godliness.*"

Jewish dietary laws, known as *kashrut*, do not deal with weight loss or physical health but with a diet of sanctity and holiness.

Kashrut

The word *kosher* means "fit" and is applied in the Talmud, for example, to a Sefer Torah or a mezuzah, which are said to be kosher if they are properly prepared. But by kosher today we generally mean food permitted to be eaten, and the dietary laws are treated under the heading of *kashrut*, the abstract noun formed from the word *kosher*.

Various reasons have been given for observing these laws; a popular one is that the forbidden foods are unhealthy, though this reason is not found in talmudic sources. The general stress in the Torah regarding these laws is on holiness.

What has holiness to do with eating? The answer is that in Judaism everything must be brought into contact with the spiritual domain, and by eating some foods and refraining from others in obedience to our religion, we elevate the act of eating, which in itself is neutral, to a vehicle for godliness. People who control their appetites because they believe God wants them to, serve God even while eating. And it must not be forgotten that just as Judaism states that to eat some foods is wrong, it also states that eating can be a religious duty, eating matzah on Passover, for instance, or dining in the sukkah on Sukkot, or partaking of festive meals on the Sabbath and festivals. No one can live for more than a few days without food. We must eat to live, but one of the effects of observing kashrut is that we do not live to eat.

Furthermore, Jewish history has something to say regarding kashrut, which, whatever its origins, has kept Jews together and made them conscious of Jewish ideals. Some of the dietary laws have acquired a special significance because Jews in the past were prepared to keep them even at the cost of their lives. In the time of the Maccabees, for example, the soldiers of Antiochus threatened death to those who disobeyed the king's order to eat pork. So that, over and above the natural abhorrence for the pig and the fact that the Torah forbids it, refraining from eating it is a powerful symbol of Israel's faithfulness even unto death. Or consider the effects of the laws of kosher killing (sheḥitah) and removing the blood from meat. These rules have over the centuries implanted in Jews a hatred of blood and have contributed to the Jewish ideal of compassion. No Jewish housewife was ever allowed to wring the neck of a chicken. The killing had to be done by a skilled and learned person who knew all the laws, never by a brutal slaughterer performing the task solely for the money. Many of the other laws have wholesome effects, though the Jew who believes that they all were God-given will keep them whether or not the reasons for them are appreciated.

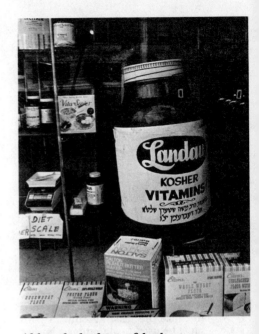

Although the laws of kashrut are detailed, there is room for interpretation.

Standards of Observance

There is no doubt that there are variations even among Orthodox Jews in their observance of kashrut. Some Jews will never eat pork but will eat meat that has not had sheḥitah. Others will not eat beef that has not had sheḥitah but will see no harm in eating chicken without sheḥitah. Others, again, will never eat nonkosher meat, but

---

Forbidden Animals, Birds, and Fish

The rules regarding which animals, birds, and fish may be eaten and which are forbidden are stated in two passages in the Torah, in Leviticus 11 and in Deuteronomy 14:3—21. Only those animals which both chew the cud and have split hooves may be eaten. These are the domesticated animals, the cow and the sheep. Various conjectures have been made as to why the choice should depend on these two factors, but they are only conjectures. No method of distinguishing the kosher from the non-kosher birds is stated, but a list is given of the forbidden birds, among them the eagle, the owl, and the raven. Here it has been suggested—though this, too, is only a conjecture—that the forbidden birds are all birds of prey that must not be eaten, in order to express our abhorrence of cruelty and the exploitation of the weak by the strong. As for fish, no names of fish are given (in fact, there are no references to the names of particular fish anywhere in the Bible) but only those fish that have both scales and fins may be eaten. Once again no reason is given but various guesses have been made. A non-Jewish commentator observed recently that fish that do not have fins and scales usually live deep down in the sea, like the octopus, and that in ancient times the sea was held to be the abode of the gods of chaos. If this is correct, the prohibition can be seen as a mighty protest against idolatrous ideas.

will not bother with separate sets of dishes for meat and milk. Still others keep a strictly kosher home but are not particular about what they eat outside the home.

From the point of view of Jewish law, all this is not admissible. The dietary laws have to be kept in their entirety. And yet variations do exist and we must not condemn them out of hand, especially since many people can find their way back to a full Jewish life only by gradual experiment.

Sheḥitah

Sheḥitah (from *shaḥat*, "to slaughter") is the method of killing animals for food that renders them kosher. No details of this are found in the Torah itself, but according to the Talmud the method enjoys divine authority because its details were given by God to Moses at

A finely sharpened knife designed to cause the least amount of pain must be used to slaughter a kosher animal (eighteenth-century engraving).

Sinai. This means, in any event, that from time immemorial that was how Jews killed animals for food.

The sheḥitah must be done with a finely sharpened knife without a single notch, for that might tear, and the animal's foodpipe and windpipe must be severed cleanly. There are many other detailed rules, so that only a person learned in the law and trained for the purpose can be a *shoḥet*. He must receive authorization from a competent rabbinic authority. Maimonides and others have called attention to what seems to be the basic idea behind the sheḥitah laws, to give the animal as painless a death as possible. Of course, all killing of animals for food involves a degree of cruelty, which is one of the reasons some people are vegetarians. Judaism does not require us to be vegetarians but when we do kill animals for food, it is to be as painless as possible. From time to time, voices are raised against sheḥitah and attempts made to ban it. But distinguished medical authorities have testified that sheḥitah involves an almost immediate cessation of consciousness on the part of the animal, so that it is the most painless method of killing animals for food. One expert declared that he wished his own end might be as painless as that of an animal killed by sheḥitah.

Terefah

Even when an animal has had sheḥitah, it must not be eaten if it has a defect that renders it *terefah*. The word *terefah* means "torn" and the prohibition against terefah meat is based on the verse: "And ye shall be holy men unto Me; therefore ye shall not eat any flesh that is torn (terefah) of beasts in the field; ye shall cast it to the dogs" (Exodus 22:30). The rabbinic tradition as recorded in the Mishnah (tractate *Ḥullin* 3:1) is that terefah refers not only to the meat of an animal torn by wild beasts but to any serious defect in the organs of an animal or bird. These defects are listed in detail, for instance, if there are perforations of the lungs. This is why the shoḥet, after performing the sheḥitah, examines carefully the animal's lungs. No further examination is required, however, on the grounds that most animals are not terefah. But whenever something peculiar is noticed about an animal or a bird, such as severe discoloration, the question is submitted to a rabbi to decide whether it is kosher.

Salting Meat

In a number of places in the Torah there is a prohibition against blood. Although it is, of course, quite impossible to draw all the blood from meat, the process of salting does remove enough to make the meat permissible. In the salting process (often done by the kosher butcher before the meat is sold), the meat is soaked in cold water for half an hour. This softens the texture of the meat, making it easier for

"Judaism holds that there is no need for us to be vegetarians but that our method of killing animals for food should be one that avoids as much pain and cruelty as possible."

the salting to extract the blood. The meat is then placed on a sloping drainboard to let the water drain away. Salt is then scattered over the whole surface of the meat, and left on it for one hour. Then the meat is thoroughly rinsed in water two or three times. Liver cannot be treated in this way. It must first be cut across in a number of places, then salted, and then roasted or grilled on an open fire. So strictly is the prohibition against blood treated that it is the general practice to discard an egg in which a blood speck is seen.

Meat and Milk

"It is forbidden to cook any meat with milk, to eat the resulting mixture or to gain any benefit from it."

Three times in the Torah it is stated: "Thou shalt not seethe a kid in its mother's milk" (Exodus 23:19; Exodus 34:26; Deuteronomy 14:21). According to the rabbinic tradition, the kid and its mother's milk are only given as examples (perhaps because they are easily found together by the shepherds in the fields) of meat and milk. According to this tradition it is forbidden by biblical law to cook any meat with milk, to eat the resulting mixture, and to have any benefit from it whatsoever (selling it to a non-Jew, for example). By rabbinic law this is extended to eating meat and milk at the same meal. It is also

Waiting between Meat and Milk

Talmudic law forbids eating meat and dairy dishes during the same meal, though one Rabbi, we are told, waited twenty-four hours after a meat meal before drinking milk. But from the Middle Ages on, Jews began to wait a given time between eating meat and milk. (When dairy dishes are eaten first, it is necessary to wait only a short period—twenty minutes to half an hour—before eating meat.) The period for waiting differs from community to community. Some wait one hour, others six hours. English Jews generally wait three hours, which seems to be a compromise between one hour and six. The reason given why a longer period is required for milk after meat, is that meat takes longer to digest. One reason suggested for not mixing meat and milk is that meat comes from a dead animal, milk from a living animal, and Judaism, as a life-affirming religion, emphasizes the difference between life and death.

Is Chicken Considered Meat?

The prohibition against mixing meat and milk is based on the verse: "You must not boil a kid in the mother's milk" (Exodus 23:19), which the Rabbis understand as forbidding the cooking of any meat with milk. The Rabbis extend the prohibition to eating meat and dairy dishes at the same meal. For this reason, two sets of dishes are required in an observant Jewish home, one for meat and the other for milk dishes. The second-century teacher R. José the Galilean argued that the reference to the "mother" in the verse implies that only the meat of mammals may not be eaten with milk. Consequently, he permitted the flesh of fowl to be eaten with milk. This opinion is not followed by the Sages, who forbade the eating of *any* meat, including that of fowl, with milk.

forbidden to cook meat in milk dishes or vice versa, which is why observant Jews have two sets of dishes, one for meat and the other for milk.

There are various customs as to how long one should wait after a meat meal before drinking milk or eating cheese. Some wait six hours, some three, and some only an hour. In observing these laws, one learns how important it is in life to make distinctions (as between milk and meat) and to be discriminating in whatever we do. Many moral failures are due to the lack of ability to discriminate between what should be done and what should not.

"Kosher-style" food is not necessarily kosher. In addition to the correct ingredients, the laws of kashrut demand proper preparation of the food.

Probability and Neutralization

Strict though the dietary laws are, there are a number of leniencies recorded in the talmudic sources and accepted as the law. First, there is the probability principle. We have already noted that it is not required that an animal be examined to see whether or not it is terefah (except for the examination of the lungs, which have a high proportion of disfunction) because it is assumed that the majority of animals do not suffer from the defects that would render them terefah.

A somewhat theoretical illustration of reliance on probability is given in the Talmud (*Ḥullin* lla–b). If, in an enclosed town, there are ten butcher shops, nine of them selling only kosher meat and one selling nonkosher, and some meat is found in the town, that meat may be eaten since the probability principle declares it kosher as it is likely to have come from one of the kosher shops.

Another principle is that of neutralization. It is, of course, forbidden to mix terefah food with kosher in order to neutralize the former, but if inadvertently some terefah food did become mixed with kosher food, then the whole mixture is permitted if there are sixty times as much kosher food as terefah, provided, naturally, that the terefah food can no longer be recognized (in which case it must be removed from the dish). This is known as *battel be-shishim*, "it is neutralized in a proportion of one to sixty." For this reason, not all canned foods are forbidden even if prepared without rabbinic supervision. If the amount of forbidden food is so small that it cannot be recognized and is one-sixtieth of the kosher food in the can, the mixture is permitted. It goes without saying that, wherever possible, foods that may contain terefah should be bought only if they have a certificate from a recognized rabbinic authority who has supervised them and declared them kosher. In the United States the law is very strict on attempts to sell nonkosher food as kosher.

Foods Damaging to Health

Besides prohibiting nonkosher food, the Rabbis come down very heavily against food that may be injurious to the health. According to rabbinic teaching, it is utterly wrong for a person to argue that his health concerns only himself, and if he wishes to eat harmful food what business is it of anyone else? The human body is given to a person in trust by God. People can serve God adequately only by being healthy and consequently it is forbidden to eat anything that may damage health. Food that can endanger health, declare the rabbis, is to be avoided even more than food forbidden by religious law.

Thus, although the probability principle applies to nonkosher food, it does not apply if there is danger to life. If there are ten cups, one containing poison and nine quite harmless, it would be forbidden to drink from any of the cups even though the probability is that an individual cup is not poisoned. In other words, it is strictly forbidden by Jewish law to play "Russian roulette." One can easily see how this would apply today. If the doctor orders someone to keep a certain diet to avoid ill health, according to the laws of kashrut, he should heed the doctor's advice. This also implies that care should be taken, say, when visiting foreign countries, not to drink the water or eat the food unless one has made sure it is safe. We are all hygiene- and health-conscious (sometimes too much so) and it is well within the scope of the Jewish teachings that we should be.

Plants and Vegetables

Apart from the prohibition of eating untithed produce, which applies only in the Holy Land, there are no bans on plants and vegetables. Everything is assumed to be kosher unless there is reason to declare it

> *"It is wrong for a person to argue that his health is of concern only to himself. The human body is given to one in trust by God."*

Vegetarianism

Jewish tradition stresses concern for all God's creatures. To cause unnecessary pain to animals is a serious offense. Yet that tradition does permit the killing of animals for food, perhaps as a concession to human weakness. The Jewish mystics even suggest that when meat is eaten by the man who tries to lead a holy life, the soul of the animal is elevated and assists in the service of God. Saadiah Gaon went so far as to say that animals will be rewarded in Heaven for the pain they suffer in this world, though Maimonides ridicules the idea of an animal Paradise. Thus, complete vegetarianism is not advocated in the Jewish tradition. But *sheḥitah,* the way set down for killing animals for food, is the method that causes the least suffering to the animal, and the trouble of preparing kosher food discourages the eating of meat.

Maimonides and Dietary Laws

Maimonides explains some of the dietary laws as a protest against idolatry. He surmises, for example, that the idolatrous priests used to boil meat and milk together and eat the mixture as a kind of magical encouragement to the gods to make the earth fruitful. Creeping and crawling things are forbidden and are called an "abomination" which a holy people must avoid. The talmudic rabbis extend the prohibition of abominable things to include even kosher food eaten in a way to promote sickness, out of dirty dishes, for example. The general principle behind it all is that the Jew must be clean in body and soul.

forbidden. For instance, when potatoes were first discovered, no one questioned that they were kosher, simply because one could think of no possible prohibition that could apply to this vegetable. However, fruit or vegetables containing worms must not be eaten until the worms have been removed.

16 Jewish Movements

Early Jewish Movements

This chapter is concerned with Jewish movements that still function in a vital way in Jewish life today. But a few words are necessary regarding earlier movements. In ancient Palestine, the Sadducean movement had many followers so far as we can tell from the sources. According to both the Talmud and the early historian Josephus, the Sadducees differed from the Pharisees in two major respects. First, the Sadducees preferred a more or less literal interpretation of Scripture and rejected the Pharisaic doctrine of the Oral Torah. Second, in the words of the Mishnah, they believed there is only one world; unlike the Pharisees, they believed that this life is all there is and had no belief in a Hereafter.

In the Middle Ages, the Karaites similarly rejected the Oral Torah, at least in its rabbinic version. The Karaites claimed to obey the plain meaning of the Bible, rejecting both talmudic interpretations and the authority of the Talmud. For instance, the Karaites took literally the Sabbath injunctions not to have a fire burning in the home and sat in darkness on Friday night; and they refused to go out of their homes or synagogues in obedience to their interpretation of the Sabbath law about staying in one's *place*. (The rabbinic interpretation is that it refers to a whole "town".)

Ḥasidic Proverbs

A Ḥasidic master who had succeeded his father as leader of his Ḥasidic group began to introduce changes into the practices of the group. He was reproached for departing from the custom of his father. "No," he retorted, "I am a faithful follower of my father for he, too, departed from some of the customs of his father. I follow in my father's tradition of change."

At the court of the Kotzker Rebbe, special honors were paid to a certain man. Rabbi Solomon Eiger, a Mitnagged whose son had adopted Ḥasidism despite his father's opposition, was curious to know why honors were paid to this particular man. "Is he a very rich man?" "No, he is extremely poor." "Is he a learned man?" "No, he can hardly read the Torah." "Is he of good family?" "No, he has very humble origins." "Why, then, is so much honor paid to him?" "Well, he is a very modest man." Rabbi Solomon laughed: "If he has neither wealth nor learning nor a good family background, he has plenty to be modest about." But when the Kotzker heard of this exchange, he declared: "A man who has neither wealth nor learning nor good family and yet manages to be modest is truly deserving of honor!"

Ḥasidic Proverbs

It was said of the Ruzhyner that he never bent his head to the food when eating but always took the food to his mouth with his head erect, and this was a token of his holiness. The Mitnagged rabbi of Lemberg laughed at this. "What is so special about that? Anyone can do it." "Try it and see," the Ruzhyner's Ḥasidim retorted. The Lemberger Rov did try for some days, but found that inadvertently he was bending his head to the food all the time. He admitted that the Ruzhyner was a holy man.

In the seventeenth century the Shabbetean movement at first convinced many Jewish communities that the Messiah had come in the person of Shabbetai Ẓevi of Smyrna. It is one of the great oddities of Jewish history that even after Shabbetai Ẓevi had converted to Islam there were still Jews who secretly believed he was the Messiah. They said he had to pretend to forsake Judaism in order to rescue the "holy sparks" residing even in the domain of falsehood!

Although all three of these movements had an undeniable influence on Jewish life and thought (the Karaites, for example, influenced the Rabbis to study the Bible more closely), they are hardly living movements today. There are no Sadducees today and no followers of Shabbetai Ẓevi. There are a few Karaites in the State of Israel, but they are not really identified with Jewish life in any positive sense. But other movements, while not necessarily as potent as when they arose, are still with us in one form or another.

"It is one of the great oddities of Jewish history that even after Shabbetai Ẓevi had become converted to Islam, there were still people who secretly believed in him."

Ḥasidism

The founder of the Ḥasidic movement was Rabbi Israel ben Eliezer (1700–1760). He was known as the *Baal Shem Tov*, "Master of the Good Name." This meant a person who, it was believed, could perform miracles of healing and other wonders by invoking the "Good Name" of God (by the power of the divine names recorded in the kabbalistic writings). But it must not be imagined that the Baal Shem Tov was a mere miracle-worker, of whom there were many at that time. He was rather a man of tremendous personal magnetism, a holy man whose thoughts were centered on God and who taught that God is to be found not only through study of the Torah by intellectuals, but by living in a spirit of dedication. After the death of the Baal Shem Tov, his disciple, Rabbi Dov Baer of Mezhirech, known as the *Maggid* ("Preacher"), attracted around him a galaxy of saintly men who became the leaders of the movement. Through their efforts Ḥasidism won hundreds of thousands of adherents throughout Poland, Russia, Lithuania, Hungary, and Romania.

There are two ideas basic to Ḥasidism. First is that of *devekut* ("attachment"). The ideal is to be "attached" to God in that one's mind is always on God; that he thinks about God and dedicates his actions to Him. Even when we eat and drink, when we conduct busi-

The emphasis in Ḥasidism is not only on a search for God through Torah study, but also on living in the world in a spirit of dedication.

ness affairs or talk with friends, our minds should be with God. According to Ḥasidic teaching, the whole universe is pervaded by God's sustaining power; indeed, for Ḥasidism the only true reality is God and all things are in God.

The result of all this is that the Ḥasid (the word means something like "saint," but in Hasidism it came to mean a member of the group, a follower of the Ẓaddik) is always joyous and happy. Even when Ḥasidim meet with suffering and tragedy, they try to see in life only the divine force which is good and good alone. This is the kindred Ḥasidic doctrine of simḥah ("joy"), not a kind of frivolous irresponsibility but a deep appreciation that the world is good because God is wholly good, however difficult it is to see the purpose of evil in the universe. And because Ḥasidim try always to live in the presence of God, they cultivate the other Ḥasidic ideal of shiflut ("humility"), which means being humble before God. No one can dare to feel proud before the majesty of God.

The second basic Ḥasidic idea, one which aroused the ire of the Mitnaggedim (the word means "opponents" and refers to the traditional rabbis who were bitterly at odds with the whole Ḥasidic movement), is that of a new type of leader, the Ẓaddik. The word Ẓaddik originally meant simply a good person, but in Ḥasidic doctrine the Ẓaddik (or the Rebbe) is the holy man, the leader of the Ḥasidic group. The ideal of devekut sounds very attractive, but if you try to have God always in mind you will see how difficult it is to attain. Ḥasidism holds that only the spiritual superman, the Ẓaddik, can attain devekut all the time, hence the Ḥasid has to attach himself to a Ẓaddik through whom he can become "attached" to God. In the course of time, after the death of the Maggid of Mezhirech, the idea developed that the son or grandson of the holy man was more fitted than any one else to be a Ẓaddik. Thus, eventually there were dynasties of Ẓaddikim, each with its own followers. The Ẓaddik's function was also to give spiritual counsel to his Ḥasidim, to pray on their behalf, to work healing for them, and to have them around his table, especially on the Sabbaths and festivals, when he spoke "words of Torah." These Torah words were generally collected by the sons or disciples of the Ẓaddik and they form the bulk of the vast Ḥasidic literature. It has been estimated that there are about 3,000 works produced by the Ẓaddikim and the Ḥasidim.

The best-known dynasties of the Ḥasidim today are: Lubavitch, Sotmar, Ger, Belz, Bobov, and Vishnitz. The special Ḥasidic garb is the long *kapote* ("cloak"), the *streimel* ("fur hat" made of sable, with thirteen tails corresponding to "the thirteen qualities of divine mercy"), the *gartle* ("belt" worn for prayer), white socks (worn by some Ḥasidim on the Sabbath), and the long beard and *peot* ("corners" of the bead, worn long and often curled). Ḥasidic prayer is generally characterized by rhythmic movements and gestures and is accompanied with melody. From time to time Ḥasidim break into dance. This is a religious exercise (not too unlike the religious dance of the "dancing dervishes"). A Ḥasidic teacher declared that in the dance at least one leg is always off the ground so that it symbolizes an attempt to rise above earthly concerns and reach out to Heaven.

It might be asked, why this was viewed with suspicion by the Mitnaggedim? Their opposition was based on a number of grounds. First, any new movement was seen as a breach of tradition. Second, the doctrine of the Ẓaddik suggested that the Jew requires an intermediary between himself and Creator, and the excessive veneration of the Ẓaddik seemed to border on idolatry. Third, the Ḥasidim, at first at least, tended to pour scorn on the traditional rabbis, who the Ḥasidim declared, studied Torah not for the sake of God but to win fame. Such an attitude, declared the Mitnaggedim, could result only in loss of respect for study of the Torah, the supreme religious duty in the traditional scheme. And fourth, the Mitnaggedim saw that Ḥasidic leaders tended to reverse the traditional priorities, placing prayer with burning enthusiasm and faith above study of the Torah.

Haskalah

Under the influence of Moses Mendelssohn and his circle in Berlin in the eighteenth century, a new movement of a kind very different from Ḥasidism arose. This movement taught the value of the ideals of Western society and became known as the *Haskalah* movement (the word means "Enlightenment;" think of the word *sekhel*, "sechel," for "common sense"). The German language, at that time the language of secular culture, was widely cultivated by the *Maskilim*, the upholders of the Enlightenment. They argued that Jews must learn to come out of the ghetto where they had been imprisoned for centuries, not just physically but also mentally and spiritually. The whole world and its culture—its literature, music, science, and education—was theirs for

> *"It was the Ẓaddik's function to give spiritual counsel to his Ḥasidim, to pray on their behalf and to work healing for them."*

Differences among the various "movements" in Judaism do not always prevent shared worship and celebration.

One of the more conspicuous innovations within the Reform movement is the equal participation of women in all synagogue functions.

"The Maskil was a person who tried to have the best of both worlds, that of Judaism and that of the European enlightenment."

the asking if only they would allow themselves to combine the new learning with the older Jewish traditions.

The Haskalah spread from Berlin to other parts of Europe. There was a particularly strong Haskalah in Galicia and in Lithuania. The movement produced a special type of Jew, the *Maskil*, who was not basically disloyal at all to any of the traditional Jewish values but who tried to have the best of both worlds, that of Judaism and that of the European Enlightenment. Nevertheless, because it was so difficult to live in two civilizations at the same time, many of the Maskilim became far more interested in the Enlightenment than in traditional Judaism, and eventually the movement became more or less secular in tone. For this reason it was vigorously attacked by both Ḥasidim and Mitnaggedim. Fierce battles ensued in which the Maskilim called their opponents reactionary, hidebound, superstitious, and irrelevant, while the opponents accused the Maskilim of heresy, secularism, lack of regard for Jewish tradition and for their fellow-Jews, and blind acceptance of a civilization that needed to be judged, not uncritically embraced.

Reform

The Reform movement, which arose in Germany at the beginning of the nineteenth century, was also concerned with the problem of the Jew facing the challenge of Western society, but, unlike Haskalah, was essentially a religious movement within Judaism. Seeing that many of the more brilliant minds were dazzled by the new cultural experience and were leaving Judaism altogether, the early Reformers wished to demonstrate that if Jewish practices and beliefs were interpreted according to Western standards, Judaism had much to offer. They wanted to show that there was no need to abandon the faith; on the contrary, Judaism would have much to teach the outside world as it had taught humanity in the past.

The earliest reforms were of a minor nature. Thus the Hamburg Temple introduced some prayers in German as well as in Hebrew, an organ to accompany the services, greater decorum than had prevailed in most of the traditional synagogues of the day, sermons in the vernacular, and (this was seen by the traditionalists as the most serious breach with tradition) omitted prayers for the restoration of the Jewish people to Zion. Eventually, however, as Reform spread, it became much more radical. The great Reform leader, Rabbi Abraham Geiger, was more moderate than his colleague Rabbi Samuel Holdheim, but even Geiger was unhappy about many of the ritual laws of Judaism while Holdheim went so far as to transfer the observance of the Sabbath to Sunday and to argue that the *get*, the traditional divorce, was no longer required and that divorce should be governed entirely by the laws of the state in which Jews lived.

Reform Judaism became prominent in the United States especially under the influence of Isaac Mayer Wise, the founder of so many of the Reform institutions in this country. Various Reform "platforms" were published opposing not only tradition but also earlier Reform positions. For instance, the Reform attitude about the return to Zion changed a good deal, so that in the twentieth century a number of prominent Reform rabbis such as Stephen S. Wise and Abba Hillel Silver were staunch Zionist leaders. But as a general principle, Reform Judaism tends to make a distinction between the religious and ethical teachings of Judaism, which are held to be binding for all time, and those rituals which are subject to change. For instance, not all Reform Jews disregard the dietary laws, but Reform does not attach the same significance to them as to, say, the laws regarding ethical conduct.

The opponents of Reform came to be called Orthodox. Originally this was a term of reproach by the Reformers—as if to say, you refuse to move forward and you stand still in reaction—but the name was eventually adopted with a kind of pride by those against whom the taunt was directed. Here, too, the attitudes hardened. Reform Jews accused Orthodox Jews of being too much concerned with the past and not enough with the present, of being far too rigid in their approach to Jewish law; of getting priorities wrong in placing so much emphasis on the ritual law; and of encouraging apostasy by presenting Jews with an either/or dilemma—either you keep everything or you might as well leave Judaism. The Orthodox countered that the Reformers were tampering with the lifeblood of the Jewish people; that they denied the divine character of the Jewish religion; that they had the nerve to change laws laid down by God Himself; and that Reform was a religion of convenience.

Neo-Orthodoxy and Conservative Judaism

Two men were largely responsible for approaches somewhere midway between Reform and Orthodoxy. The first was the nineteenth-century Rabbi Samson Raphael Hirsch. Hirsch accepted the values of Western society but denied that this demanded any "reform" or even any basic change of attitude to the completely divine character of traditional Judaism. The attitude of Hirsch has been called Neo-Orthodoxy; it is Orthodox in that it holds fast to the doctrine that the Torah in all its details is God-given and can never be changed, but "Neo" ("new") in that it encourages the study of secular sciences and of languages other than Hebrew and urges its followers to embrace that which is good in Western civilization. Hirsch's slogan, adapted from *Ethics of the Fathers,* was: "Torah and Derekh Eretz." For Hirsch, *Derekh Eretz* (literally, "The Way of the Land") means living a Jewish life within the terms of Western life in general—a devout Jew, intensely observant and yielding to none in the belief that the Torah is divine, can, at the same time, be a European literary figure or a banker or a scientist or a professor at the university or another cultured person enjoying, say, the music of Beethoven or Mozart and the writings of Goethe and Schiller.

Another nineteenth-century teacher developed a middleway

"In general Reform Judaism tries to distinguish between the religious and ethical teachings of Judaism on the one hand and its particular rituals on the other."

Rabbis Dennis and Sandy Sasso, ordained by the Reconstructionist Movement, were the first husband-wife rabbi team in history.

"The school founded by Zacharias Frankel stressed the binding character of traditional Judaism."

"The Musar movement demanded of its followers a ruthless self-criticism leading to sound ethical conduct."

The Havurah Movement is Judaism's most recent new group. Here, Havurah Jews on New York's Upper West Side, observe Tashlikh along the Hudson River.

philosophy. Rabbi Zacharias Frankel saw Judaism as a historical religion that changes gradually in response to various challenges but organically, not by violent interruption of Jewish growth and development. The school he founded (which was continued in the United States as the Conservative movement, led especially by Rabbi Solomon Schechter) stressed the permanent binding character of traditional Judaism. It supported Sabbath observance in its traditional form and the dietary laws in their entirety, but believed in natural growth and change as well as in a less rigid approach to Jewish law. This school, unlike that of Hirsch, is more open to modern critical studies on the Bible and the Talmud. According to this school, the Jewish student can have an open mind on the origins of various Jewish beliefs and institutions. He might, for example, conclude that the dietary laws had their origin in certain primitive ideas. But—and here lies the new approach of this school—that ought not interfere with loyalty to these laws and their continued observance since they have become part of Judaism and the way by which God guides Israel. All the laws are consequently seen as God-given, not necessarily in direct communication but through the experiences of the Jewish people in its long historical quest for God.

Musar

The word *Musar* means "instruction," "reproof," "calling attention to the need for a better life." The word is found, for instance, in the verse: "Hear, my son, the instruction (musar) of thy father" (Proverbs 1:8). During the Middle Ages, many Musar works were produced, such as Baḥya's *Duties of the Heart,* with the aim of improving the Jewish character through the constant admonition to obey the voice of conscience and of duty. But the Musar movement proper was founded in the nineteenth century in Lithuania by Rabbi Israel Lipkin (who lived in the town of Salant and is therefore known as Israel Salanter).

The Musarists, the followers of Rabbi Israel, studied the older Musar literature but introduced a completely new note. Rabbi Israel believed (to some extent he anticipated Freud) that people have forces in their souls that lie beneath the level of the conscious, rational mind and that these really influence our lives. It is no use, he taught, merely to read the Musar literature, because that will not have a lasting effect on conduct. In order to get down, as it were, into the subconscious mind, a constant repetition of Musar themes is needed. If, for example, a person is becoming proud and vain, to irradicate these traits he must repeat over and over again verses about the folly of pride and vanity. By chanting these repeatedly in a melancholy voice, an abhorrence of these undesirable traits becomes habitual and one becomes more humble. The Musarists met in special little houses (called Musar stiebels), where the members encouraged one another in character improvement. The Musar movement demanded of its followers a ruthless self-criticism leading to sound ethical conduct.

A *Musar* saying: The world says: If you cannot go over, you must go under, but Musar says if you *cannot* go over, you *must* go over.

A man asked Rabbi Israel Salanter: "I have only half an hour a day in which to study the Torah; which subjects should I study?" "Study Musar," replied Rabbi Israel, "and you will find another half hour."

Rabbi Israel's disciples expanded the movement. Despite strong opposition from traditionalists, the movement, though elitist, catering to the few, managed to spread. Nowadays the Musar attitude is shared by the traditional Yeshivot in the United States and in the State of Israel.

New movements have a way of arousing opposition and the Musar movement was certainly no exception. The traditional rabbis objected to the implication of the Musarist claim. If, they argued, the human character can be improved only by means of these new methods, does this not cast doubts on the traditional view that the Torah itself is healing for the soul and the best assurance of good living? Again, the Rabbis objected, to have special groups to study Musar smacks of sectarianism, as if the Musarists wish to have a little elitist enclave in which they can feel superior to other Jews. The Maskilim attacked the Musarists for what they saw as a morbid insistence on sin and guilt. Too much introspection of the kind the Musarists engaged in could damage a person's self-confidence and wreak havoc with one's inner life. The Musarists retorted that in this day and age, when there are many challenges to Jewish tradition, the "fear of Heaven" must be cultivated in this new, intensive way if traditional Jews are to remain firm in their belief. It should be noted that in our day the study of the Musar movement has been largely overlooked, partly because of the great interest in the more colorful movement of Ḥasidism. The movement did not produce much literature (it was chiefly an oral doctrine) but what little it did produce is worthy of study as an attempt to get beyond mechanical observance and to promote a more spiritual approach to traditional Judaism.

Zionism

There is little need to say very much here about the Zionist movement, since the establishment of the State of Israel has overtaken Zionism! To put it another way, Zionism has been realized beyond the wildest dreams of its founders, even of the practical dreamer Theodor Herzl, who introduced the concept of modern, political Zion-

"Zionism has received its expression in a form beyond the wildest dreams of its founders."

"I believe that a wondrous generation of Jews will spring into existence. . . . The Maccabees will rise again." Theodore Herzl

ism. It needs only be said that traditionalists as well as Reformers opposed Zionism; the former on the grounds that we must wait for the coming of the Messiah to establish a home for the Jewish people in the Holy Land; the latter on the grounds that the Messianic hope is to be realized not in Zion but in Europe and the United States, with greater freedom and better educational opportunities for all. History has a way of making nonsense of many of our tidy schemes. The establishment of the State of Israel removed at a stroke all opposition to Zionism, so that today only a tiny and totally unrepresentative group of Jews still persists in reproducing the old arguments. We shall examine all this in greater detail in the chapter on the State of Israel.

17

The Holocaust

Anti-Semitism and the Nazis

Anti-Semitism as a political instrument emerged in the nineteenth century. At that time various political leaders sought to capitalize on people's dislike of the unfamiliar by claiming that Europe's economic and social ills were caused by Jews. Nazi anti-Semitism was entirely irrational—suggesting, for example, that on the one hand Jews were all capitalists exploiting the workers and, on the other hand, were part of a Communist conspiracy to overthrow capitalist society! No canard was too base to issue against the Jews by the anti-Semites. The bigger the lie, declared Hitler, the more likely it is to be believed. A number of thoroughly unscientific racist theories were advanced, declaring the Jews belonged to an inferior race which had to be subjected to the purer races, chiefly the Aryan.

In Tzarist Russia, anti-Semitism was responsible for the terrible pogroms in which the mobs were encouraged to attack innocent Jewish men, women, and children. The Dreyfus case in France was the outcome of the French version of anti-Semitism. And so it happened in other countries as well, until the Nazis in Germany introduced the horrible anti-Jewish persecutions culminating in the so-called "final solution" of the Jewish problem, the total extermination of the Jewish people. In all, six million Jews, a third of the Jewish people, were

"The murder of six million Jews, unparalleled in all Jewish history, is what is now called the Holocaust."

149

A painting entitled "Expulsion of Jews from a Russian town" illustrates anti-Semitism decades before the Holocaust.

murdered in concentration camps, in gas chambers and in the ghettos of Poland. This event, unparalleled in all Jewish history, is what is now called the Holocaust. For many young people it all belongs to the past, and young people are not generally responsive to events which took place before their time. For many of the young, Hitler is almost as remote a figure as Pharaoh or Haman. But to those of us already grown to manhood and womanhood in the Holocaust period, it has seared so deeply into our souls that our whole outlook is affected. In the past, Jews have not chosen to dwell on the excesses of Jew-haters, arguing, generally, that what has been done is now over and we should turn in optimism toward the future. But such an attitude is impossible with regard to the Holocaust, because it challenges the continuation of a Jewish philosophy of life.

The Devastating Challenges

The belief on which Judaism has stood from the beginning is that of a benevolent Creator who works out His purposes through human history and has a special role for the Jewish people in His scheme. All this was challenged tragically and overwhelmingly and when it became apparent, as the facts became known after the war, that God had allowed fiends in human form to hurl living children into gas ovens, to torture people merely because they were Jews. How can Jews go on believing in the goodness of God, and in His special purpose for the Jewish people, after this catastrophe?

The problem of evil is acute even when a single innocent child suffers, and various attempts have been made to deal with that problem in the light of Jewish faith. But never before has the whole

"How can Jews go on believing in the goodness of God now that the catastrophe of the Holocaust has come about?"

scheme of things been so called into question as it has when a third of the Jewish people has been wantonly murdered. We have a duty to face the problem squarely, even if tempted to throw up our hands in horror and declare that we can never hope to understand this mystery, and can hold on to faith in God and in His plan for Israel and humanity only because the alternative—that there is no God—makes even less sense of our experience. For the person of faith, our very questioning in the name of the good means that we feel in our souls that there is a good in whose name we issue the protest, and how can there be unless there is a God, the ultimate Source of goodness?

Knowing Our Value from Our Enemies

In a way it is possible to gain some degree of hope and to wrest meaning from chaos by the fact that the foul torturers and murderers saw the Jews as their greatest enemies. Hitler and his followers have paid us a tribute without knowing it. If these monsters were the enemies of humanity, as it is now clearly seen, it follows that they must have been sane enough to recognize where goodness resided.

Evil attacks the good. The Nazi hatred of the Jew is therefore a perverse acknowledgment that Judaism contains the seeds of goodness and that its continued existence requires the continued existence of the Jews. For if everything simply evolved of lumps of matter, why do we condemn Hitler and the Nazis for being what they were? We do not condemn lifeless matter. We do not blame an avalanche for sweeping innocent people away or a storm for wrecking an airplane. Professor Emil Fackenheim has stated very forcefully in his writings that it is the supreme obligation of Jews not to let Hitler have the last word. One can go further and state that if there is no God, there is no last word to be uttered because "a word" suggests meaning and without God what sense are we to make of "meaning"?

Is It Morbid to Dwell on the Holocaust?

Is it morbid to dwell on the terrible tragedy? Yes, it is but, unfortunately, life in the twentieth century has been often unhealthy and morbid and we cannot behave like children who try to hide from the unpleasant. It will not all go away simply because we refuse to think about it. It is both right and necessary that we study the Holocaust for two reasons. The first is that already, only forty years since it happened, there are those who insult the memories of the martyrs who died by claiming, despite the overwhelming evidence, that it did not happen. Second, Judaism bids us mourn for the slain. Maimonides, in a famous passage, states that if a member of a family dies and the others fail to mourn the loss adequately they are cruel. Why cruel? Because it is natural for human beings to grieve their losses and if

"The Nazi hatred of the Jew is a perverse acknowledgment that Judaism contains the seeds of goodness in its very nature."

Philosophers have asked, "Can God create a stone which even He cannot pick up?" Many have echoed this question, asking, "Where was God during the Holocaust?"

Formerly inmates together for three years at Auschwitz, two women meet for the first time in thirty-five years at Yad Vashem, Israel's official memorial for victims of the Holocaust.

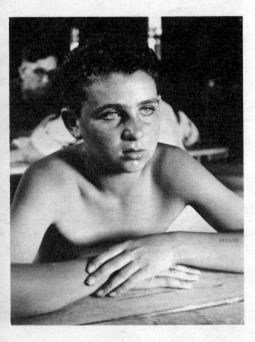

there is no mourning it can only mean that the loss is not really felt. A person who does not experience a profound grief when a near relative dies is unfeeling, insensitive and cruel.

It is true that Judaism discourages mourning for the dead more than a year. This is because the dead are at peace in Heaven and because life must go on as the dead would have wished. But that cannot apply to an event so catastrophic as the Holocaust. The Jewish people calls those who perished in the Holocaust *kedoshim* ("holy ones"), the name traditionally reserved for martyrs. It is good that we remind ourselves of those kedoshim, that we pray for the repose of their souls, above all that we remind ourselves and the world that these unbelievable things did happen and can happen again unless humanity determines to fight against hatred, racism, prejudice, and intolerance.

We Are All One

One of the effects of the Holocaust on sensitive Jews has been to remove the barriers between Jews of differing philosophies. This does not mean that there is no room for differences. As honest men and women we are obliged to work out honestly our philosophy of life and to defend it. What it does mean is that Jews can no longer afford to read whole classes of Jews, with whom we happen to disagree, out of Judaism and the Jewish people. Hitler made no distinction between one Jew and another. Our sense of Jewish loyalty, our protest against Hitlerism and anti-Semitism demand that we stick together, despite heated differences, as "one people upon the earth." Those of us who are left have decided not to give Hitler the last word but to rebuild Jewish life, and this holy task requires the efforts of all Jews.

We Have Resolved to Live on

A very superficial and totally unacceptable explanation of the Holocaust is that it brought about the State of Israel. Stated thus baldly it seems to suggest that God could not permit Jews to establish the State of Israel before they had paid Him the price of the six million. This is worse than no explanation at all. It is to see God as a Being who demands the sacrifice of millions of His creatures before He will help the remainder. This concept has no place within Judaism. Only the pagan god Moloch demands human sacrifices. How God could have allowed the Holocaust we do not know, but our faith in Him must postulate that basically it was "against His will." A more profound understanding of the connection between the Holocaust and the establishment of the State of Israel is that much of the impetus for the rehabilitation of the Jewish people and for the building of the State came from resolve of the survivors of the Holocaust that Jews must not yield to despair, but must build again.

"Above all we remind ourselves and the whole world that these unbelievable things did happen and can happen again."

They Kept Judaism Alive and So Must We

Some of the stories, all of them true, that have come out of the camps and the ghettos are among the most poignant and yet the most inspiring narratives in the whole Jewish saga. In the most desperate circumstances, Jews studied the Torah at the risk of their lives; met for prayer, scraped together their pieces of dry bread in order to "celebrate" the Sabbath. There are tales of nonreligious Jews risking their lives to save Scrolls of the Torah from desecration; of believers singing songs of praise to God even as they went into the gas chambers; of scholars writing down ideas they had discovered in Torah learning on whatever scraps of paper they could find in the hope that one day they would be found; of rabbis rendering decisions in Jewish law even when the next hour might be the end of both questioner and decider. It was all based on the conviction that come what may, people must do all in their power to continue to embrace the Torah of life.

This heroism and this determination to be Jews even in the valley of the shadow, has resulted in a powerful and holy resolve on the part of Jews alive today to revive Jewish life and learning, to

Praying during the Holocaust

A pious Jew in the Kovno ghetto, compelled to do forced labor by the Nazis, asked Rabbi Oshry, the Rabbi of Kovno, how he could recite the daily benediction "Blessed art Thou, O Lord, who has not made me a slave," since he was a slave. Must he not be honest when speaking to God? Rabbi Oshry reassured him. It was the Nazis who were the real slaves, abandoned as they were to their fearful wickedness. But a person who can freely rise in the midst of such torture to pursue the ideals of integrity when speaking to God, is no slave but a truly free person.

refuse to allow the torch of the Torah to be extinguished, to strengthen Jewish educational establishments, to study Judaism and to live Jewishly. If the destruction was greater and more terrible than anything that had hitherto happened, Jews everywhere have spontaneously declared their sacred resolve to rebuild more strongly than ever before. Judaism is indestructible. This is the maxim Jews today have determined to make true. Out of the ashes of the Holocaust, faithful Jews have kindled a new fire; the fire of Jewish optimism when all seemed lost; the fire of trust in the God of Israel even when, in the language of tradition, He seemed to be hiding His face; the fire of hope and learning, of renewal and growth and freedom.

The Prayer of the Jewish Saint

The famous medieval Jewish moralist, Baḥya Ibn Pakuda, tells of a Jewish saint, who had suffered indescribable torments, offering this prayer to God: "My God, Thou hast given me over to starvation and poverty. Into the depths of darkness Thou hast plunged me, and Thy might and strength hast Thou taught me. But even if they burn me with fire, only the more will I love Thee and rejoice in Thee." Only a great saint can offer such a prayer and during the Holocaust there were many such great saints who did not falter in their love of God and their trust in Him even when they were literally burned in fire. It would be a gross impertinence for those of us who have been spared to pretend to this kind of faith and courage. All we can and should do is thank God for keeping us alive and conclude that it must be for a purpose and that purpose cannot be other than to continue to live as Jews.

No Retreat into Reactionary Attitudes

It is very tempting to argue, as some Jews have, that if the lesson of the Holocaust is that we must live more convincingly than ever as Jews, it means that we should give up caring for others and should retreat into a new ghetto of our own making. But such a response must be resisted in the name of Judaism. One of the reasons why Jews did not on the whole oppress others is because their history has made Jews realize how bitter it is to be victims. A passage in the Midrash says that when God was about to bring the people of Israel out of Egypt He first made them promise that if they ever owned slaves, they would set them free as soon as possible. Knowing the degradation of slavery from firsthand experience they were expected not to subject other human beings to it.

On the whole, Jews have, in fact, been ready to extend the lesson of the Holocaust to include freedom from terror and violence to all peoples. Jews, the sufferers from oppression and injustice, must fight oppression wherever it rears its head and practice justice even when it does not seem to pay. Allied to this is the very difficult

---

"If oppression is so hateful and justice so magnificent, then Jews must fight oppression wherever it rears its head."

Retelling the story of the Holocaust has resulted in a powerful and holy resolve on the part of the Jews today to revive Jewish life and learning, to refuse to allow the torch of Torah to be extinguished, and to strengthen Jewish educational establishments.

Anne Frank

The poignant story of Anne Frank (1929–1945) and her diary has survived the Holocaust. Anne's parents escaped from the Nazi persecution in Germany, where Anne was born, to Amsterdam where she was educated. When the Nazis took Holland, teen-aged Anne and her family went into hiding to avoid certain death. Their concealment was at first successful, and friendly non-Jews helped them with food and other needs, but eventually their hiding place was discovered. Anne fell ill in Bergen-Belsen and perished there. She was barely sixteen. Her diary, discovered later, reveals the reflections of a youthful, creative writer who poured out her thoughts and fears. Anne's diary was published and translated into many languages. The diary of Anne Frank occupies an honored place in the tragic Holocaust literature, for the insights of a highly-gifted young girl and because it expresses the torments of innocent children in a world gone mad.

The Warsaw Ghetto

On April 19, 1943, a German force entered the Warsaw Ghetto for the purpose of continuing the mass deportation of Jews to the death camps. At this time there was an organized group of underground resistance movement fighters. Though they had few arms, the Warsaw Ghetto fighters managed to repulse the Germans, inflicting heavy losses. The Germans returned and set fire to the Ghetto. The Ghetto was destroyed, but the desperate Jewish fighters showed the world that Jews could fight and die with heroic dignity. Sporadic resistance continued until August, 1943. The Warsaw Ghetto uprising became the symbol of the Jew fighting back against his tormentors, refusing to go meekly to his death. It inspired a whole generation to realize that courage is a Jewish virtue and to hope and pray that their sacrifice would not be in vain.

resolve not to blame the whole non-Jewish world for the crimes committed by the Nazis. It is not only that many non-Jews risked and even gave their lives to save Jews during the Holocaust, but that the Jewish sense of fairness should prevent wholesale condemnation of, say, the German people. Nor should we be too ready to see the Holocaust as evidence of the total collapse of Western values. After all, the whole Western world was not directly guilty (though it is now generally acknowledged that there was too much indifference to the fate of Jews on the part of civilized countries like the United States and Great Britain), and the West did wage a war in which millions died fighting the Nazis.

Jews have rightly taken to heart the fact that if Jews will not help themselves, very few others will. It is not much good deploring this, since that is how things are. So it is perfectly correct for us to have a sense of priority and to give precedence to Jewish needs. Jews have sacrificed themselves on the altars of good causes long enough to see that if this is at the expense of Jewish survival it pays no dividends. Yet the other truth remains that Judaism has never allowed

Halakhic Questions During the Holocaust Period.

A quota of young boys was collected for extermination in one of the death camps. The father of one of the boys knew that he could bribe a guard to free his son but that the guard would have to make up the quota by adding another boy. Was the father justified in saving his son's life by indirectly causing the murder of another boy? The rabbi to whom the question was addressed broke down and declared himself incapable of rendering a decision.

A *shofar* was smuggled into the camp. Were those Jews who wished to hear the shofar blown on Rosh Hashanah permitted to risk their lives by arranging a short service at which the shofar would be sounded? The rabbis permitted it, since life was constantly at risk in any event and the psychological effects were immeasurable.

A Jewish girl, compelled to pander to the lusts of the Nazis, had the word for prostitute tattooed on her arm. After her freedom she asked the rabbi whether she should have the tattoo erased. The rabbi replied that she must not do this, for it would suggest that she was to blame. The tattoo would serve as a permanent reminder of Nazi bestiality.

The Jews in the Kovno ghetto had no wine for the Passover Seder. How could they carry out the *mitzvah* of drinking the four cups of redemption? The rabbi replied: "Carry it out with four cups of sweet tea."

Jewish indifference to the fate of the rest of humanity. Freedom and justice are indivisible. If we want these for ourselves, we must want them for all people. Living in a world in which constant choices have to be made between our own interests and those of others, we must try somehow to further our own without turning away from the cry of the hungry and persecuted and enslaved of those who are not Jews.

18

The State of Israel

The Dream of Zion

From its beginnings Judaism has centered not only on a people but on a land—*Eretz Yisrael*, "The Land of Israel," or *Eretz ha-Kedoshah*, "The Holy Land." After the destruction of the First Temple, although the exiles in Babylon were far from unfortunate in their new surroundings, they looked upon themselves as "exiles." The Psalmist, speaking of this period, begins his lament: "By the rivers of Babylon, There we sat down, yea, we wept, When we remembered Zion" (Psalm 137:1). He repeats the oath: "If I forget thee, O Jerusalem, Let my right hand forget her cunning, Let my tongue cleave to the roof of my mouth, If I remember thee not; If I set not Jerusalem above my chiefest joy" (Psalm 137:5–6).

The joy of the return from the Babylonian captivity under Ezra and Nehemiah was expressed by the Psalmist when he sang: "When the Lord brought back those that returned to Zion, We were like unto them that dream. Then was our mouth filled with laughter, And our tongue with singing" (Psalm 126:1–2). After the destruction of the Second Temple, in the year 70 C.E., the hope of another return was never dimmed. Many of the standard prayers spoke of this hope; the poets expressed it in their liturgical compositions; the codifiers continued to rule that it is a religious duty for the Jew to reside in the Holy Land, even though, many of them said in the Middle Ages, the duty could not be fulfilled because of the dangers on the way. There was a constant settlement of the Jews in Palestine. Judah Halevi and Naḥmanides, Joseph Caro (author of the *Shulḥan Arukh*) and the Safed mystics, and many other famous Jewish teachers, made their lives in Eretz Yisrael. With the rise of modern Zionism the old dream of a return looked close to becoming a reality, and in 1948 the new State of Israel was, in fact, established. The old dream has come true.

Why a Land?

That the State of Israel has provided a home for the homeless; that it has enabled three million Jews to find security and relief from persecution and oppression; that it has helped to heal to some extent, at least, the wound of the Holocaust; that the Hebrew language and Jewish thought and literature have through it acquired a new lease on life—all this is ample justification, if such were needed, for the exis-

157

Why Israel?

We read at the end of tractate *Ketubbot* in the Talmud: "When Rabbi Zera went up to the land of Israel and could not find a ferry wherein to cross over the river into the Holy Land, he seized hold of a flimsy rope bridge and crossed over. A Sadducee sneered at him: 'O hasty people, you are always so impetuous.' Rabbi Zera retorted: 'The spot which Moses and Aaron were not worthy of enter-ing who could have assured me that I would have been worthy of enter-ing?' Rabbi Abba used to kiss the cliffs of Akko. Rabbi Ḥanina used to repair the roads of the Holy Land. Rabbi Ḥiyya bar Gamda rolled him-self in its dust, for Scripture says: 'For thy servants take pleasure in her stones, and love her dust' (Psalm 102:15)."

"It is the notion of a sacred soil, a holy land, that some find difficult to accept."

Traditionally, Jews place a *mizrach* on the wall of their home that faces Jerusalem, orienting the observer toward the center of the Jewish world.

tence of the new State. But Jews and the Jewish tradition generally go much farther when they talk of the holiness of the land, as if the very soil is sacred. The Talmud tells us that some travelers to Palestine would kiss the soil when they landed in Eretz Yisrael. Some find this notion of a sacred *soil*, a holy *land*, difficult to accept, especially from the religious point of view. If God is everywhere and can be wor-shiped wherever people give their hearts to Him, why should a spe-cial piece of land be particularly sacred?

Basically this is the same kind of problem as that of the Chosen People. We tend to think in generalities and are a little embarrassed by any particularistic claims. But all the great achievements of hu-manity have been made through the particular rather than the gen-eral. The special sanctity of a spot on earth may be compared to the sanctity of the synagogue. What do we mean when we say that God is especially present in the synagogue? Is He not present everywhere? The answer is that, of course, He is, but we are not in the mood to sense His presence everywhere and it is we who require a special place where He can be met. Many devout Jews have, indeed, under-stood the idea of the Holy Land in some physical sense. These Jews would speak of the mysterious interaction between the physical and the spiritual. For example, the soul does inhabit the physical body, though when we start to think of what "inhabit" means in this con-nection, we find the idea very hard to pin down. The soul certainly does not reside in any particular part of the body but is present there-in somehow.

But others would prefer not to think of the sacredness of Eretz Yisrael in a physical sense. They would rather think in terms of asso-ciation. The very fact that the tremendous creations of the Jewish spirit were the product of this piece of land and no other; the very presence of the Hebrew prophets on this soil and on no other (with the exception of Ezekiel); the natural longing of the exiles for a return to their homeland and the prayers they poured out toward Jerusalem —all these have made the land holy. This is one of the reasons, from the religious point of view, why the Bible speaks of "going up" to the Holy Land and why we still speak of it as *aliyah* (literally "a going up"). The Rabbis say that the land of Israel is higher than all other lands, meaning, presumably, higher spiritually.

"The rabbis say that the land of Israel is higher in spiritual status than all other lands."

The Beginning of the Redemption

Precisely because the establishment of the State of Israel constitutes the partial realization of the ancient dream, it has seemed to many to have something messianic about it. And here lies a problem. The State of Israel has achieved wonders in its short existence: a fair and just society has been created; the soil has been reclaimed; democratic processes have been set in motion; universities have been established and they flourish; the Hebrew language has become a flexible tool and a fine literature has been produced; science and medicine have made contributions to the health of the world; tourism has been encouraged so that millions of people now visit the antiquities and the numerous other interesting sites; there is complete religious freedom for the adherents of Christianity and Islam. In short, the State of Israel is a huge achievement. But it is a modern State in an imperfect world, which means that it needs an army to defend itself against attack; a police force to protect its citizens against crime. It has to face the threat of war, economic and political problems, and the Arab question. It must balance the claims of the religious against the freedom demanded by the nonreligious. This is to be expected, and most unbiased observers would agree that, with all its faults and problems (most of them inseparable from modern Statehood and to be found among the most advanced and privileged countries), the State of Israel is the great miracle of the twentieth century.

So, while the old dream and the religious quality of the State demand a messianic interpretation of what has happened, sober reality and sane assessment make it only too clear that the Messiah has still not come. A popular answer offered by many religious Jews, is to draw on rabbinic sources which speak of a gradual dawning of the messianic age, a paving of the way, so to speak. This has been called, using an old Aramaic expression, *atḥalta de-geulah*, "the beginning of the redemption"; that is to say, the messianic age has not yet arrived and the world is still unredeemed, but neither is the State of Israel to be seen in purely secular terms as yet another state, albeit a hopeful one with much to its credit. In this way, the religious meaning of

The Messianic Age

Those who see the creation of the State of Israel as *atḥalta de-geulah* cite a number of midrashic statements that the messianic age will dawn gradually and that human effort will precede divine intervention.

A favored theme is that, according to the Midrash, the fire on the Temple altar came down from Heaven, but not until the priests had kindled the altar fire by human hands.

statehood is safeguarded without encouraging a never-never-land attitude which prefers escapism to a grappling with real problems.

A Jewish State

The establishment of the State of Israel took place so rapidly that there has not been time for any profound assessment as to what a Jewish State should be, how its Jewishness should be expressed. Already there are the obvious tokens of Jewishness—the use of Hebrew; the growth of synagogues and yeshivot; the enormous amount of Jewish books published; newspapers in Hebrew; the influence of Jewish law on the legal machinery of the State; the official celebration of the Jewish festivals and the Sabbath as the day of rest; the observance of kashrut in hotels; the rebuilding of ancient ruins; the coming alive of the great biblical sites; and the reinvestigation of all the classical Jewish sources as well as the study of the Bible by young and old. But the influence of Judaism is also seen in more subtle ways; for instance, in the pursuit of justice and compassion. When, to take a well-known example, the Knesset debated, soon after the establishment of the State, whether or not capital punishment should be abolished, the abolitionists won the day because they were able to point out that this had long been the trend in Jewish thought, so that to abolish capital punishment was to act Jewishly. Again, with hardly any exceptions, the conduct of the soldiers in the wars with the Arab armies has been exemplary, with no looting and no rape, and with sincere desire to avoid so far as humanly possible the loss of civilian life, all in obedience to the teachings of classical Judaism. The problem so far unsolved is the role of the Jewish religion in the State of Israel.

Religion in the State of Israel

"Laws of personal status are entirely in the hands of the rabbis who administer traditional Jewish law."

A modern democratic State, which Israel is, cannot tolerate religious coercion. Each individual citizen must be free to choose how much religion he or she is prepared to accept, or whether to accept any religion at all. The problem of safeguarding this freedom in a State based on a particular religious outlook is the problem of many states in the modern world. In the United States the problem has been lessened, if not entirely solved, by the doctrine of complete separation between Church and State. In Great Britain the doctrine is not accepted to the same degree. The Queen is still the Head of the Established Church and the Bishops are appointed officially by the Prime Minister. Sunday is the official day of rest and many public facilities do not operate on that day. On the other hand, British law does not interfere with rights of individuals in matters of religion; though in a recent case, a heavy fine was imposed for the ancient offense of blasphemy when a scurrilous attack was made on the Christian religion.

In the State of Israel the problem is still acute. For instance,

The Jews of modern Israel have transformed dry sand into a land "flowing with milk and honey." Here, a carefully planned forest grows up out of the once barren desert.

laws of personal status are entirely in the hands of the rabbis who, in this area, administer the traditional Jewish law so that, for example, a kohen cannot marry a divorcée, there is no civil marriage, and Reform and Conservative conversions to Judaism are not recognized. In addition, only accredited Orthodox rabbis can officiate at weddings, and all official rabbis are civil servants employed by the State. Public transport does not run in most Israeli cities on the Sabbath. The religious parties in the Knesset influence the way the machinery of the law is developed.

Is this a good thing? Many religious Jews, and some who are not so religious, would reply in the affirmative, arguing that the Jewish character of the State must be preserved at all costs so that the State of Israel will not become just another Middle Eastern state. Other Jews feel that the cause of Judaism would be better served if there were greater freedom for the individual, and so the debate continues. In any event, one unfortunate result of the present situation is that the term *dati* (from *dat*, "law"), meaning "religious," is now applied only to those who follow the Orthodox way, with the result that many Israelis who are not too observant but who are religious in outlook are said to be irreligious or even anti-religious. Perhaps the solution lies in a greater stress by religious leaders on the quest of the individual for God. Judaism is not only a means of group survival; it has much to say to the individual soul. And there are hopeful signs that this is being done increasingly, though it would be a rash person who does not see difficulties ahead.

Israel and the Diaspora

The vast majority of Jews outside Israel give unconditional support to the State. They contribute toward its maintenance; seek to influence

The Wailing Wall, ca. 1900.

their own countries in its favor; visit Israel regularly and, perhaps, study there for a time; rally to Israel's support whenever it is attacked; and look upon themselves as partners in the work being done in Israel. They appreciate that there is no equal partnership between Israel and the Diaspora. After all, the Israelis have to bear the full burden of building up the State and their lives alone are at risk when danger threatens.

It has sometimes been argued that the attachment to Israel on the part of Diaspora Jews has created dual loyalties. Is this true? One supposes that it is. Jews loyal to Israel and at the same time loyal to their own native countries do have a dual loyalty. What is wrong with that? It is possible to have more than one loyalty, just as a person might be loyal to both parents and children. It can be a problem only when the two loyalties are in conflict, an event that is extremely unlikely nowadays in the United States and, to perhaps a somewhat lesser extent, in Great Britain, and Europe. Conflict is one thing, tension another. There can be tensions between our love for our own country and our love for Israel. Apart from political issues, we may have such a strong affection for our native land that it overrides the attractions of Israel, or we may be so inspired by the realized dream of Israel that we tend to overlook the call of our native land. The point is that tensions do exist in life and we must learn to live with them. There may be tensions, say, between love for one's parents and love for one's children. A sensible person will not try to ignore the tensions but will consider carefully how to reconcile the two loyalties.

An idea that has emerged views the Jewish people as a unit, with Israel as its center. The Zionist philosopher, Aḥad ha-Am, had this concept of Israel (not yet established in his day) as a spiritual center. He envisioned that the intense Jewish life and the cultivation of Hebrew and Jewish learning in Israel would affect Jewish life everywhere. That has, indeed, happened. But there is also a two-way traffic. Israeli thinking has benefited from Jewish thinking in other lands. Israeli achievements would not have been possible without the support and encouragement of Diaspora Jews.

But what of the future? Ben Gurion suggested the "liquidation of the *Galut*," the eventual immigration of all Jews to Israel. The possibility of all Jews packing up and leaving for Israel is simply not practical. And if Jews are to continue to live outside Israel as Jews, they must build for the future in Jewish terms outside Israel, too. The more realistic picture seems to be one in which Israelis and Diaspora Jews share the task of rebuilding Jewish life, with the State of Israel naturally occupying a central but not an exclusive role.

The Ingathering of the Exiles

It is astonishing how Jews have been gathered together in Israel from the most diverse communities and welded into a united people. There are still divisions—Jewish individuality and self-confidence being what it is, how could it have been otherwise?—but there is also the

A second Lieutenant in the Israeli Air Force, this young woman helps to defend Israel from its enemies while creating a safe haven for the "ingathering of the exiles."

"Israelis and Diaspora Jews share the task of rebuilding Jewish life."

The Law of Return

The Law of Return in the State of Israel, which permits every Jew to claim the right to live in Israel, gave rise to the question: Who is a Jew? In reality, the halakhic position is clear: The child of a Jewish mother or a person converted to Judaism is a Jew and never loses his Jewish status. But it is not the halakhic question that is at stake but the intent of those who framed the Law of Return. What did they mean by a *Jew*? Thus, in the case of Father Daniel (a Jew who had become a Christian monk and demanded to immigrate to Israel under the Law of Return) it was decided that, although halakhically he had not lost his Jewish status, those who framed the Law of Return hardly intended it to apply to a Jew who had converted to another religion. Another problem is whether conversions of non-Jews, conducted by non-Orthodox rabbis, are recognized. The Israeli Rabbinate has generally taken the line that such conversions are not valid either because non-Orthodox rabbis are not considered eligible to preside over conversions or because the conversions have not met requirements of the Halakhah (i.e., immersion in a *mikveh* and undertaking to keep all the precepts).

closest cooperation. Fortunately, and in obedience to traditional Jewish law, serious attempts have been made to preserve the special character of the various communities—Sephardim are still very different from Ashkenazim in the State of Israel, Ḥasidim from Mitnaggedim, Litvaks from Galitzianers, South Africans from Germans, Americans from Bokharans, Hungarians from English. Many scholarly studies are yielding new information about the rich variety of Jewish cultures. It is no accident that one of the keenest students of Jewish cultural variety and the customs of far-flung Jewish communities was Yitzḥak Ben-Zvi, a former president of the State of Israel.

The ingathering of the exiles also has a cultural and intellectual angle. The State of Israel appreciates how important it is now to preserve the Jewish knowledge of the past, reclaiming classics in danger of being lost and finding a home for them and other works of the Jewish genius. The Dead Sea Scrolls are an exciting example of this gathering in of "exiled" or lost works. Huge encyclopedic works have been undertaken in Israel. Among them are the massive *Hebrew Encyclopedia*; the English language *Encyclopaedia Judaica*; the *Encyclopedia Talmudit*, a digest of the vast legal literature of the Talmud and rabbinics; the publishing of texts found hitherto only in manuscript; and the amazing spate of reprints of works long out of print and now available at reasonable prices. This is besides the new dictionaries of the highest scholarly standards; the fine textbooks on all Jewish subjects; the digests of Jewish teachings; and new editions of the Bible, the Talmud, the Midrash, and the philosophical and mystical classics.

"In the State of Israel today there is an appreciation of how important it is to gain vast summaries of the Jewish knowledge of the past."

Israel and Peace

The right of Israel to exist within safe and secure borders is paramount. Beyond that there can hardly be an Israeli or a Jew anywhere who does not wish Israel to be at complete peace with its neighbors. Here, too, the Jewish tradition has molded public opinion that war is an abomination and peace the supreme blessing. The wish for peace is contained in both the Jewish and the Arab greetings. All our important prayers conclude with a prayer for peace. And peace is possible if enough people of goodwill are to be found. It would bring advantages of every kind not only to Israel but to all the peoples in the area.

19

Love Thy Neighbor

"How can anyone be commanded to love? And how can we be commanded to love others as much as we love ourselves?"

Is It Possible to Love Our Neighbors as Ourselves?

"Love thy neighbor as thyself" is the usual translation of the Hebrew *ve-ahavta le-reakha kamokha* (Leviticus 19:18). Abraham Lincoln once said that it was not the passages in the Bible he did not understand that bothered him, but the passages he understood only too well. Presumably, he meant that some biblical passages made very heavy demands on him, which he felt he ought to accept but which he found extremely difficult to act upon. "Love thy neighbor as thyself" is surely one such passage. We all appreciate that it is good and proper for us to love others, but when we try to put the rule to work we run into problems.

Thus, how can anyone be *commanded* to love? Love is a spontaneous reaction, not something that can be willed. Either we already have this love, in which case no command is required, or we do not have it, in which case no command will have any real effect on our feelings. Indeed, it can have the opposite effect, since it is natural for human beings to refuse to be told how they should feel emotionally. Again, even if a command to love our neighbor makes sense, how is it possible to love others as much as we love ourselves? Moreover, since the term *neighbor* includes people we do not know at all, how can we

166

possibly love them? Does not love imply a relationship with someone we know? And does the rule mean that we must like everyone? How can we control our feelings of dislike of some folks, often, we must admit, for reasons of which we are unaware, as in the little jingle:

> I do not like thee Dr. Fell,
> And why it is I cannot tell,
> But this I know and know it well,
> I do not like thee Dr. Fell.

The result is frequently that we torture ourselves for failing to live up to a challenge we are told is at the heart of Judaism. There has been a good deal of discussion of the problem by the great Jewish teachers. The following presents the meaning of the verse from Leviticus as understood by many of these teachers.

Acting Lovingly

First, we must note that the rule does not appear in Leviticus in isolation, but as part of a larger verse. The verse reads in full: "Thou shalt not take vengeance, nor bear any grudge against the children of thy people, but thou shalt love thy neighbor as thyself: I am the Lord." The correct translation, then, of ve-ahavta is: "*but* thou shalt love" (the letter vav here means "but") and this part of the verse is connected with the first part. The verse, in fact, is saying: Do not practice revenge, do not try to get even with someone who has wronged you, but behave toward that person as if no wrong had been done. The talmudic rabbis give these illustrations in order to define "taking revenge" and "bearing a grudge." If you ask someone to do you a favor and he refuses, and later asks you to do a favor which you refuse, you are taking revenge. If, on the other hand, when he asks you for a favor you do it, but recall that you are not acting like he did, you are bearing a grudge. The point is that the verse is not thinking of feelings or emotions but of actions. Furthermore, the Hebrew word (ve-ahavta) le-reakha, with the preface *le*, really means "*to* thy neighbor." The meaning is: "love *to* thy neighbor," instead of the usual form: *ve-ahavta et reakha*. Thus, the meaning of the verse now be-

"Love thy neighbor as thyself" advises us to behave toward others as we would like them to behave toward us.

The Hillel Story

There is a well-known tale told in the Babylonian Talmud, tractate *Shabbat* 31a. A man who wished to be converted to Judaism declared that he wished to be taught the whole of the Torah during the time he could stand on one leg. The teacher Shammai would have nothing to do with such an unreasonable request, but Hillel said to the man: "That which is hateful unto thee do not do unto thy neighbor. This is the whole of the Torah. The rest is commentary. Go now and learn (more about it)." This story (whether it is legend or fact is irrelevant for our purpose) supports our contention that the "golden rule" is a challenge to us to *act* decently to our neighbors as we would wish them to act to us.

comes much clearer. It means: "Do not engage in vengeful acts or in acts which demonstrate that you bear a grudge. Rather, perform loving acts (acts such as are directed to one who is not hated, but loved) to thy neighbor." The verse does not demand that we whip up spurious emotions in order to pretend something we do not really feel. It simply cautions us to behave toward others (whether we like them or not) as we would like them to behave toward us. The verse is an appeal to proper actions, and actions can be commanded.

Action Has an Effect on Character

It should be added, however, that in much of Jewish teaching there is the idea that actions can change character, so that if we perform loving actions to others, we will come to have greater love for them. For instance, the Book of Deuteronomy says that if one sees a neighbor's beast struggling under its burden, one should help the neighbor. But suppose there are two neighbors in difficulty, one an enemy and

A Ḥasidic Tale

The Tzanzer Rebbe once broke down in tears. "It is known that a man may study the Torah," he said, "lead a holy life and pray regularly and still belong to the *Sitra Aḥra*" ("The Other Side"), the Zoharic name for the demonic, unholy side of existence. "Perhaps," said the Rebbe, "for all my learning and prayer I really belong to the Sitra Aḥra." But then he found reassurance. "The Sitra Aḥra is incapable of love. It is selfish and grasping, thinking only of itself. I do have love for others in my heart, so, for all my failings, I cannot really belong there."

the other a friend. To whose assistance should one go first? The natural response would be, of course, to the friend. The Rabbis say otherwise. You already love the friend. Force yourself to attend first to the needs of your enemy and you will become better disposed toward him and he toward you.

Thy Neighbor Is as Thyself

It has also been suggested that the word *kamokha*, "as thyself," does not refer to "thou shalt love" but to "thy neighbor." The correct translation should be: "love thy neighbor who is as thyself." Martin Buber has elaborated on this in terms of his "I-Thou" philosophy. Buber argues that the verse means that we should treat our neighbors not as things to be used, but as persons like ourselves. Other human beings are not objects we can use, either by manipulating them for our own selfish ends or even to satisfy our need to be helpful. Rather they are persons in their own right. A Jewish teacher in the Musar movement in the last century said that we should not think to ourselves, before helping others, that we are performing a mitzvah, obeying God's command. To do this would mean that we have not, in fact, carried out the mitzvah. The command is to be a special kind of person who does not need the spur of a divine command in order to act lovingly to others.

Who Is Thy Neighbor?

A question now to be considered is the precise meaning of *reakha*, translated as "thy neighbor." A better translation would be "thy fellow." Does this term mean a fellow Jew, or does it refer to all human beings, Jews and Gentiles? Since the first half of the verse speaks of "the children of thy people" it seems clear that the word *reakha* in the second half of the verse means a fellow Israelite, which would limit the golden rule to Jews. And yet what a narrow view this would be, and how could such a view be reconciled with Judaism's teachings that God created *man* in His image, that all human beings are embraced by God's special concern and regard? In the context the reference is to a fellow Israelite. Any law code of a nation, when it refers to those governed by the law, means those who belong to that nation. But that does not mean that the law should be applied only to Jews. The law code in Leviticus, of which our verse is a part, is a kind of constitution for an ideal Jewish state and is thus addressed first to Israelites in their dealings with fellow Israelites, much as the United States Constitution is addressed to its citizens in their dealings with each other. When, however, Jews are called upon to apply the ideal to non-Jews, they are expected to extend the original interpretation of the law and to apply it to all people. We cannot be expected to have loving feelings for all people. Indeed, we are not called upon to have

We are commanded to behave lovingly to all people (opposite page).

Rabbi Akiva said: Love thy neighbor as thyself—this is the essence of the Torah.

"The Mishnah teaches that whoever destroys a single human life is as if he had destroyed a whole world."

such feelings toward all Jews. We can and are commanded to *behave* lovingly to all people.

Each Person Is a World

In the Mishnah (tractate *Sanhedrin* 4:5) there is an interpretation of why, in the biblical narrative in the Book of Genesis, one man, Adam, and his wife Eve are the parents of the whole human race. This is to teach us, says the Mishnah, that whoever destroys a single human life is as if he had destroyed a whole world, whereas whoever saves a single human life is as if he had saved an entire world. Since the example is Adam, it follows that the teaching refers to every human being and is not to apply only to Jews. It is true that in some texts of the Mishnah the words "of Israel" are added, so that the meaning is, whoever saves a single *Jewish* life. But, as a host of Jewish scholars have noted, this reading is not found in any of the ancient texts of the Mishnah and contradicts the whole tone of the Mishnah with its reference to Adam. The limitation was added much later by a less tolerant copyist, perhaps, to be fair to him, one who had suffered persecution at Gentile hands, which often happened, alas, in the Middle Ages. Whatever the reason for the addition, it is not authentic and belies the true message of Judaism.

When My Interests Conflict with My Neighbor's

The golden rule instructs us to act lovingly to others. What is to happen when their interests conflict with our own? Take the example recorded in the Babylonian Talmud, tractate *Bava Metzia* 33a: My animal has gone astray and so has my neighbor's. I have an obligation to recover my neighbor's animal if I can, but if I go after his animal I

Loving One's Neighbor

Loving thy neighbor is a high religious imperative, but what is the law if more than one neighbor needs help? Are there rules of precedence? There are many such rules in the Talmud. In one halakhic discussion a man is faced with two people in difficulty. One of them, his enemy, is struggling to load a burden on his animal, while the other, his friend, is struggling to unload a too-heavy burden from his animal. Normally, preference should be given to the man who is unloading because both human being and animal are in distress. Nevertheless, the Talmud states, he should give preference to his enemy. Every act which turns an enemy into a friend and which encourages neighborly feeling, even toward those one dislikes, is to be preferred over a simple act of good neighborliness.

am likely to lose my own. Which takes precedence? Or, to quote another example, I have a small sum of money for my needs and my neighbor requires a similar sum for similar needs. Do I have to give him the money and deprive myself of it? The answer given in the Talmud is interesting. The Talmud states that logically my needs and my animal must come first. Otherwise everyone is called upon to help his neighbors at his own expense, and that would be of no ultimate benefit to anyone. Thus, the Talmud rules, "Your own comes before that of every other man." And yet the Talmud goes on to add that anyone who is too rigidly insistent on his rights all the time will suffer from it. He will find that he is always in need. An acute observation! We all have rights and privileges but if we are to lead healthy lives in society we will not get very far if we always insist on our rights and are never prepared to forgo them when occasion demands. For instance, if I want a book that my friend wants too, I am certainly not bound to buy it for him if by so doing I deprive myself of it. Yet if I know he needs it more than I do, that it will be of greater use to him, or if I wish to help him more than I want to have the book, then I would be doing a good deed and acting within the full spirit of our verse if I bought it as a present for him.

A Famous Case

A famous debate is recorded in the Talmud, tractate *Bava Metzia* 62a. Two men are journeying through a desert. One of them has a jar of water sufficient to keep him alive until he reaches civilization, while the other has no water and so will die. The teacher Ben Petura holds that the man with the water is obliged to share it with his companion so that both will survive for a time but eventually both will perish. Rabbi Akiba disagrees, holding that it is unreasonable for both to die if one is able to survive. Consequently, Rabbi Akiba rules, the man who has the water has no obligation to share it with the other. He can hold on to it and survive, even though his companion will die at once.

This debate has often been misunderstood. Its concern is with

the question of whether the man with the water must share it with his companion. Here Ben Petura holds that the man with the water has a present obligation to share the water rather than witness the death of his companion. He must share the water and thus carry out his present duty even though to do so will eventually result in his own death. Rabbi Akiba refuses to see this as an obligation. What is not discussed at all is whether the man is obligated to give all the water to his companion. It would be absurd to argue that he is, because the companion, once he has the water, would have the same obligation to return it.

Nor do the two teachers discuss the very different question, whether the man with the water may give it entirely to his companion so that he will die but his companion will survive. Supposing the man with the water is single, while his companion has a wife and family who depend on him; or he believes the other man's life is of greater value than his own and he wishes to make the supreme sacrifice, may he do so? Some commentators have argued that he may not do so, because it is always wrong for a man to give his life for another. But this is by no means certain. During the terrible days of the Holocaust, there were numerous instances of people's risking their own lives and even giving up their lives so that others would be spared. In a town in Poland, for instance, the Nazis had issued an order that a Ḥasidic rebbe be arrested and tortured, whereupon a follower of the rebbe put on the rebbe's clothes and took his place. It would be rash to argue that he was doing a wrong according to Jewish teaching. Surely most of us would applaud his sacrifice and see him as a saintly person who gave his own life for the life of a man he revered and who could bring the teachings of Judaism to a much wider circle than he could ever do.

May One's Life Be Saved at the Expense of Another's?

Judaism is emphatic that in no circumstances is one permitted to save his own life by taking another's. The Talmud in tractate *Pesaḥim* 25b records a case decided by the fourth-century Babylonian teacher Rava. A local tyrant ordered a Jew to kill another man, or be killed. This man, who wished to obey Jewish law, asked Rava whether it is permitted to commit murder in order to save one's life. Rava ruled that he must allow himself to be killed rather than kill the other. "How do you know," declared Rava, "that your blood is redder? Perhaps the blood of that man is redder." In other words, how do you know that your life is of greater value.

The great French commentator Rashi explains it in this way: Normally a crime or a sin may be committed in order to save life, but this cannot apply to murder because the crime itself involves the taking of a life. The sole justification for taking one life in order to save another would be that one life has more value than the other. But no human being can know whose life is of greater value and it

"No human being can know whose life is of greater value."

must follow that murder is never permitted, not even to save one's own life. Some later authorities remark that this ruling of Rava's would apply even if the would-be murderer is a renowned scholar and saint while the intended victim is a person of no account. Who is to say that another is of no account? It may well be that in God's eyes the ne'er-do-well counts more than the scholar and saint since he may be living a better life.

Self-Defense

In that case, it may be asked, why is one permitted to kill in self-defense? Judaism does teach that if someone wishes to kill you and there is no other way of saving yourself than by killing him you may do so; indeed, you are duty-bound to save yourself. The answer is that an attacker with intent to kill has taken the initiative. This is totally different from Rava's case where the intended victim is innocent. Why should one innocent person be murdered to save another innocent person? But when the attacker, of personal choice, decides to kill someone else, he has become a would-be murderer and it is right for an intended victim to defend him- or herself. The Talmud goes further. Not only is the intended victim duty bound to defend himself but witnesses to the attack are obliged to rush to his defense, saving him even if the only way is by killing the attacker. The Talmud does, however, qualify this by stating that it applies only if the intended victim can only be saved no other way. If he can be saved by merely maiming the attacker, it would be wrong to commit murder.

Thus far we have dwelt mainly on what might be termed the negative aspects of loving one's neighbor. But, of course, Judaism stresses particularly the positive acts of benevolence, kindliness, and encouragement through which the love of one's neighbor is expressed. It is to these that we turn in the next chapters.

20 Compassion

Rahamanut

The Hebrew word for compassion is *rahamanut* (in the Yiddish form, *rachmones*). This word has the same root as the word *rehem*, "womb," and denotes, perhaps, the tenderness and pity a mother has for her child. Compassion is, for Judaism, one of the highest values. The Rabbis state that compassion is one of the three distinguishing marks of Jews (the other two are benevolence and modesty). This does not mean that compassion is peculiar to Jews. Non-Jews are also compassionate, and when a Jew is compassionate it is not as a Jew but as a human being. Compassion is part of human nature. By saying that compassion is a Jewish virtue we mean that Jews should be true to this basic element in the human character and that failing to means failing in their obligations as Jews. The Torah trains people in the way of compassion so that the Rabbis also say that the ancestors of a person lacking in compassion did not stand at the foot of Sinai; that is, does not really belong to the people of the Torah. The ideal is, according to the Rabbis, for humans to resemble their Maker. God is described in the Bible as compassionate so people, too, should be compassionate and in this way be God-like.

What Is Compassion?

"To be compassionate is to feel for the sufferings of others, to be moved by the pain others experience."

To be compassionate is to feel for the sufferings of others, to be sorry for them in their troubles, and to be moved by their pain to do something about it. Rahamanut is the tear shed for the sick and the poor; the hand stretched out in friendship; the concern for the handicapped; the commiseration with the failure; the prayer for humanity groaning in despair. Although rahamanut should result in action, it is in itself a desirable element in the character. It is what we mean

---

A Midrash on God's Compassion

After the Egyptians had pursued the escaping Hebrew slaves, the sea parted for the slaves, who were saved, and then engulfed the Egyptians. At that time, the angels on high wished to sing the praises of God, but He protested: "My creatures, the work of My hand, are drowning, and you want to sing My praises!"

---

when we say a person is kind and sympathetic. Its exact opposite is cruelty and indifference to others.

The Importance of Compassion

The importance Judaism attaches to compassion can be gauged from the many references in the classical Jewish sources to God as compassionate. The phrase commonly used in the Talmud for "God states" in Scripture is: "The Compassionate (Raḥmana) says." In the second benediction of the Amidah, God's compassion for His creatures is described: "Thou sustainest the living with lovingkindness, revivest the dead with great compassion (be-raḥamim rabim). Thou supportest the falling, healest the sick, loosest the bound, and keepest Thy faith to them that sleep in the dust." One of the names of God in the prayers and in Jewish parlance generally is: Av ha-Raḥamim, ("Father of Compassion"). The Grace After Meals speaks of God as feeding the whole world "with goodness, with grace, with lovingkindness, and with compassion." The prayer for peace at the conclusion of the Amidah refers twice to God's compassion: "Grant peace, welfare, blessing, grace, lovingkindness, and compassion unto us and unto all Israel, Thy people. Bless us, O our Father, even all of us together, with the light of Thy countenance: for by the light of Thy countenance Thou hast given us, O Lord our God, the Torah of life, lovingkindness and righteousness, blessing, compassion, life and peace." (Among Eastern Jews it is not unusual for a child to be given the name Raḥamin.)

To be compassionate is to feel for the suffering of others.

The Extent of Compassion

In the Jewish ideal, compassion is to be extended to all God's creatures. The prophets castigate non-Israelites for their lack of compassion to one another, not only to Israelites. Jeremiah speaks of the people from the north country who "lay hold on bow and spear, they are cruel, and have no compassion" (Jeremiah 6:23). Amos pronounces God's verdict of doom on those nations who committed atrocities against one another, among them Edom who "did pursue his brother with the sword, and did cast off all pity, and his anger did tear perpetually, and he kept his wrath for ever" (Amos 1:11).

Compassion must be shown even to animals. Tza'ar baaley ḥayyim, "causing pain to living creatures," is a serious wrong, according to the Rabbis (tractate Bava Metzia 32b). We have noted in the chapter on the dietary laws, that according to some Jewish teachers, the purpose of sheḥitah is to adopt as painless a method as possible when killing animals for food. Many Jewish teachers see humanitarian reasons for other prohibitions in the Torah: against muzzling the ox while ploughing (Deuteronomy 25:4); yoking an ox with an ass (Deuteronomy 22:10); taking the young before sending away the mother bird (Deuteronomy 22:6–7); and killing an animal and its

"Many Jewish teachers see the reason of other prohibitions in the Torah as avoiding unnecessary pain to animals."

young on the same day (Leviticus 22:28). Of this last prohibition, the Zohar (III, 92b) remarks in its own mystical vein: "Thus if a man does kindness on earth, he awakens lovingkindness above, and it rests upon that day which is crowned therewith through him. Similarly, if he performs a deed of mercy, he crowns that day with mercy and it becomes his protector in the hour of need. So, too, if he performs a cruel action, he has a corresponding effect on that day and impairs it, so that subsequently it becomes cruel to him and tries to destroy him, giving him measure for measure. Israelites are withheld from cruelty more than all other peoples, and must not manifest any deed of the kind, since many watchful eyes are upon them." There is even a Jewish custom of not wishing "wear it in good health" to one who puts on leather shoes or a fur coat, because they were obtained by killing an animal.

Are We Ever Permitted to Be Cruel to Animals?

"People are more important than animals because we alone can worship God."

If the above is correct, it might be asked, why does Judaism allow us to kill animals for food and why is vivisection permitted? The answer is that people are more important than animals because we alone can worship God (and, indeed, feel compassion). Judaism does, therefore, permit the use of animals for human benefit, but lays down two conditions. First, pain must be kept to a minimum and must be vital to human health and well-being. For instance, many authorities refuse to permit the force-feeding of geese to improve the quality of their livers, since it is not essential and the cruelty is excessive and unnecessary.

Second, the pain must be caused reluctantly. There must be no gloating over an animal's suffering. The Talmud tells an astonishing tale about the great teacher Rabbi Judah the Prince (tractate *Bava Metzia* 85a) who saw a calf being led to the slaughter. The calf sought protection under Rabbi Judah's cloak, whereupon he said: "Go, for

God's Compassion for Animals

Moses and David, says the Midrash, were at first shepherds. Why? Because they could not lead their people until they had shown compassion to dumb animals, seeking out every lost sheep and bringing it back home safely.

There are two laws in the Book of Deuteronomy regarding the treatment of animals. One forbids the muzzling of an ox while it is ploughing, so that it cannot eat; the other forbids yoking together an ox and an ass. The Rabbis say that the first prohibition extends to "muzzling verbally" (i.e., by shouting at the animal to stop eating). As for the second law, many commentators see it as pity for the ass, obliged to toil together with a more powerful animal. But the French commentator, Ḥazkuni, suggests that the reason is pity for the ox, a noble beast which must be yoked with the inferior ass.

There is a lovely talmudic legend about a rabbi who asked Elijah the prophet to show him men in the marketplace who were destined for Paradise. Elijah pointed out to the rabbi two jesters, men of little religious sensibility but whose job it was to bring a smile to the faces of those in distress.

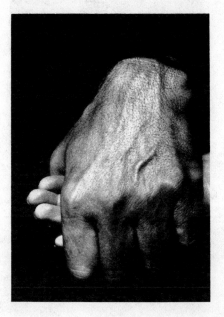

this you were created." As a result, Rabbi Judah was punished with great suffering. Some time later he saw his maidservant sweeping out a nest of weasels from a corner of his palace. "Let them stay," ordered Rabbi Judah, " 'And His tender mercies are over all His works' (Psalm 145:9)." Thereupon his suffering left him.

It should be noted that the tale is not told in favor of vegetarianism. There is no suggestion here that it was wrong to kill the calf for food. But a great teacher like Rabbi Judah should not have said: "Go, for this you were created" as if it mattered little to him that one of God's creatures was to be killed. Rabbi Judah had to atone for his sin by showing extreme compassion, making up for his unfeeling attitude though no wrong would have been done had he allowed the maidservant to proceed with her work.

Those in Special Need of Compassion

Judaism teaches that those whom fate has treated harshly are to be the special objects of our compassion. For instance, the stranger, the widow, and the orphan are especially singled out for kindly treatment in many a biblical passage (see, for example, Exodus 22:20–23; Leviticus 19:9–10; Leviticus 23:22). According to the Rabbis (tractate *Bava Metzia* 58b) it is utterly wrong to suggest to those who mourn or otherwise suffer that their sufferings are a punishment for their sins. That would be to pour salt on their wounds. This in spite of the fact that generally the Rabbis do encourage people to attribute their sufferings to their sins and to examine their deeds when they suffer.

But the distinction is clear. One has to be hard on oneself at times but this does not permit a harsh attitude toward others. Self-discipline, even of a severe kind, is religiously sound. But religious people must always resist the temptation to be as hard on others as they are on themselves. Women, say the Rabbis, are easily moved to tears, so a man should be especially careful not to shout at his wife or otherwise offend her.

Rabbi Israel Salanter, founder of the Musar movement, counted every one of his words in obedience to his ideal of self-control. And yet he once conversed at length on trivial matters with a man who had experienced much sorrow. Rabbi Israel felt it his duty to bring a little cheer into the poor man's sorry existence.

"One has to be hard on oneself at times, but this does not permit a harsh attitude toward others."

The Compassionate Do Not Cause Embarrassment to Others

In addition to showing pity, the ideal of compassion involves taking great care not to put others to shame. In what is no doubt rabbinic hyperbole but still a very serious treatment of a very serious matter, the Rabbis declare that whoever puts another to shame in public has no share in the World to Come. To insult others is also a serious offense. Again no doubt using hyperbole, the Rabbis say that a man who calls another wicked should be deprived of a livelihood, and one who calls another a bastard should be flogged. Sinners who have repented of their sins must never be reminded that they were once sinners, and converts from idolatry to Judaism should never be reminded that their parents were idolators. If someone has an ugly nickname it is forbidden to call him by that name. It is wrong to laugh when a person makes mistakes when saying the prayers, or whenever someone unwittingly exposes his ignorance.

One should avoid anything that causes distress to others. An example in the Talmud says that in the presence of the family of a criminal who has been hanged for murder, one should not say that something is "hanging" from the ceiling. Even when it is necessary to rebuke someone, it should be done with tact and without embarrassing him. However, where an offense has been committed by one of a group of people and it is not known who is responsible, it is the duty of the guilty person to own up, so as not to put the others under suspicion. But if he does not own up, it is forbidden for someone else to expose him. All these ideas are found in the classical rabbinic sources and are based on feelings of delicacy and concern for the dignity of humankind.

Are There Any Limits to Compassion?

From all that has been said until now it might be concluded that there are no limits whatsoever to compassion. Such a conclusion is unrealistic. The Jew is not called upon to be mawkish or to confuse compassion with sentimentality. On the whole, the Jewish tradition does know of two instances where compassion should be rejected. If a judge comes to the conclusion that A is in the right and B in the wrong, it is a perversion of justice if, because of feeling sorry for B, the judge decides in his favor. This is what the Rabbis mean when they say: "There must be no compassion in a law suit (*Ketubot* 84a). A moment's thought enables us to see that this must be so if justice is to prevail. The law must be clear and decided objectively. Only chaos can result if decisions are made by judges on the basis of their feelings. There is, of course, nothing to prevent the judge, who may feel strongly about it, from compensating B with personal funds after the decision has been given. What the judge must never do is to bend the law through a misapplication of compassion.

Raḥamanut is the tear shed for the sick and the poor; it should result in action.

"It is wrong to laugh when a person ignorant of Hebrew makes mistakes when saying the prayers."

Compassion is also evil, when it is shown to people who are cruel and utterly lacking in compassion. When this is done it really shows both lack of compassion and faulty reasoning, since if compassion is a virtue it can be furthered only by total rejection of its opposite. A rabbinic saying (*Yalkut*, Samuel paragraph 121) puts it thus: "Whoever has compassion on the cruel will in the end be cruel to the compassionate." The proof quoted from Scripture is from the narrative about King Saul. Saul was commanded to kill the cruel king Agag whose vicious sword had made widows of many poor women, but Saul was sorry for Agag and spared him (I Samuel 15:9). And yet later on Saul slew the priests of Nob because they had given shelter to his foe David (I Samuel 22:17–19). One of the reasons given in Scripture for excluding the Ammonites and Moabites from the congregation of the Lord (Deuteronomy 23:4–5) is that they refused to give the hungry and thirsty Israelites bread and water. The commentators explain that those lacking elementary decency and compassion cannot become members of the people of Israel, whose distinguishing mark is compassion.

A Heart of Flesh

We say that a cruel, unfeeling person has a heart of stone. This idiom is taken from the book of Ezekiel: "And I will remove the stony heart out of their flesh, and will give them a heart of flesh" (Ezekiel 11:19). What a remarkable metaphor! The "heart of stone" does not allow anything to penetrate it willingly. The stony-hearted person is really lacking in imagination, always failing to put himself in the other's shoes. He is never moved by human torment, although not directly responsible for it. But he is indirectly responsible, since evil people would not be so bold if they did not know they could rely on the indifference of others. The one with the "heart of flesh," on the other hand, will always try to see things from the other's point of view. If someone wrongs him, the wrong will be forgiven both because he realizes how much it must have cost the other to ask for forgiveness, and because he knows no one is perfect and that it would be hypocritical to ask God for His compassion and forgiveness while being personally unforgiving. Jewish moralists write that all devout Jews, before going to bed at night, should say aloud that they bear no grudge against anyone and that they forgive anyone who has wronged them during the day.

Compassion is one of the shining virtues. Unlike some other virtues it does not really make severe demands on our nature. On the contrary, as Judaism sees it, it is an appeal to us to realize what we know we want to realize. Who does not admire the compassionate person, and how rarely do we speak of compassion as being too difficult? Judaism believes that it is the stony heart that is unnatural to humanity and that people want to have the "heart of flesh."

"Compassion can be evil when it is shown to people who are themselves cruel and lacking in compassion."

21
Benevolence

"Benevolence expresses in practice the attitude of compassion."

Compassion and Benevolence

Compassion (raḥamanut), is closely connected to benevolence (gemilut ḥasadim). Compassion leads to benevolence. The one is an attitude, the other its practice. It is possible for a hardhearted person to perform acts of benevolence, as a momentary whim, perhaps, or because he is ashamed to do otherwise. Conversely, it is possible for a compassionate person to fail miserably in practical benevolence by being too easygoing or too lazy to act out personal feelings. The Jewish ideal is to be both compassionate and benevolent; to have a good heart and to do good deeds. A Ḥasidic master gave a fine turn to the passage in the Amidah: "Thou sustainest the living with lovingkindness, revivest the dead with great compassion." His interpretation is that, by giving living men and women the opportunities for practicing lovingkindness, God "sustains" them in life. He makes their life worthwhile, for what kind of living can it be if there is no benevolence? Similarly by endowing people with feelings of compassion, God "revives" the dead; the hardhearted person is like a corpse, unfeeling and completely insensitive, and when he is moved it is like reviving the dead.

Two Concepts

There are two related concepts in the Jewish tradition: (1) benevolence (gemilut ḥasadim, literally "bestowing lovingkindness"); (2) tzedakah, "charity." This second term has had an interesting history. The word tzedakah in the Bible means "righteousness" and is synonymous with the word mishpat, "justice." But by rabbinic times the

True Kindness

A penetrating old rabbinic comment on Jacob's request that his son Joseph bury him in the Holy Land notes that the aged partriarch speaks of a "true kindness" (Genesis 47:29). The comment is that kindness shown to the dead is *true* kindness. When we benefit the living our motives may not be entirely altruistic, since we may hope secretly that one day they will repay the kindness. When, on the other hand, we are kind to the dead, we know that they will never be able to repay us, and our kindly act is in no way tainted by any ulterior motive.

word had assumed the meaning of "charity," "alms-giving." By that time, the concept had developed that "righteousness" does not only mean being just, but also being charitable or, rather, being just by being charitable. The poor are entitled to our help, it says. God has so ordered His world that the poor have a "right" to assistance and if we are charitable we are merely doing our duty.

The Talmud states that there are three main differences between *gemilut ḥasadim* ("benevolence") and *tzedakah* ("charity"). Tzedakah is for the benefit of the poor, while gemilut ḥasadim is for the rich as well. One cannot give charity to a rich person who already has enough. One can be kind and benevolent to a rich person as well as a poor one. Second, tzedakah refers to a contribution of money. The poor person needs *financial* assistance. But gemilut ḥasadim implies the giving of oneself to help others, by a friendly act or a compassionate word. Third, tzedakah is given to the living. One cannot give charity to the dead, whose financial cares are over. But gemilut ḥasadim can be extended to the dead, by burying them and attending their funerals as well as by reciting prayers in their memory.

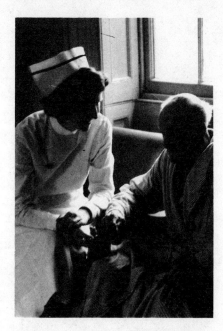

An example of benevolence? Speaking a word of encouragement and praise.

Benevolence

Many examples of benevolence (gemilut ḥasadim) have been recorded in the rabbinic literature and in the works of the Jewish moralists. Prominent among the acts of benevolence is "visiting the sick," which means far more than a mere occasional visit. It means caring for the sick and doing all one can to heal them. A whole section in the *Shulḥan Arukh* is devoted to the rules for visiting the sick, and these display considerable delicacy of feeling. For instance, it is ruled that, while the more visits one pays the more meritorious he is, care should be taken not to visit at inconvenient times or to weary the sick person and the family, or when the patient suffers from an embarrassing illness. Similarly, it is tactless to visit an enemy who is sick. Even though the visitor may wish to let bygones be bygones, the sick person may imagine he has come to gloat. The Rabbis say that the Divine Presence is with the sick person because God shares in his suffering. Consequently, one must sit in a respectful attitude when visiting the sick. Prayers should be offered for his recovery, both at the bedside and in the synagogue. Medieval authorities discuss whether it is right to pray for a merciful release for someone suffering from an incurable and painful disease. The conclusion is that it is right and proper for friends to do so, but not for the patient's family since, subconsciously, they may wish him to die not for his own sake but so they can be spared the strain of looking after him.

Comforting mourners is another example of gemilut ḥasadim. In talmudic times it was the custom to take gifts of food and especially of wine to mourners to bring a little cheer into their lives. To attend a funeral is also an act of benevolence, paying the last respects to the departed and accompanying them to their rest. Other examples are

"It is tactless for someone to visit an enemy who is ill. The sick person may imagine the other has come to gloat."

lending money to help tide someone over a financial difficulty; speaking a word of encouragement and praise; lending books or other needed articles; greeting others warmly; helping the aged and infirm. Hospitality to guests is stressed. The prime example is Abraham, who made his guests so very welcome (Genesis 18:1–8). According to the Midrash, Abraham had a door at every side of his tent so that strangers could quickly find refuge. In Eastern Europe Jews used to say that the house of a hospitable person had "Abraham's doors." The Musar movement particularly emphasized kindly behavior. Rabbi Nathan Finkel, the Musar leader of the Yeshiva of Slobodka early in this century, used to go to the railway station to help people with their baggage when no porters were available. He once accompanied a team of gypsies and sang with them to cheer them on the way.

The Importance of Benevolence

The Rabbis wax eloquent in describing the virtue of benevolence. The usual rabbinic description of the good person is of one who studies the Torah and practices benevolence. On the other hand, they say that students of the Torah who have no acts of benevolence to their credit have no Torah to their credit either! Why? Because Torah study that fails to result in good deeds does not have much value and cannot be very profound. Benevolence, it is stated in *Ethics of the Fathers* (1:2), is one of the three things upon which the world stands. The world cannot endure for long unless people are kind and helpful to one another. And the Mishnah (*Peah* 1:1) states that there is no

Helping the aged or the infirm is a prime example of the Jewish view of benevolence.

Charity

In the town of Brisk in Lithuania there was a man renowned for his charity. But the rabbi of the town, Rabbi Ḥayyim Soloveichik observed that the man was not really generous, because he loved to give charity so much that he would hate to see poverty abolished!

limit to benevolence and that it is one of the things for which a person is rewarded by God in this life, as it is the capital stock of the reward stored up for the Hereafter. The Midrash applies the verse: "mingled with oil" (Numbers 7:19) to the study of Torah, which is significant only if "mingled" with the oil of good deeds, the practice of benevolence.

Relief for the Poor

Tzedakah, "charity," is, as we have noted earlier, the giving of money to help the poor. There should be an element of benevolence (gemilut ḥasadim), say the Rabbis, in all tzedakah. The poor should be spoken to gently and kindly, and whatever is given should be offered with a good heart without being patronizing. The English saying "as cold as charity" does not apply to the Jewish attitude. It is better not to give at all, say the Rabbis, than to give in a way that shames the poor.

> *"Charity should be given with a good heart, without being patronizing."*

Over 1,500 years ago in talmudic times there was an elaborate system of relief for the poor. Charity overseers, who were among the most respected members of the community ("If you can," a talmudic saying goes, "marry the daughter of a charity overseer"), made two separate collections from the townsfolk. One was for a weekly distribution to the poor of that town. The other was for daily distribution to the poor who were passing through the town. Jewish communities had a number of societies, each with its own charitable purpose. There was a society for helping the poor financially, another for providing dowries for poor brides, still another for giving interest-free loans to the needy, and so forth. The education of poor children and other religious needs of the poor were taken care of, such as food and wine for Passover. Long before adequate social provision was made for the poor in European lands, the Jews had worked out a system of relief for the poor that is among the glories of Jewish history.

Who Qualifies and How Much?

The Rabbis knew that there existed professional beggars who made a good living by pretending to be poor, thus taking advantage of the good-hearted. The Mishnah (*Peah* 8:9) warns people who fake lameness or blindness in order to trick others into helping them, that if

they persist, they will eventually become really infirm and crippled. On the other hand, really poor people who make do with their lot without asking for help will be blessed by God in that one day they will become rich enough to support others. Still, the Rabbis did not view kindly a person in dire circumstances who refused to ask for assistance. An old Yiddish saying has it: "He did not die of hunger; he died because he was too proud to ask."

What is the definition of "poor"? How poor does a person have to be to qualify for relief? Obviously, poverty is a relative matter, but the Rabbis did try to lay down hard and fast rules. Thus, they state, someone who has 200 zuz in ready cash or 50 zuz invested in a business enterprise can no longer be considered poor and entitled to public aid. A person who has a smaller amount does qualify even for a substantial donation; since he meets the terms of the law and he is entitled to whatever is being given the poor. In a somewhat humorous vein the Rabbis comment that "a cunning wicked man" is one who gives a poor person who has 199 zuz the extra zuz that removes him from the category of the poor. On the face of it, the donor is giving charity, but he is really depriving the needy one of the right to a much larger donation.

How much charity is a person obliged to give? The official rabbinic reply is a tenth of one's income when there is a need for relief. To this day there are many pious Jews who set aside a tenth of their annual earnings for charity. But the Rabbis frown on people giving more than a fifth of their income to charity because they themselves might become poor and have to throw themselves on the mercy of others. However, the Ḥasidic master, Rabbi Shneur Zalman of Lyady, states that if a sinner wishes to atone for his sins by giving charity, he may give far more than a fifth, just as a person will be ready to give away much wealth when physical health is at stake.

Precedence

The Rabbis also tried to work out detailed rules as to who comes first when there is not enough for distribution to all the poor. Where it is a question of food, a man should be given before a woman because he has a family to support. If it is a question of clothing, on the other hand, a woman comes first because she suffers greater embarrassment if she has no proper clothes to wear. Similarly, if a man and a woman are held for ransom by bandits, the woman should be ransomed, if there is only enough money to rescue one, because her suffering can be far greater than a man's. A man must help his own poor relatives before he helps other poor people. Similarly, the poor of one's own town come before poor of another town, and the poor of one's own country before those of other countries. However, the poor of Eretz Yisrael are to be treated as the poor of one's own town for this purpose.

A *pushke* (charity box), Vienna, 1868.

In Praise of Charity

Just as we saw the Rabbis praise benevolence, they praise charity most highly. Charity is the distinguishing mark of our father Abra-

---

Maimonides' Eight Degrees of Charity

Maimonides' famous statement in his great Code of Law on the eight degrees of charity is given in ascending order (Maimonides formulates them in descending order but the following arrangement is more convenient for our purpose):

1. A man gives, but is glum when he gives. This is the lowest degree of all.

2. A man gives with a cheerful countenance, but gives less than he should.

3. A man gives, but only when asked by the poor.

4. A man gives without having to be asked, but gives directly to the poor who know therefore to whom they are indebted, and he, too, knows whom he has benefited.

5. A man places his donation in a certain place and then turns his back so that he does not know which of the poor he has benefited, but the poor man knows to whom he is indebted.

6. A man throws the money into the house of a poor man. The poor man does not know to whom he is indebted but the donor knows whom he has benefited.

7. A man contributes anonymously to the charity fund which is then distributed to the poor. Here the poor man does not know to whom he is indebted, neither does the donor know whom he has benefited.

8. Highest of all is when money is given to prevent another from becoming poor, as by providing him with a job or by lending him money to tide him over a difficult period. There is no charity greater than this because it prevents poverty in the first instance.

"Israel can only be redeemed from exile as the result of the charity Jews give."

ham, say the Rabbis. Israel's throne is established only through charity—without it, Judaism cannot survive. Furthermore, Israel can be redeemed from exile only by the charity Jews give. No one ever becomes poor through giving charity and no one ever suffers harm from giving. On the contrary, the more merciful a person, the more mercy will God show to him. Just as an idolator is called a "scoundrel" so, too, is the person so lacking in faith and generosity that he gives nothing away. Scripture states that God hears the cry of the poor (Job 34:28). It is therefore essential not to cause the poor to cry out in their distress. Job is the example of the man who not only gives to the poor but also commiserates with them. Job boasted with justice: "If I have not wept for him that was in trouble, and if my soul grieved not for the needy" (Job 30:25). A person should bring some cheer into the lives of the poor, as did Job: "And I caused the widow's heart to sing for joy" (Job 29:13).

Justice and Love

A number of Christian thinkers—and the Jewish writer, Aḥad ha-Am as well—have suggested that, from the ethical point of view, the difference between Judaism and Christianity is that Christianity is based on love while Judaism is based on justice. Where this description of the two religions is accepted, the inevitable result is that Christian thinkers try to show that an ethic of love is superior, because it comes from the heart and is not bogged down by rules and regulations, while Jewish thinkers try to show that an ethic of justice is superior, because it is less subject to fancy and more sane and realistic.

The truth is that there is little truth in the alleged distinction. It is not for us to point out that Christianity also knows of justice, but we can and should point out the absurdity of the generalization regarding Judaism, as if the classical Jewish sources were not full of the concept of love! If there were any lingering doubts about this, it is hoped that they were dispelled by the chapters of this book on compassion and benevolence. What is correct is that Judaism does attach the utmost significance to justice. We saw in the chapter, Love Thy Neighbor, that the command to love is understood by the Jewish teachers as demanding concrete, practical expressions of love, which can be only in terms of justice. The two words which appear as synonyms in the Bible—*tzedek* ("righteousness") and *mishpat* ("justice") —both mean "justice" and the demand to practice justice. A commonly used term for the same concept in the rabbinic literature is *din* ("law," "judgment"). And what are the great law codes produced by the legal masters if not statements of just principles in action? To this day, if a devout Jew wishes to know how to behave in a given situation, he asks: "What is the *din*?"

> *"The command to love demands concrete expression in terms of justice."*

A Mishnah Tale

This case is recorded in the Mishnah. A's ox gores B's cow and a dead calf is found beside the cow, it being known that the cow had been carrying the calf. B consequently demands compensation not only for the cow but also for the calf, which the cow may have lost through the goring by A's ox. But A counterclaims that the calf may have been dropped by the cow before the cow had been gored by the ox and no compensation is due for the loss of the calf. There is thus a doubt whether or not A has to compensate B for the calf, and since A has possession, he does not have to pay for the calf.

Claims in Conflict

Justice is called into operation whenever there are two conflicting claims. For instance, A claims ownership of a piece of land because he inherited it from his father; but B, while admitting that the land was once A's, claims he bought it from A and produces evidence to prove it. A denies ever having sold the land to B and rejects B's evidence. Both A and B cannot be right. The two claims are in conflict and the most strenuous efforts must be made by the courts of law (there can be no justice without detailed law and law courts) to determine which of the two is telling the truth. For the court to decide in favor of the rightful owner is to practice justice. If they mistakenly decide in favor of the wrongful owner, both judged and judge are guilty of injustice.

Naturally, there are many instances where, on the evidence available, it is simply not possible to establish the truth. But even here there is a just solution. Jewish law gives the benefit of the doubt to the one who is in possession of the disputed property. This is a procedural matter and is not based on any ideas that a person holding some property is necessarily its rightful owner. What the rule means is that in the absence of any real evidence, the court would not be *justified* (it would not be a just act) in removing the property from where it is, for they would be deciding, without sufficient cause, in favor of one of the parties. Where the evidence is insufficient they have no right to decide in favor of either party, so that the only fair procedure is to leave the property where it is unless further evidence is available.

Similarly, in matters of control of crime and punishment for crime, justice means weighing the claims of society against the conflicting claim of the criminal. In a just society, the right of the criminal to prey on others must be rejected in favor of the right and duty of society to protect itself. However, justice is further involved when society has to weigh carefully how far to punish the criminal in order to protect itself. So far as the punishment affords this protection, it is just. But if it exceeds the degree of protection required, it is unfair and unjust to the criminal who, as a human being, also has rights. Of course, people of good will can debate endlessly the extent of the protection society requires against the criminal and the degree of rights the criminal possesses, but when they do they are discussing justice and, since their debate may lead to practical consequences, they are practicing justice in the very debate.

"In a just society, the claims of the criminal to prey upon others must be rejected in favor of society's right to protect itself."

Courts of Law

There can be no justice without the establishment of proper courts of law to administer justice. The Rabbis hold that one of the demands made by the Torah even on non-Jews—one of the "seven mitzvot of the sons of Noah"—is to have a satisfactory system of justice in the land. The Hebrew for "court of law" is *Bet Din*, "house of justice." For

"No judge should sit in a case where one of the contestants is a dear friend or a fierce enemy."

civil cases a Bet Din is made up of three judges learned in the law, and the decision of the majority is followed. (The Talmud states that it is forbidden for the judge in the minority to tell one of the contestants: "I decided in your favor, but what could I do?") The judges must be entirely unbiased. No judge may sit in a case if one of the contestants is a friend or an enemy. The laws regarding the judges are given in the Book of Deuteronomy (16:18–19): "Judges and officers [the Rabbis explain this as a police force] shalt thou make thee in all thy gates, which the Lord thy God giveth thee, tribe by tribe; and they shall judge the people with righteous judgment. Thou shalt not wrest judgment; thou shalt not show partiality; neither shalt thou take a bribe; for a bribe doth blind the eyes of the wise, and pervert the words of the righteous." And there follows the marvelous verse with its passion for justice: "Justice, justice [note the repetition] shalt thou pursue, that thou mayest live, and inherit the land which the Lord thy God giveth thee" (Deuteronomy 16:20). Taking a "gift" (shoḥad) means first of all that the judge must never take bribes, but the Rabbis go further and apply it to any gift, even from the contestant he considers in the right. As the verse says, the "gift" blinds the judge, exerts a subconscious influence in favor of the giver. One of the Rabbis in the Talmud refused to act as a judge in a case because one of the contestants had brushed a feather from the judge's cloak. Even this trivial act, he felt, biased him in the man's favor.

Interestingly enough, in the Book of Exodus we read how Moses was instructed in the proper arrangement of the courts by his

The Bet Din in Operation

Many of the larger Jewish cities have a *Bet Din,* a court of arbitration to which Jews bring complaints against others. It is considered a point of honor to prefer to consult Jewish judges rather than resort to secular courts. If, however, one of the parties to a dispute refuses to attend the Bet Din, the other is permitted by the Bet Din to bring his case to the general court.

The most famous case in all legal history is that of Solomon and the two women, each of whom claimed the same baby to be hers. Solomon ordered his soldiers to cut the baby in half, giving half to each woman, whereupon, the true mother said that the baby should be given to her rival.

Freud has something to say about the psychology of the false claimant. Of what use to her was half an infant? But, said Freud, she did not really want the infant. All she cared about was that the other woman would have a baby while she had none!

The seventeenth-century halakhist R. Joshua Falk, author of the work *Meirat Eynayim* on Jewish law, was summoned to the Bet Din by another man. The judge decided against Rabbi Falk. When the decision has been given, Rabbi Falk asked the judge for his reasoning. The judge replied that in the work *Meirat Eynayim* he had found the correctness of his decision. Rabbi Falk realized that he himself, in his book, had shown that he was wrong, but so strong is self-interest that he had forgotten what he himself had written, and had believed, incorrectly, that he had a case.

non-Israelite father-in-law Jethro. When Jethro saw Moses taking on the whole burden himself, he urged Moses to appoint judges under him to deal with the many cases that came up (Exodus 18:13–27). It is as if the Torah is saying that justice is for all people and can be appreciated by all people, not only Israelites, so that Jews should learn from the advice of non-Jews, too. Still, once the Torah had been given, the Rabbis frowned upon Jews bringing their cases to Gentile courts if they could bring them to Jewish courts. To do so would suggest that they thought the laws of the Torah were not as just as those of the Gentiles. Jethro tells Moses: "If thou shalt do this thing, and God command thee so, then thou shalt be able to endure, and all this people also shall go to their place in peace" (verse 23). There is a powerful rabbinic comment on this to the effect that when justice is done, *everyone* finds peace, even the loser. No one can feel at peace knowing an injustice has been done. Therefore the Rabbis comment: "If a man has lost a cloak in a law suit (because the judges have decided against him) let him go out of the courthouse singing."

> "Anyone who has a bad reputation in money matters is disqualified from acting as a witness."

Witnesses in a law suit have to be perfectly respectable people who can be relied on to tell the truth. Anyone who has a bad reputation in money matters is disqualified from acting as a witness. Fascinating is the law that no near relative can be a witness in any circumstances. Of course, one cannot be a witness in favor of a relative since there is bias, but why should a father, say, be disqualified from testifying *against* his son? One reason given by the commentators is that family quarrels can sometimes be very vehement and the father, in a fit of temper, may rush to the court to punish his son by testifying harshly against him. But other commentators explain that even if the father is telling the truth, the Torah does not think it right for a father to be the instrument of justice against his own son, or a son against his own father. It would be justice attained in an unjust way.

In Praise of Justice

The first chapter of *Ethics of the Fathers* concludes with the saying of Rabban Simeon ben Gamaliel: "On three things the world rests: on justice (*din*), truth (*emet*), and peace (*shalom*)." The verse quoted is: "These are the things that ye shall do: Speak ye every man the truth with his neighbor; execute the judgment of truth and in your gates" (Zechariah 8:16). The commentators remark that where there is truth, there is justice and where there is justice, there is peace. A peace based on injustice is no peace and will not last. On the basis of this, Rabbi Mordecai Jaffe (d. 1612), in his introduction to his great law code *Levush Malkhut*, gives a very fanciful but profound interpretation of the verse: "And God said: Let the earth put forth grass" (Genesis 1:11). Rabbi Jaffe notes that the initial letters of the words *din* ("justice"), *shalom* ("peace"), and *emet* ("truth") form *deshe*, the word

used in the verse for "grass." Right at the beginning of creation, God declares that if the earth is to grow and endure, if civilization is to prosper and not to collapse, there must be a growth of justice, peace, and truth.

Application in Daily Life

It is not only in the law courts that justice must be practiced. Judaism demands that people be just in all their dealings with one another. The relationship between employer and employee, for example, must be based on fairness. The employer must give employees a fair wage, listen sympathetically to their complaints, and pay their wages on time. In return, employees must put in a fair day's work. The Talmud permits workers to recite the Shema on scaffolding because to go down would be to waste their employer's time. On the other hand, for prayer, which requires greater concentration, they must be given time by their employer to descend.

According to the rabbinic interpretation of the Deuteronomic law (Deuteronomy 23:25) workers in a vineyard are allowed to pick as many grapes as they wish to eat. It would be unfair to them to have to work in a luscious vineyard and not eat. But they must not "put any in thy vessel," that is, they are not allowed to take any grapes home without paying for them, for that would be unfair to the employer.

Shopkeepers must charge fair prices and not take advantage of their customers. They must have just weights and measures. In Eastern European communities it was not unusual for the rabbis, when they saw that the fishmongers were charging exorbitant prices, to issue a ban on fish for the Sabbath (even though it is traditionally a special Sabbath delicacy) in order to bring down the price. In talmudic times it was considered a great offense to attempt to corner the market in life's essential commodities.

There is an interesting debate between the second-century Palestinian teacher Rabbi Judah and his colleagues (Mishnah *Bava Metzia* 4:12). Rabbi Judah held that it is not permissible for a shopkeeper to distribute nuts to children in order to encourage them to buy at his shop when sent to buy commodities by their mothers. He held that this is unfair competition with the other shopkeepers. The sages, Rabbi Judah's colleagues, disagreed, holding that the other shopkeepers could do the same or go even better by distributing even choicer delicacies to the children. In the same passage another debate is recorded. Rabbi Judah, anxious to protect the interests of the other shopkeepers, held that it is forbidden to sell wares below market price. This would be unfair competition, he said. But the sages held that, on the contrary, he should be encouraged, since if the shopkeepers compete in lowering prices, the customers will benefit. In other words, the sages and Rabbi Judah were debating whether it is more in accord with justice to protect the shopkeepers or the community.

Going beyond the Letter of the Law

It is a principle in Judaism that one should not always insist on his legal rights but should sometimes go beyond the letter of the law (*lifnim mi-shurat ha-din*). The Talmud tells of a rabbi who hired some porters to carry casks of wine for him. The porters were negligent and broke the casks. According to the strict letter of the law, he could charge the porters for the loss of his wine and he was certainly under no legal obligation to pay them their wages. Yet another rabbi urged him not to insist on compensation, and moreover to pay them their wages, not because this was the law but because he should set an example of going beyond the letter of the law.

The point to be noted here is that to go beyond the letter of the law is itself a requirement of the law, but it is up to the individual when to implement it. It obviously cannot be expected that all individuals in all circumstances must forego their rights. If they did, every dishonest person could become rich at the expense of others.

From the Talmud

The Talmud tells of certain extremely pious men (ḥasidim) who would bury any pieces of broken glass so deep that no amount of ploughing in the field could ever bring them up again. The law requires only that reasonable care be taken. But these saintly people wished to avoid even the remotest possibility of anything of theirs causing harm to other people.

There are times when it is right to insist on the strict application of the law, and times when the proper thing to do is to relinquish one's rights—depending on the goodwill, sense of fair play, and the circumstances of the individual.

"To go beyond the letter of the law is itself a requirement of the law!"

Gratitude and Ingratitude

An important aspect of justice is gratitude for favors rendered. We owe it to others to thank them for any kindnesses they have done, and certainly not to repay them with ingratitude. One of the most remarkable verses in the Bible is: "Thou shalt not abhor an Egyptian, because thou wast a stranger in his land" (Deuteronomy 23:8). Many generations after the Exodus, Egyptians were to be treated with respect because their ancestors' had offered the children of Israel hospitality. Joseph and his brethren had been welcomed by Pharaoh and the Egyptian people so that, even though the Egyptians later oppressed the Israelites, their original kindness was never to be forgotten.

A popular proverb quoted in the Talmud (*Bava Kama* 92b) has it: "Into the well from which you have once drunk water, do not throw clods of earth." That is, one must be grateful even to inanimate things; how much more to human beings? The Midrash remarks that when Moses had to perform his wonders he was never commanded to stretch out his staff over the river Nile (as with wonders that proceeded from the earth) because when he was a tiny babe, the placing of his ark in the Nile had saved his life. Aaron had to use the rod on the Nile, not Moses, for whom it would have been an act of ingratitude. Joseph Ibn Migash (1077–1141) tells of his teacher Rabbi Isaac Alfasi, who fell ill. A certain man looked after him, giving him medicinal baths in his home. Later the host fell heavily into debt and was obliged to have his bathhouse evaluated in order to pay off his creditors. Alfasi refused to be a judge in the case. There are two reasons why a friend of one of the contestants in a law suit may not act as a judge. The first is that people are biased in their friends' favor. But in addition, if honesty compels us to decide against our friend who has helped us in the past, we will be guilty of ingratitude. If this applies to human beings, concludes Ibn Migash, how much more should we be grateful to God, the source of our life, and never depart from obedience to His will.

No Advantage to Be Taken of the Helpless

Justice requires that one should never take advantage of someone's helplessness. The biblical verse states "Thou shalt not curse the deaf, nor put a stumbling block before the blind, but thou shalt fear thy

The Rabbis strictly forbid willfully giving someone bad advice (right).

Shopkeepers must charge fair prices and must not take advantage of their customers (below).

God: I am the Lord" (Leviticus 19:14). The commentators explain that it is wrong to curse anyone, but a deaf person cannot retaliate and to curse him adds the offense of taking advantage of someone's weakness.

The same applies to placing an obstacle in the path of a blind person. Besides the offense of causing harm if the blind man falls, the very placing of the obstacle in his path is an offense in itself! The Rabbis extend this to cover every instance of causing harm, physical as well as spiritual, to another by allowing someone to err through a weakness. For instance, the Rabbis strictly forbid giving advice one knows to be bad, such as advising someone to go into a business with a person known to be unscrupulous. The innocent party is like a blind person who cannot see the danger. Again, the Rabbis think of someone who wishes to sin to be like the blind. Consequently, to encourage him in his blindness by providing the opportunities to sin is misleading the blind.

Compromise

The Rabbis say that if both parties to a dispute are willing to compromise, each giving way a little, this is itself a form of justice, since both are satisfied. It is especially commendable in a complicated case where it is unlikely that all the right is on one side. In marital disputes, for example, Rabbis who try to make peace between husband and wife generally can do so only by pointing out to both that they are right in some respects but wrong in others. There are some people whose sense of justice is so overwhelming that they cannot compromise. It is a matter of principle, they declare. (The Israelis call them "principle-nudniks"). To be sure, we must have our principles and live by them, but often we must realize that compromise is also a principle and that justice is best served when both give way a little.

Honesty and Integrity

To be honest, is naturally, an important aspect of justice. "Thou shalt not steal" in the Ten Commandments refers, according to the Rabbis, to the most serious kind of theft of all, kidnapping; but it and other biblical verses condemn all kinds of theft. The thief is under an obligation to return the stolen article to the victim and cannot simply offer to pay its value, unless it is damaged or lost. If a person has stolen from many people and does not know the identity of the victims, say the Rabbis, he should, in order to make good the thefts, create something from which the public can benefit, such as a public garden and fountain. "Thou shalt not steal" includes plagiarism, stealing another person's ideas and passing them off as one's own. The Talmud is full of exact attribution of teachings, who said what and in whose name. Religious objects gained through theft are useless. A stolen lulav, for example, cannot be used on Sukkot, and it is considered a form of blasphemy to recite Grace over stolen food. How can the thief give thanks to God for providing food if the food was "provided" by theft? Honesty implies that one's word be kept. Even when there is no legal contract, a promise to buy or sell should be honored. And double-talk should be avoided. "Let your 'yes' be 'yes' and your 'no' 'no'," say the Rabbis. The Jewish ideal is to be completely honest in all one's dealings.

"There are some people whose sense of justice is so powerful that they always refuse to compromise."

23
Holiness

What is Holiness?

Because holiness (*kedushah*) by any definition points to an intangible world, to the spiritual, it is an elusive concept. Most of us have some idea of what is meant by saying that something is "sacred" or "holy" but we find difficulties when we try to put it into words. A working definition of holiness is given in the Hebrew Encyclopedia, entitled *Otzar Yisrael*, under the heading "Kedushah." The definition is: "That which is elevated above any material concept and distinguished from any secular concept or is separated for the name of the Lord." Holiness, in other words, is a religious concept. A person whose life is conducted on a purely secular plane might be a good person but neither he nor others would refer to him as "holy."

In the Bible "holiness" is a characteristic of God Who is apart

Holy Objects

Judaism knows of holy objects and sacred places. The *Sefer Torah*, for example, is holy, as are *tefillin, mezuzah* and other Torah writings. Interestingly enough, objects used in carrying out the precepts, such as *tzitzit* and the *shofar*, are not treated as holy objects. The difference is that holy objects must be treated with the utmost reverence and may not be used for any other purpose. For example, one may use tzitzit, removed from the *tallit*, as a bookmark, but may not use a mezuzah for that purpose. Examples of special holy places are the Land of Israel, the site of the Temple, Jerusalem in general, the synagogue and the house of learning.

The word *kedushah*, "holiness," comes from a root meaning to set apart (i.e., certain places and objects have been dedicated to the service of God). There are, on the whole, two ways of understanding the sanctity of these objects and places. One, favored by many Jewish teachers, is that somehow a supernatural quality, a kind of flow from the Divine, actually resides in the object or place, just as the soul occupies the human body. It is "there" but not in any easily detected spatial sense. Others understand the concept of holiness as being a matter of association. The fact that it has been dedicated to God's service causes it to be treated differently.

Certain persons, too, are held to be holy, generally because they lead pure, ascetic lives and do not have ugly traits of character. Especially among Ḥasidim, but not peculiar to them, the holy person, because he is attached to to the spiritual realm, may become inspired by the holy spirit (*ruaḥ ha-kodesh*) and guide others, even performing miracles through the power of his prayers.

196

from the universe and beyond its limitations. The song of the *serafim* is: "Holy, holy, holy, is the Lord of hosts; The whole earth is full of His glory" (Isaiah 6:3); that is to say, God is apart from everything in the material universe, yet in that universe there are intimations of His holiness—"The whole earth is full of His glory." Anything dedicated to God is called "holy," the Temple, Bet ha-Mikdash, for example, or the synagogue, which is called a *makom kadosh*, "holy place." The implication is that to be near to God it is necessary to be holy, and this is expressed in the key verse: "Speak unto all the congregation of the children of Israel, and say unto them: Ye shall be holy; for I the Lord your God am holy" (Leviticus 19:2). The verse is addressed to "all the congregation of the children of Israel" so it must be something possible for all. And this is where a difficulty arises, since by "holy people" we usually refer to hermits or very unworldly persons and this is hardly an ideal for everyone; or, as far as Judaism is concerned, for anyone!

Holy People

In fact, Judaism awards the title *kedoshim*, "holy ones," to very few. Only a handful even of the great teachers of the past are usually referred to as kedoshim—Rabbi Judah the Prince is called *Rabbenu ha-Kadosh*, for example. Martyrs are called kedoshim both because they have "sanctified God's name" by giving their lives for His sake and because they have demonstrated that the spiritual world means more to them than anything this material world has to offer.

Significantly, Jewish communities are called "holy"—a community is referred to as *kehillah kedoshah*; implying that where Jews are gathered together for sacred purposes, even if as individuals they are far from the ideal of holiness, collectively, holiness is present. The holiness ideal is, then, not for the few saints but for men and women living normal lives in the physical world. How can they be holy? The Jewish reply is by keeping in touch as much as possible with spiritual things. This involves, a certain readiness to give up too much attachment to worldly things, a degree of separation from material pleasure, though not its denial. On the verse: "And ye shall be holy men unto Me" (Exodus 22:30) the Kotzker Rebbe commented: "Be holy but not in a wild, inhuman way. Be holy but be *men* at the same time." Martin Buber observed that Judaism demands that we be "humanly holy."

Self-Control

This leads us to consider how far Judaism believes in self-denial. It is too easy to reply that Judaism does not believe in any kind of self-denial except of things actually forbidden. The Rabbis say: "Sanctify yourself by denying yourself even something of that which is other-

The Jewish concept of holiness includes self-control. But each individual must decide how to exercise restraint.

"The implication is that to be near to God it is necessary to be holy."

wise permitted." What this means is that self-control must be exercised even when doing that which the Torah permits. That which the Torah forbids, it forbids to all. At the same time, the Torah permits many things, but it is not a blanket permission. The Torah does *not* say, "As long as it is not technically forbidden, you can do whatever you wish." Indulging in things permitted can be so gross and unrefined that it is a block to holiness. Take, for instance, a person who never eats forbidden food or food gained by illegal methods, never goes with anyone other than his or her own spouse, never eats or drinks on Yom Kippur, never sleeps when it is time to be up and about; and yet spends most leisure time eating and drinking, having sex, and sleeping. He is far from the Torah ideal of a person who not only obeys the laws, but who has a "Torah character."

Naturally, there can be no detailed laws about such matters, but it *is* a Torah law that each person must exercise self-control. Just as the ideal of going beyond the letter of the law in financial matters is itself a law that is left to individual discretion, so is the religious ideal of holiness. Its necessity is a law, but how it is applied is a matter for free but honest choice. What for one person is gross indulgence is essential to the health of another. It is left to each individual to decide how much self-control should be exercised so that worldly pleasure and enjoyments are not a barrier to appreciation of spiritual things. To do this is to be holy.

Holiness a Gift

Rabbi Moses Ḥayyim Luzzatto (1707–1746) says that, according to Jewish teaching, the attainment of holiness is not possible through one's own efforts alone, but is ultimately a gift from God. He quotes the talmudic rabbis who say that a person who makes a little effort to be holy is given much holiness from on high. The effort means keeping aloof from whatever is grossly material. After all, says Luzzatto, a person is a physical being, merely flesh and blood, so that to become really holy, God must impart to him some of His holiness.

We are at this point considering something more than the holiness required of "all the congregation of Israel." This is religion at its most intense form, and while it is good to know that many Jews have striven to be holy in this superior way, for most of us it belongs more to a vision or remote ideal than to practical Jewish living. In fact, Luzzatto states this only at the conclusion of his work *Mesillat Yesharim*, "Path of the Upright," which is a treatise describing humanity's ascent through various stages of the spiritual life until becoming so holy as to attain the "holy spirit" (*ruaḥ ha-kodesh*), to become inspired. Luzzatto's famous work follows the "path of the upright" mapped out by the second-century teacher Rabbi Phinehas ben Yair (tractate *Avodah Zarah* 20b). Rabbi Phinehas ben Yair outlines the progress people can make in holy living, beginning with obligations

"Luzzatto remarks that the attainment of holiness is not possible through a person's own efforts but is ultimately a gift from God."

The Talmud teaches: "Knowledge of Torah leads to watchfulness, watchfulness to zeal, zeal to cleanness, cleanness to abstinence, abstinence to purity, purity to saintliness, saintliness to humility, humility to fear of sin, and fear of sin to holiness."

every Jew has and going on to much higher things, which, to be honest, are probably beyond the majority of us today.

Here is the statement of Rabbi Phinehas ben Yair: "The knowledge of the Torah leads to watchfulness, watchfulness to zeal, zeal to cleanness, cleanness to abstinence, abstinence to purity, purity to saintliness, saintliness to humility, humility to the fear of sin, and the fear of sin to holiness. Holiness leads to the holy spirit and the holy spirit leads to the resurrection of the dead." From this last clause, too, we see he is teaching a rare stage akin to what we usually refer to in English as "saintliness" of the highest degree.

For Lesser Mortals

Having gone far above our normal grasp, we should now return to consider what approach to holiness is possible for ordinary people (although the Jew who strives to be holy is not really "ordinary," but distinguished). Judaism knows of many aids to holiness, the means of bringing a person closer to the divine even when living fully in the material world. Prominent among these are the "holy days"—the Sabbaths and festivals when secular concerns are put aside and there is time for spiritual refreshment as well as the many opportunities for eating and drinking as sacred acts, in the Sabbath and festival spirit.

Yom Kippur in particular is called in the Jewish tradition *Yom ha-Kadosh*, "*the* Holy Day," the special day when the needs of normal physical life are transcended and the Jew is especially near to God. The classical works of Judaism are called "holy." By studying these "holy books," even if, as in the case of Luzzatto, they take us further than we are ready to go, we learn that there can be a sacred dimension to human life.

And there are the numerous symbols of the Jewish religion, many of which are reminders of holiness—tefillin, the Sefer Torah, and the mezuzah are obvious examples. On the negative side, there is the need to avoid, so far as possible, the opposite of the holy. It is called, in the Jewish tradition, *tumah*, "uncleanness", "contamination." The best-known of the "negative" reminders are the dietary laws. According to rabbinic teaching, forbidden food "contaminates" the soul, that is, keeps a person far from the divine. Without over-stressing it, one can think of books and magazines which can hardly be conducive to holiness. Another powerful symbol of holiness is fire. From earliest times, fire and light have been seen as pointing to something higher and not of this world, because of their brightness and the way they dispel darkness. In Judaism there are a number of fire symbols—the Sabbath lights, the Havdalah candle, the Ḥanukkah lights, the eternal lamp in the synagogue. The Zohar, seeking to explain the Jewish custom of swaying during prayer, suggests that it is like a little candle placed near a great flame. As the candle is drawn toward the flame, the human soul in prayer is drawn toward the divine fire, causing the body to sway to and fro.

One can think of books and magazines which are hardly conducive to holiness.

"By studying the holy books we learn not to forget that there can be a sacred dimension to human life."

Excess of any sort breaks the
bounds of holiness.

*"How can one be Holy?
The Jewish reply is by
keeping in touch as much
as possible with spiritual
things."*

Preserving a Sense of Balance

The Talmud (tractate *Taanit* 11a) records two opinions on self-denial.
One Rabbi said that people who deny themselves are sinners (presumably because they reject the legitimate gifts of food and drink God
has given to them). But another Rabbi said that, on the contrary, such
people are holy. There has been much discussion of these two opinions in the moralistic literature, and various attempts have been
made to reconcile them.

Many of the later Jewish teachers hold that it all depends on
motive and temperament. If a person is really sincere in the quest for
God and truly appreciates how necessary it is to forgo many of life's
pleasures in order to get nearer to God, he is holy. But if his reasons
are a hatred of life or a morbid disposition or, worst of all, a wish to
demonstrate superiority to lesser beings in the practice of self-control,
he is a sinner, guilty of using religion to satisfy selfish desires.

There is nothing so unwholesome as false piety because it de-
grades the whole concept of religion. That is why we must be ex-

Flying Horses

There is a Ḥasidic tale about the
horses of the Baal Shem Tov, the
founder of the Ḥasidic movement.
Whenever the Baal Shem Tov wished
to get quickly from place to place,
he entered his carriage and uttered
certain words by whose magic
power the horses were able to fly
through the air with the carriage.
While the Baal Shem was flying miraculously through the air, the Ḥasidim who tell the tale wryly observe,
they began to imagine that the
horses were angelic beings, far
above ordinary creatures down on
the ground. But when the Baal Shem
Tov reached his destination he would
lead the horses into the stable and
feed them hay. Then the disciples
knew that the creatures were no
more than horses.

tremely cautious when we approach the tremendous subject of holiness. It is all too easy for us to pretend to be what we are not. Judaism advocates holiness; it does not hold with priggishness. Basically, it is all a matter of preserving a proper balance. The ideal of holiness must never be absent, but we must be honest with ourselves, always trying to have the right motivation and not trying to overreach ourselves.

In Praise of Holiness

Very numerous are the statements in the rabbinic literature in praise of holiness. Before carrying out the mitzvot, the Rabbis rule—and this is still the practice today—it is essential to recite the benediction:

While God is remote from human understanding, He can be very near to us if our hearts are ready for Him.

"The ideal of holiness must never be absent, but we must be honest with ourselves."

Where Is God?

A Hasidic tale answers the question. Two little boys, who later became famous Ḥasidic masters, were being taught by their Torah teacher. The teacher asked them: "Where is God?" One of the boys replied: "Where is He not?" But the other boy, with deeper insight, replied: "Wherever He is allowed to enter, there He is." Holiness, then, means making the human heart ready for God to enter.

Where is God? Wherever He is allowed to enter, there He is.

"Blessed art Thou, O Lord our God, King of the universe, Who has *sanctified* us with His commandments." Through observing God's laws we become holy. The usual name for God in the rabbinic literature, when He is spoken of in the third person, is *Ha-Kadosh Barukh Hu*, "The Holy One, blessed be He." One of the Rabbis was praised as *benan shel kedoshim*, "son of holy ones," because he never gazed at the emperor's figure on a coin (either because the emperor was worshiped or because there were idolatrous symbols held by him on the coin). Total rejection of anything that savored of idolatry was seen as a particular sign of holiness.

There are degrees of holiness and one must always go higher in matters of the sacred, never lower. Thus it is permitted to sell a copy of one of the prophetic books in order to buy a Sefer Torah with the money, but not the other way around. The Sabbaths and festivals should be welcomed by observing them a little earlier than they actually begin, and their departure should be postponed a little in order to allow the holy to encroach on the profane. The sanctity of the Sabbath is, in miniature, like the sanctity of the World to Come. According to the Rabbis, when God gave Israel the Sabbath, He gave them a foretaste of the holiness of Paradise. Holiness is so problematical to attain completely while a person is still alive and subject to temptation that, the Rabbis say, God calls no righteous person holy until he is dead and buried. The Zohar states that of all holy things, none is holier than the Torah, and that both students of the Torah and those who help them to study are entitled to be called holy.

Dwelling in Their Midst

"The great mystery of the Jewish religion is that God, who is so remote, can yet be so very near."

"And let them make Me a sanctuary (*mikdash*), that I may dwell among them" (Exodus 25:8). An ancient comment to this verse helps us understand the concept of holiness. The Israelites were told to erect a sanctuary for God to dwell in. But the comment says that since God is everywhere, the purpose of the sanctuary (and this applies to all aids to holiness) is to awaken holy feelings, which then cause God to "dwell among *them*," that is, in their hearts. The great mystery at the center of the Jewish religion is that God, Who is so remote from all human understanding, can yet be very near to us if the necessary conditions are prepared.

Jewish Ethics

Jewish Ethical Ideas

Many volumes have been written on the classification of Jewish ethics. The little gem of a work, *Ethics of the Fathers*, is part of the *Mishnah*, though the correct Hebrew title is simply *Avot*, "Fathers," and the word "Ethics" does not appear in the title. The work is really an anthology of ethical teachings by the "fathers," the great teachers of the past, those who flourished in the mishnaic period (up to the year 200). Each teacher gives a brief statement, generally in three parts, of certain religious and ethical ideas and each is introduced with "He used to say." This is highly significant for a study of Jewish ethical values. Each teacher *used to say* that which his age particularly required. Ethics is not as hard and fast as law. There are various responses to ethical living, and much depends on the needs of a particular age and culture. Some ethical problems of the past, for instance, bear little relevance to our age, but we have our own ethical problems to face. The following is a brief statement of some of the ethical values in the Jewish sources that seem particularly relevant to the modern Jew.

"There are various responses to ethical living, and much depends on the needs of a particular age and culture."

Human Dignity

Judaism considers humanity as being of the utmost significance in God's plan for His universe. All people are created in the image of God and, therefore, every human being is entitled to respect as a part

Ethics of The Fathers

Here are a few typical sayings from *Ethics of the Fathers*:

"Do not be as servants who serve their master in order for him to reward them but rather be like servants who serve their master unconditionally."

"Provide yourself with a teacher, acquire for yourself a companion and judge all men favorably."

"If I am not for myself, who is for me? But if I am for myself only, what am I? And if not now, when?"

"Never keep yourself apart from the community."

"If you have studied much Torah, do not imagine that you are deserving of great praise, for it was for this purpose that you were created."

203

The foundation of Jewish ethics includes the belief that every human being is created in the image of God and is therefore entitled to respect.

"In our day, Jewish learning will only win the support it deserves and will only be encouraged if learned Jews are held in high regard."

of humanity. The rabbinic term for this is *kevod ha-beriot*, "respect for (God's) creatures." The word *beriot* refers to all human beings, Gentiles as well as Jews. All people are entitled to respect by virtue of their basic humanity. Nevertheless, some people have to be paid more respect than others; some are especially singled out and have to be accorded extraordinary dignity.

The obvious example is that of parents. The fifth commandment is "Honor thy father and thy mother." Old folks and students of the Torah are entitled to special regard and honor, too, the former because they have lived through so much and are rich in experience, the latter because they bear the dignity of the Torah they have studied. The Rabbis go so far as to say that although it is meritorious to restore a neighbor's lost animal, this duty is not binding on a scholar if it is beneath his dignity to lead an animal through the streets. Scholars must respect their own learning and must not degrade themselves in any way. Their clothes for example, should always be clean and neat. Rabbinic hyperbole has it that a scholar who goes out into the street with stained garments deserves to die!

In our day, Jewish learning will win the support it deserves and will be encouraged only if learned Jews are held in high regard. Other people who are to be treated with special respect are pious men and women, the charitable, and the benevolent. The otherwise strange talmudic saying, that Rabbi Judah the Prince used to show special honor to the rich, probably refers to rich people who were liberal to the poor.

The Rabbis are very strict about any attempt at improving one's own image at the expense of another's. They call this "gaining honor through another's disgrace." For instance, it is wrong to expose another person's ignorance in order to parade one's own superior knowledge. Similarly, if a friend wishes to perform a service that might be considered undignified, such as carrying a heavy piece of

baggage, that he would not normally carry, the service should be refused. It is wrong to say one is better in some respect than another person, even if the other is not present and suffers no embarrassment.

With delicacy of feeling, the Rabbis state that although it is meritorious to refuse, at first, an honor that is given, if it is offered by a great person it should be accepted on the spot without further ado, as if to say that there can be no greater honor than to be honored by a great person. Similarly, when two people are about to enter a room it is good, if one knows that the other has more learning or more good deeds, to let him go in first. Interestingly enough, this is limited to a room that has a mezuzah, as if to say there is no particular honor in entering a room whose door is not dignified by having God's name affixed to it.

A communal leader should have respect for the community, listening to others' opinions and never lording it over them. Respect for the community also involves never doing anything degrading or shameful in public, not only out of self-respect but out of respect for the public. A remarkable rabbinic comment on the law that a thief who steals a lamb has to pay fourfold restitution, while one who steals an ox has to pay fivefold (Exodus 21:37), says that the Torah respects even the dignity of a thief. The thief who had stolen an ox suffered no loss of dignity, but the thief who had stolen a lamb, which had to be carried because it could not walk by itself, suffers some loss of dignity.

"Respect for the community also involves never doing anything degrading or shameful in public."

Humility

Moses, the greatest Jewish leader, is described as the most humble: "Now the man Moses was very meek, above all the men that were upon the face of the earth" (Numbers 12:3). Abraham, the father of the Jewish people, protests: "Behold now, I have taken upon myself to speak unto the Lord, I who am but dust and ashes" (Genesis 18:27). When Saul was chosen as the first king of Israel, he was discovered "hidden . . . among the baggage" (I Samuel 10:22), an expression that is still used by Jews to describe one who shuns the limelight. The Torah is compared to water, say the Rabbis, because just as water always flows downward so, too, the Torah which comes from on high, flows into the heart and mind of only the lowly person.

Not that humility is easy to attain. Everyone knows how easy it is to be guilty of false modesty, of being proud of not being proud, of being untrue to oneself by imagining that humility means that one should be unaware of self-worth and should, therefore, claim no credit. The great thirteenth-century teacher Naḥmanides writes as follows in a letter to his son: "Accordingly I will explain to you how to become accustomed to humility in daily life. Let your voice be low, and your head bowed; let your eyes be turned earthwards and your heart heavenwards. Do not gaze into the face of anyone you speak to. Every man should be in your eyes greater than yourself. If he is wise or wealthy it is your duty to show him respect. If he is poor and you are richer, or if you are wiser than he is, think to yourself that you are more deserving of blame than he is because if he sins it is out of ignorance while if you sin it is with intention." Naḥmanides thus advises his son to cultivate humility by considering all others his superiors.

Even if a person knows himself to be superior he has no reason for pride, since the superior person is more responsible for his failings than one who knows no better. On the deeper level, this means that, since God alone can know someone's true worth, and how he is acquitting himself within the limits imposed by background and temperament and ability, there is no cause for pride. It is not naive for the great person to think the ignoramous or sinner may be superior. For all anyone knows, it may well be so in God's eyes!

But in Ḥasidic thought in particular, humility does not mean that a person feels inferior or unimportant. It means rather that when confronted with the majesty of God, he does not think of the self at all. A person may be fully aware of his personal achievements and talents and may be prepared to fight for his point of view, but nonetheless should be humble because it is all as nothing compared with the only true reality—the glory of God. Jewish tradition has it that we bow in prayer and then straighten up again. Symbolically this expresses the idea that we should be aware of how insignificant man is and yet, once we realize this, hold our heads high because all our gifts are from God, and for this we can be thankful without claiming any merit for ourselves. This is why it it is a serious mistake to confuse humility with a lack of self-respect. Or to put it another way, the Rabbis say that the Torah was given on the lowest of all mountains, Sinai, to teach that the student of the Torah should be humble. But it has to be realized that neither was the Torah given in a valley. A person has to be great in order to be small. The Torah was given on a lowly mountain but it was, nonetheless, given on a mountain.

"To have a religious outlook on life we should be aware of how insignificant man is; yet once we realize this we can hold our heads up high!"

The Rabbis compared the Torah to water: both flow downward. The Torah descends from on high, flowing into human hearts and minds.

Ethical Principles

R. Moses Sofer once heard a man protesting his complete unworthiness, stating that he was unlearned and unworthy of respect. R. Moses Sofer looked at the man and said: "You are not so great that you can afford to be so small."

The Ḥafetz Ḥayyim came to the town of Navaradok to obtain approval for his book on the evils of malicious gossip from Rabbi Y. M. Epstein, the rabbi of that town. Rabbi Epstein sent two brilliant young students to the Ḥafetz Ḥayyim's lodgings to engage the author in conversation. For over two hours they tried to provoke him into making disparaging remarks about this or that rabbi or communal leader, but the Ḥafetz Ḥayyim did not say one slighting word. When they told Rabbi Epstein, he wrote in his recommendation: "This author practices what he preaches."

Truth

"Truth is God's seal," say the Rabbis. Rashi has a novel explanation of this saying. The word for "truth" is *emet*, which is formed from the letters *alef*, *mem*, and *tav*—the first, middle, and last letters of the alphabet. The whole of the alphabet and, therefore, the whole of the Torah, which is recorded in the letters of the alphabet, is a matter of truth. It is a Jewish ideal to pursue truth throughout life. Jews are expected to be true to God, striving always for religious sincerity and intellectual honesty. Jews are expected to be true to others, both in loyalty to friends and neighbors and by never tricking or defrauding them or telling them lies. And Jews are expected to be true to themselves by realizing the best of which they are capable and by not fooling themselves by being less than honest in self-scrutiny.

Important though truth is, the Rabbis do not consider it wrong to tell a "white lie," a lie for the purpose of promoting sound human relations. For example, the Rabbis say, it is permitted to tell a lie if that is the only way to avoid strife and contention. Aaron the priest, the prototype of the promoter of peace, is depicted as reconciling two

Ethical Principles

His disciples asked Rabbi Israel Salanter how they could best make the necessary preparations on Friday for the coming of the Sabbath. He replied: "Help your wives with the housework and speak especially gently to them."

A Ḥasidic master once gave a coin to a beggar with a bad reputation. His disciples asked him: "How can you give a coin to such a bad man?" The saint replied: "Is he worse than I, to whom God gave it in the first place?"

The Belzer Rebbe, R. Arele, once heard a rumor that a little boy had fallen into a deep pit. He cried out: "I hope it is not one of my children." All his days the Rebbe grieved at having, even in a moment of stress, implied that as long as his own family was safe it did not matter what happened to others.

enemies by telling each one that the other had expressed regret at the quarrel and wished to make it up. Of course, common sense must guide us as to when to depart from the truth. It is all too easy to excuse falsehood on grounds of expediency.

The ideal of truth also requires the rejection of hypocrisy. The rabbinic expression for the hypocrite is "one whose inside is not like his outside," that is, one who presents a front to the world that is contradicted by his inner life, by what he really believes and feels. A rabbinic saying is that the ark containing the two tablets of stone was made of "gold, within and without" (Exodus 25:11) to teach that a scholar whose "inside is not like his outside" is no true scholar (tractate *Yoma* 72b). It is perhaps worth noting that the Rabbis, in their hostility to hypocrisy, urge that one's "inside" be like one's "outside," not the other way around. Nowadays, many young people, in their reaction to what they consider to be the hypocrisy of their elders, refuse to pay lip service to virtue and argue that they must act out what they feel "inside," even if their feelings are base and unworthy. External conventions, if based on sound Jewish ideals, should be observed, say the Rabbis. Hypocrisy is avoided and integrity achieved by making the "inside" conform to the "outside."

"A scholar whose inside is not like his outside is no true scholar."

Lashon Ha-Ra and Rekhilut

Rabbi Israel Meir ha-Kohen (Kagen), who died fifty years ago, devoted a major part of his life and work to combating malicious talk which he considered destructive in the communities of Lithuania, where he lived. He wrote a book on the subject which he entitled *Hafetz Ḥayyim* ("Desirous of Life"), and he is now referred to simply as "the Ḥafetz Ḥayyim." The title is derived from the Book of Psalms (34:13–14): "Who is the man that desireth life, and loveth days, that he may see good therein? Keep thy tongue from evil, and thy lips from speaking guile." The Ḥafetz Ḥayyim lived to be nearly a hundred years of age, which his disciples cited as proof that the Psalmist's words are true. In rabbinic and subsequent Jewish terminology, to speak evil of another, even though it be true, is to be guilty of the offense of *lashon ha-ra* "the evil tongue." There is another offense of speech known as *rekhilut* ("talebearing") based on the verse: "Thou shalt not go up and down as a talebearer (*rakhil*) among thy people" (Leviticus 19:16). An example of *rekhilut* is seen when one person tells another that a third party has spoken badly of him or done him harm. People do sometimes find a kind of perverse joy in dwelling on the faults of others or in stirring up trouble and creating mischief. Perhaps their motive is to demonstrate their superiority. Perhaps they are bored and have nothing better to do. Some people even say that they enjoy a good gossip. But Judaism, knowing the harm it can do, sets its face strongly against all evil talk.

Some of the rabbinic teachings say one should not praise a person to his enemies because that will encourage the enemies to speak ill of him; that if a secret has been imparted, it should not be told to others; that it is forbidden to say: "Do not speak about So-and-so, I do not want to talk about that one," implying that something is known to his or her discredit; that one should not denigrate whole classes of people (like "the blacks" or "the Jews" or "women" or "men"). The Ḥafetz Ḥayyim points out that many people never speak ill of the dead but see no harm in speaking ill of the living. The reverse is true, says the Ḥafetz Ḥayyim, since evil talk cannot disturb the repose of the dead, but the living are all too easily hurt by it. Nevertheless, there is an ancient ban on speaking bad things about the dead. What if the only way a person can be prevented from suffering injury is to speak ill of someone else? Suppose, for instance, someone is about to become a partner in a business venture with a person you know to be a crook; should you tell? Or, suppose you know that a young man who suffers from mental illness is about to marry a young lady who knows nothing of his medical history. Should you tell? The Ḥafetz Ḥayyim argues that you must tell in order to prevent the suffering of an innocent person. He quotes the conclusion of the verse: "Thou shalt not go up and down as a talebearer among thy people; *neither shalt thou stand idly by the blood of thy neighbor*" (Leviticus 19:16). Although it is normally wrong to tell tales, it is right and proper to do so if otherwise harm will result to the innocent.

Anger

When one is quick to lose one's temper, say the Rabbis, his life is not worth living since he is always upset and miserable and sorry for the hurtful things said in anger, to say nothing of the harm he may have done to others. If someone is so uncontrolled as to break things in a fit of temper, he is like an idolator carried away by nonsensical whims. Very boldly, the Rabbis point out that when Moses lost his temper, his wisdom departed from him. Even the greatest of people become a little less wise when they so forget themselves, even under severe provocation, as to fly into a rage. The Rabbis call a bad-tempered person "one in whom all kinds of Hell rule," one who knows no serenity and is as if he is in Hell, never knowing the Paradise of the serene in spirit.

In a talmudic tale, Elijah the prophet appears to one of the

"Many people never speak ill of the dead but see no harm in speaking ill of the living."

According to the Rabbis, a person who is quick to anger is not worthy to be alive. When Moses lost his temper, the Rabbis say, his wisdom departed from him.

"There are times when we only get really angry with people we love precisely because we love them."

Rabbis to tell him: "Never get drunk and you will not sin: never lose your temper and you will not sin." What, then, is a parent or a teacher to do if there is good cause to be displeased with children or pupils, and displeasure must be shown them? Otherwise how can they ever learn to do better? The Rabbis answer that one should pretend to be angry but should be serene in heart. Naturally this does not refer to the sadistic parent or teacher who punishes in a cold calculating way. Better than this is the parent or teacher who occasionally does allow anger to get the upper hand, particularly since too serene a disposition in these matters may reflect indifference. There are times when we get really angry only with people we love, precisely because we do love them. The Rabbis also say that we should not try to appease a person who is in a rage. The stupidest thing we can do is to tell someone who has just lost his temper: "Do not lose your temper." We should allow him to calm down and then, if we are to blame, say we are sorry.

Envy

The Rabbis speak of the envious person as having an "evil eye." This means that, unlike the person with the "good eye" who loves to see people happy, he cannot bear to see someone else enjoying success. In its worst form, envy is what the Germans call *Schadenfreude*, "enjoying other people's misery," but in its less virulent form, envy is the attitude of mind that cannot bear to see another person doing better than oneself. It is different from covetousness. The difference can be put in this way: if A has nothing and B has something of value, then if A is covetous he will wish to have that object also; but if A is envious, his real wish is that B should not have it either. The Rabbis advise parents not to show favoritism to one of their children because it makes the other children envious. Look what happened, they say,

Envy causes misery. The Rabbis urged us not to be ostentatious with wealth and possessions so as not to cause others to be envious.

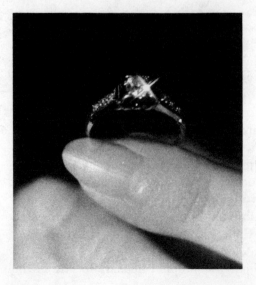

The Evil Inclination

Rabbi Ḥayyim, head of the great Ye-shiva of Volhozhyn, once saw two of his students busily engaged in con-versation. "What are you talking about?" Rabbi Ḥayyim asked. "We are discussing how to control the *yetzer ha-ra* (the "evil inclination"). "Yes," said Rabbi Ḥayyim, "the yetzer ha-ra says: I do not care if you speak about how to control me. I am safe as long as you do not study the Torah at that time." But Rabbi Israel Salanter declared that this was true only in the days of Rabbi Ḥayyim. Now-adays the yetzer ha-ra says: "I do not care if you study the Torah. I am safe as long as you do not talk about how to control me."

when Jacob showed favoritism to his son, Joseph! Similarly, one should not be so ostentatious with wealth or possessions as to cause others to be envious. If someone refuses to be envious of others, not only is his life happier but he will be rewarded for his disposition and for his trust in God Who provides for each person's needs. The Rabbis point out that Aaron was always ready to be Moses' second in com-mand, even though he was the older brother, with the result that God made him the High Priest.

One kind of envy, however, the Rabbis not only tolerate but advocate. This is envy of those who study the Torah and practice its laws. "The envy of scribes increases wisdom" is a rabbinic saying to justify a teacher of Torah setting up a rival school in circumstances that might otherwise be considered unfair competition.

The Ethical Character

In brief, the Jewish ideal is not only for a person to behave ethically, important though this undoubtedly is, but to have an ethical *charac-ter*. The Torah teaches us not only how to behave but also how to become better people. Some Jewish teachers talk in this connection of self-perfection. "Perfection" is a pretty high-sounding word and no human being can ever be perfect. God alone is perfect. Self-improve-ment is another matter. Difficult though it is, it is the task of the good Jew to strive all his or her life to be an even better Jew. "There is no rest for the wicked." Yes, Judaism does say this, but in another sense, "There is no rest for the righteous." The good person can never rest content but must ever strive to do better and to make further progress toward the goal: the nearness of God. *Ethics of the Fathers* sums up the ethical character (5:19): "Whosoever has these three attributes is of the disciples of Abraham our father, but whosoever has three other attributes is of the disciples of Balaam the wicked. A good eye, a humble mind and a lowly spirit are the marks of the disciples of Abraham our father; an evil eye, a haughty mind and a proud spirit are the marks of the disciples of Balaam the wicked." The passage continues that the "disciples of Abraham our father enjoy this world and inherit the World to Come."

25

Marriage and The Family

The Family

It is not too much of an exaggeration to say that the unit around which Judaism centers is the family. Since the biblical period, the people of Israel was counted according to its families. The word *mishpaḥah*, "family," occurs again and again, in the Book of Numbers, for example. In Chapter 10 of the Book of Genesis the whole human race is thought of as a great collection of separate families who are, nonetheless, related to one another. Pride in one's family has been a characteristic of Judaism. It is obvious that this idea of *yiḥus*, "family pride," can be overdone. If a child is born into a less than noble family but through his own efforts becomes a worthy human being, it would be absurd and wrong to cast aspersions on his background. Righteous children of unrighteous parents are not to be discredited, as the prophet Ezekiel (Chapter 18) taught long ago, but are especially deserving of credit. Still, Jews have seen much point, when choosing a life partner, in considering carefully the family of the intended spouse.

Marrying out of the Faith

"What kind of Judaism will the children experience if only one of their parents has any feeling at all for the faith?"

One of the most important rules about marriage, as Judaism sees it, is not to marry out of the faith. This is a rule at times difficult to follow, and yet a rule which allows no compromise. It is easy to see why Judaism has been so insistent on this matter. How can there be a proper Jewish home, close to the synagogue and its ideals, with a real Jewish atmosphere, if husband or wife is not Jewish? What kind of Judaism will the children experience if only one parent has feeling for the faith? These children will be bound to question the truth and validity of Judaism since one parent is admittedly indifferent, if not positively hostile. Conflicts between parents and children become more intense than in any normal family and inevitably affect the children's attitude toward Judaism. That is why, painful though it may be, Judaism does ask its young people to marry a member of their own faith.

Nowadays, fortunately, none of us is called upon to give his life for Judaism. Martyrdom is not demanded in the age in which we happily live. But when we recall how our ancestors, in a less tolerant age, sacrificed their lives rather than be disloyal to Judaism, we can appreciate that the limitation of marrying only within the faith is not too much to ask of us. Actually, it is a sacrifice only for those already deeply in love with a non-Jew. For the majority, there is a full awareness that a happy marriage and a sound Jewish home are attained by marrying within the faith.

Polygamy

Although there are biblical references to a man having more than one wife, polygamy was never the Jewish ideal. The Bible permits polygamy (one reason apparently because a woman without a husband was, in those times, utterly defenseless) but it never advocates it. Hardly any of the famous Jewish teachers had more than one wife. If polygamy were the normal thing, the creation story in the Book of Genesis would not have told of Adam and Eve, one man and one woman, but of Adam and his wives. And the prophets describe the relationship between God and Israel in terms of a monogamous marriage, God devoted to Israel and Israel to God, just as a husband forsakes all other women to be loyal to his one wife, and a wife gives up all other men to be loyal to her one husband.

The family is the basic unit of Judaism, and the Jewish People as a whole should see themselves as one family.

Marriage a Duty

When a man and woman marry it is, as Judaism sees it, for life. Although Judaism does permit divorce, the ideal is for husband and wife to strive to make their marriage work, remaining in love with one another and devoted to one another as long as both of them live. If, however, a marriage has really broken down, Judaism sees no point in both partners' remaining tied to each other. If husband or wife dies, Judaism sees no reason not to remarry. Judaism also sees no advantage in a man remaining a bachelor all his life or a woman a spinster, even if the motive is the better to serve God and humanity. Only very occasionally do we find in Jewish literature the idea that a

Weddings

It was the custom of the Belzer Hasidim, when a marriage was celebrated in their family, to invite to the wedding the souls of their deceased ancestors.

R. Levi Yitzhak of Berditchev used to write in the wedding invitations of his family: "The wedding will take place on . . . at five o'clock in Jerusalem, the holy city. But if, God forbid, the Messiah will not have

come by then, it will take place in Berditchev."

The Talmud observes that it is as difficult for marriages to be made in Heaven as was the miracle of the parting of the Red Sea. In other words, there is something miraculous when a man and woman from different backgrounds and with different temperaments become one as man and wife.

man (like the second-century teacher Ben Azzai) was right to remain unmarried because "his soul was in love with the Torah." Such an attitude was very rare, so that there is nothing in Judaism to correspond to the hermits, monks and nuns of other religions.

The Wedding Ceremony

In ancient times there were two distinct stages in a marriage. The first was the betrothal (kiddushin), the bride and groom being formally married but the bride remaining in her father's house for a short time. The second stage was when the bride came to her husband's home and the couple entered the marriage chamber, known as the ḥuppah ("canopy" or "cover"). Nowadays the two stages are combined and an actual canopy, under which bride and groom stand, is set up to represent the original ḥuppah. The cantor welcomes the bride and bridegroom with a blessing. The rabbi then recites the benediction for wine over a cup of wine and the special benediction in which God is praised for sanctifying His people Israel through the institution of marriage. (This part of the marriage service is the original "betrothal" or kiddushin). The parents of the bride and groom, who stand with them under the ḥuppah, hand the cup of wine to the couple and each takes a sip of the wine. The groom then places the wedding ring on the index finger of the bride's right hand while he recites: "Be thou consecrated unto me with this ring according to the law of Moses and Israel." (In talmudic times any object of value was used for this purpose, but from the Middle Ages onward it has become the universal custom to use only a wedding ring.) In Reform congregations the bride also gives a ring to the groom, while she recites: "Be thou consecrated unto me."

A Jewish marriage document, called a *ketubah*, is essentially a contract, protecting the wife in case of divorce.

The *ketubbah*, the marriage lines (from the root *katav*, "to write") is then read aloud by the rabbi. Basically the ketubbah is a marriage settlement, a legal document in which the groom undertakes to support his wife, and to provide for her if they are later divorced, or if he dies before her. Nowadays, except in the State of Israel, we follow the laws of our own country in these financial arrangements so that the ketubbah is only a formality (which is why the amount declared is the purely formal one of 200 zuzim) but it should not be omitted since it is hallowed by tradition as an important step forward in the struggle for women's rights. It is interesting to note how the tradition is not averse to introducing purely legal considerations into a romantic ceremony. A degree of realism, as well as romance, is called for in marriage.

After the reading of the ketubbah another set of benedictions is recited by the cantor over a cup of wine, and again the couple take a sip when the cup is handed to them by their parents. (This corresponds to the second stage of the original ceremony, the ḥuppah.) These benedictions, seven in number (hence the name, *sheva berakhot*) speak of joy and delight, of love of bridegroom for bride and of bride for groom, of God's placing Adam and Eve in the Garden of Eden, and praying that the newlyweds enjoy some of that bliss. A glass is broken at the end of the ceremony. Various explanations have been given for this curious custom but the official reason is that it is to remind bride and groom of the destruction of the Temple. On the happiest day of their lives the young couple are encouraged to think not only of themselves, but also of the fate and destiny of their people. By building a faithful Jewish home, they will help rebuild the ancient ruins.

Children

According to Jewish teaching it is a mitzvah to have children. Naturally, some couples are not blessed with children and it is not their fault. But Judaism teaches that children are a blessing and that it is wrong for people who can have children not to produce at least a boy and a girl, the School of Hillel taught 2,000 years ago, while the School of Shammai taught, at least two boys. Soon after their birth, children are given Jewish names. A girl is named in the synagogue on the Sabbath as soon after the birth as possible. A boy is named at the circumcision, the *brit*.

"Judaism teaches that children are a blessing and that it is wrong for people who can have children not to have them."

Circumcision

The word *brit* means "covenant." Circumcision is known as "the covenant of Abraham our father" (based on Genesis Chapter 17). It is a "sign in the flesh" that the child will be brought up as a faithful member of the covenant people. A covenant is a kind of pact between two persons; here a promise by God never to forsake Israel, never to substitute any other religion for Judaism, and a promise by Israel to be faithful to God's laws. The reason why the brit is expressed in this particular way has not been stated clearly in the Bible, but Jewish teachers have tried to offer reasons.

Some teachers have suggested, for example, that it is appropriate for the sign of Israel's loyalty throughout all *generations* to be on the organ by means of which future generations are created. Others have made the interesting suggestion that the foreskin serves no useful purpose and is even unhygienic, so that an uncircumcised male lacks perfection. In that case, why does God create a man with a foreskin and then expect him to remove it? These teachers reply that it is to stress, right from the beginning, the Jewish idea that God has left work for people to do. God does not create a perfect world or perfect men. Instead he creates an imperfect world which people, by their own efforts aided by God, can make better. In the words of the talmudic rabbis, one should be a partner with God, or as George Elliot put it, God cannot make a Stradivarius violin without Stradivarius. But whatever the reason behind circumcision in its particular form, Jews carry it out because that is how it has been since time immemorial and because they are obeying the will of God and furthering His purpose.

Bar Mitzvah

The term *Bar Mitzvah* means literally "a son of the mitzvah," one old enough to be obliged to carry out the mitzvot (a child cannot be expected to have responsibilities and obligations). In the rabbinic tradition a boy reaches the age of responsibility when he is thirteen. But a girl, who, according to the ancient rabbis, is more morally and spiritually mature than a boy, reaches the age to become *Bat Mitzvah* when she is twelve. The present-day celebrations with the boy reading the portion in the synagogue and the special party did not arise until the Middle Ages. In some congregations, nowadays, there is a similar celebration for girls.

Parents and Children

Jewish parents have obligations to their children. They must care for them, educate them, teach them Judaism in the home and arrange for them to be educated Jewishly in schools or Hebrew classes. One of the talmudic rabbis declared that if a father does not train his children so that they can earn a living when they grow up, he teaches them, as it were, to be dishonest. Another talmudic rabbi said that parents should give their children swimming lessons because to know how to swim can save lives. Parents are obliged to provide a happy home so that the children can grow in health of mind and body.

"Parents are obliged to provide a happy home for their children so that the children can grow in health of mind and body."

The Talmud obliges parents to teach their children how to swim.

Jewish parents are notoriously easygoing with their children, but the Jewish teachers remind parents that a degree of discipline is required in bringing up children. Parents who are too soft with their children, who tolerate nasty behavior and fail to rebuke it, do good neither to themselves nor to their children. For parents to be weak is only to encourage bad conduct and character.

Children and Parents

Children, too, have their obligations. "Honor thy father and thy mother" is the fifth commandment. That commandment goes on to say "that thy days may be long." According to one interpretation, children who respect their parents have a proper appreciation of life and see life as a blessing. There are children who say, "Why should I respect my parents? I did not ask to be born." But only a person who has little regard for life and its blessings will ever say this. Most of us are glad we were born. Life, for all its difficulties, is good, and we should be grateful to our parents who brought us into the world and cared for us until we were able to care for ourselves. As the Rabbis put it, there are three partners in the creation of a child—the father, the mother, and God.

How does one honor parents? Judaism replies: by acting respectfully toward them, by pleasing them, by helping them, and, if necessary by supporting them. Above all, Jewish parents are honored when their children are good Jews. Nothing gives a true Jewish parent more *naches* (the word *naḥat* means "to be easy," "to be satisfied with one's lot") than to see children following in the Jewish way. However, the Rabbis declare that parents should not be too insistent on their rights. Some rabbis argue that if parents wish to relinquish the honor that is due them they may do so. Very revealing is the talmudic rule that it is forbidden for a father to strike his grown-up son. In happy Jewish homes, parents appreciate that children, too, have their rights and are personalities who are entitled to their own opinions.

Must Children Obey Their Parents?

The fifth commandment does not necessarily mean that children must always obey their parents. If parents instruct their children to do something wrong, they should not be obeyed. A number of Jewish authorities rule that if parents order a son not to marry the girl of his choice (provided, of course, that she is Jewish) or a girl the boy she chooses, they need not be obeyed. In all these matters, much tact is required. But people of good will, whether parents or children, will try to develop their own personalities without hurting other members of the family who also have their rights.

Honoring Others

In the Jewish tradition the fifth commandment is extended to others besides parents. Respect is to be paid to grandparents, stepparents, older brothers and sisters, and teachers. Respect for the Jewish tradition is included because just as our parents shape our character, so do our traditions. Respect for old men and women is also demanded by Judaism, especially for people over the age of 70. The Talmud tells of Jewish teachers who would help even old pagans because they are rich in life's experiences.

In other words, there are two ways by which wisdom is acquired. The first is through learning and study, which is why people learned in the Torah are to be especially revered. The second is through life's experiences. Not all old people are wise. Some can be very foolish! Someone has said that it is possible to grow old without growing up. But on the whole, life has a way of teaching us. We learn how to correct our mistakes and eventually acquire the ability to warn others how to avoid the mistakes we have made. Young people are often impatient with the old, and sometimes they have a right to be. Progress would be impossible if we never went beyond the past. Yet it is a foolish person who believes that there is nothing to learn from those who are rich in years.

There is a well-known order of the ages of humanity, found in *Ethics of the Fathers* (5:21): "The age of five for the study of the Bible. The age of ten for the study of the Mishnah. The age of thirteen for

"Eventually we hope to attain the ability to warn others of how to avoid the mistakes we have made."

the carrying out of the mitzvot. The age of fifteen for the study of Talmud. The age of eighteen for marriage. The age of twenty to begin to earn a living. The age of thirty brings strength. The age of forty brings understanding. The age of fifty gives the right to advise others. The age of sixty brings old age. The age of seventy brings advanced old age. The age of eighty is reached by those who are specially strong. The age of ninety brings a stooping posture. At the age of a hundred it is as if one is no longer alive." Naturally, this passage, compiled about 1,700 years ago, reflects its period. Few men and even fewer women of sixty today will admit to feeling "old" and the usual age for marriage, nowadays, is in the twenties rather than at eighteen. Many of us begin to earn a living before we reach twenty. What the passage does demonstrate is that people generally grow wiser and better equipped to guide others as they grow older. It is also typically Jewish in its insistence that right at the beginning of life's pilgrimage the Jew should study and study again.

Adoption

What of adoption? It is rather odd that Jewish law does not know of legal adoption. However, adoption of a child is referred to in the Bible, for example, in the story of Moses who was adopted by Pharaoh's daughter (Exodus 2:10), and Esther who was adopted by Mordecai (Esther 2:7). The talmudic rabbis state that whoever adopts an orphan is considered as if giving birth to that child. Consequently, an adopted child becomes as much a part of the family and as dear to the husband and wife as their own children, and is treated as a child of the family in every respect.

The Family and the Outside World

A problem in every family is how much its members should center their lives on the family and to what extent they should find their interests and development outside its limits. It is impossible to state

Servants

If there are servants in the home they should never be made to feel inferior or insulted. The ideal is for the servants to be seen, in a sense, as part of the family. Job declares that he would have deserved his punishment "If I did despise the cause of my man-servant, or of my maid-servant, when they contended with me" (Job 31:13). There is a tale about a Ḥasidic master whose wife had a quarrel with her maid, and summoned the maid to a lawsuit. When the wife saw her husband putting on his overcoat to go to the courtroom, she said: "You do not have to go. I can plead adequately myself." Whereupon the master said: "I am not going along to plead on your behalf but on behalf of the maid," and he quoted the verse from Job (31:13).

hard and fast rules because circumstances vary and what is good for one family is not necessarily good for another. Judaism would have us strike a balance between the narrow approach, in which only one's own family matters—that is far too stifling and selfish—and the attitude of the person we all know, who is an angel outside the home but a devil inside. In the matter of charity, for instance, the Rabbis teach that a rich person's first duty is to his family's poor relations. The ideal is for the family to the outward-looking but not to the neglect of one another. There is much wisdom in the old Chinese saying: "If there is peace in the heart there is peace in the family. If there is peace in the family there is peace in the community. If there is peace in the community there is peace in the world."

"The family should be outward looking, but not to the extent that its members neglect one another."

The Jewish Home

A Jewish home should be a friendly place and those who live in it hospitable. There is a rabbinic saying that to welcome guests into the home is greater than to meet the Divine Presence. The proof is from Abraham (Genesis, beginning of Chapter 18) who, although God was conversing with him, ran to meet guests he saw approaching. If finances permit, the Jewish home should be a place of beauty. Another rabbinic saying is that a beautiful home and fine furniture broaden the mind. It goes without saying that the home should be clean and tidy, and to be a true Jewish home should contain an adequate supply of Jewish books. In short, a family living in the best Jewish tradition can create a home in which there is happiness, light, and spiritual strength. The key to this in the Bible is found in the Book of Numbers (24:5). There we are told that when the heathen prophet Balaam, who had come to curse Israel, saw their "tents," their homes, he was compelled to proclaim against his will:

> How goodly are thy tents, O Jacob
> Thy dwellings, O Israel!

26 The Messianic Idea

A Developing Idea

Maimonides lists the belief in the coming of the Messiah as one of the thirteen basic principles of the Jewish faith. It is, indeed, a principle of the religion that has been extremely strong throughout the ages and which, after the destruction of the Temple especially, offered hope to the Jewish people in its darkest days. Jews suffered and bore the sufferings of exile believing that one day God would redeem them and bring them back, from wherever they had been dispersed, into the Holy Land. They also believed that, as a result of the redemption, the whole world would become perfected, war would be banished from the earth and the kingdom of God established.

This belief is expressed in its noblest form in the Rosh Hasanah prayer, in which, at the beginning of the New Year, God is entreated to bring this joyous state about speedily, and in our days. The prayer reads in part: "Now, therefore, O Lord our God, impose Thine awe upon all Thy works, and Thy dread upon all that Thou hast created, that all works may fear Thee and all creatures prostrate themselves before Thee, that they may all form a single band to do Thy will with a perfect heart. . . . Give then glory, O Lord, unto Thy people, praise to them that fear Thee, hope to them that seek Thee, and free speech to them that wait for Thee, joy to Thy land, gladness to Thy city, a flourishing horn unto David Thy servant, and a clear shining light unto the son of Jesse [David's father] Thine anointed [*Messiah* means "anointed one"], speedily in our days. Then shall the just also see and be glad, and the upright shall exult, and the pious triumphantly rejoice, while iniquity shall close her mouth, and all wickedness shall be wholly consumed like smoke, when Thou makest the dominion of arrogance to pass away from the earth."

Like many other important Jewish ideas, the messianic idea has had a growth and a history. Scholars point out various stages in the development of this idea. For instance, the name *Messiah* for the person who will be sent by God to usher in this glorious age is not found, in this form, in the Bible. What seems to have happened, according to most historians, is something on the following lines. After the death of King Solomon, when the kingdom was divided into two, the promises made to David that his descendants would reign forever seemed more doubtful of fulfillment. Consequently, the belief grew that one day, albeit in the future, God would make the promise come

"Jews bore the sufferings of exile believing that one day God would redeem them and bring them back to the Holy Land."

221

"For the earth shall be full of the knowledge of the Lord, as the waters cover the sea." (Isaiah 11:9)

"There is a miraculous, supernatural quality about the Messiah and his rule, though in Judaism the Messiah is not a divine figure."

true and a king would arise, a "son of David," (that is, a descendant of David) who would reign over all Israel as did David and Solomon.

In the prophetic writings, this was further extended to include the idea of a blessed age in which peace would reign in the land and "nations shall beat their spears into pruning hooks." We read in the Book of Isaiah:

And it shall come to pass in the end of days,
That the mountain of the Lord's house shall be established as the top
   of the mountains,
And shall be exalted above the hills;
And all nations shall flow unto it.
And many peoples shall go up and say: 'Come ye, and let us go up to
   the mountain of the Lord,
To the House of the God of Jacob;
And He will teach us of His ways,
And we will walk in His paths.' For out of Zion shall go forth the law,
And the word of the Lord from Jerusalem.
And He shall judge between the nations,
And shall decide for many peoples;
And they shall beat their swords into plowshares,
And their spears into pruning-hooks;
Nation shall not lift up sword against nation,
Neither shall they learn war any more (Isaiah 2:2–4).

Almost the same words are found in the book of the prophet Micah (4:1–4), which can mean only that this vision was very widespread. Some of the prophets stress the glorious age but have little to say about the Davidic leader; others emphasize the leader; while still others stress both concepts.

In the postbiblical period, the full messianic doctrine came to fruition—the Messiah, son of David, will be sent by God and will bring about, a new age of peace in which all people will recognize the truth, and in which the people of Israel will be vindicated.

Natural and Supernatural

There is no doubt that when the messianic idea had become fully developed it contained both natural and supernatural elements. For instance, the idea of a Messiah sent by God was something very different from a great political leader who would help the Jewish people to return to its land. There is a miraculous, supernatural quality about the Messiah and his rule, though in no version of Judaism is the Messiah a divine figure. The Messiah is a human being, but one endowed by God with special spiritual gifts. However, in the history of Messianism, there were times when the natural elements were stressed. Maimonides, for example, refused to believe that the Messiah would perform miracles such as raising the dead. Maimonides also pointed out that many of the legends about the messianic age— that bread would grow on trees and the like, or that wild animals would become tame—are either figurative or pure speculation with no binding force for Jewish belief. In the third century the famous

Babylonian teacher, Samuel, taught that all the visions of the prophets regarding the "end of days" refer to the World to Come (the Afterlife), but that in the messianic age there would still be poverty and other ills, except that Israel will be free from domination by other nations and will live securely in its own land.

A good example of the two differing interpretations is provided by the comments on the vision of Isaiah (Isaiah 11). The prophet speaks of the wolf dwelling with the lamb and the leopard with the kid, and so forth. Some of the commentators take this literally—that wild beasts will no longer prey on weaker animals. But thinkers like Maimonides take it figuratively. The fierce nations, bent on oppressing the weak and on persecuting Israel, will become more civilized. They will no longer be as devouring wolves, but will learn to live in harmony with the mild and meek, who are like the lamb. Again, Maimonides believes that in the messianic age the Temple will be rebuilt, but by human means, whereas the supernatural view has it that the Temple is already built on high, as it were, and will drop down from Heaven.

The Orthodox View

But whether the emphasis was on the natural or the supernatural, the traditional view, still the Orthodox view today, is that we must hope daily for the coming of a human Messiah, a descendant of King David who is alive and waiting to be sent by God, one who will be recognized as such and who will reestablish the Davidic kingdom in the Holy Land. The Temple will be rebuilt; the exiles gathered "from the four corners of the earth"; the sacrificial system will be restored (there are still pious Jewish scholars who study the laws of the sacri-

Tradition teaches that after the coming of the Messiah, all the dead will be resurrected, and will be judged by God for what they did with their lives.

"There will be abundant leisure time and freedom from care and sorrow."

fices so that they will know the procedures when the Temple is built). There will be abundant leisure time and freedom from care and sorrow and oppression, so that all will have time to study God's Torah and mankind will not only live in peace, but will develop into a higher order that pursues goodness for its own sake. History as we know it will come to an end and a totally different era will begin, of human fulfillment as servants of the One God. People will live far longer than they do at present, and although they will still die of old age, it will be a very ripe old age, perhaps of hundreds of years. After a long period, all the dead will be resurrected, (brought to life again) and will be judged by God for what they did with their lives. The righteous will live forever, enjoying the bliss of being ever closer to God. An Orthodox thinker like Rabbi A. I. Kook believed that the theory of evolution, which he accepted, shows that humanity and, indeed, the whole of creation, has been moving toward ever greater heights of wisdom and morality, and that it all culminates in the messianic age.

Here we should note that the doctrine of the Messiah means that human history will find its fulfillment, on this earth, that there is "an end of days" in which injustice will be abolished and wrongs put right for all humanity *here on earth.* If it be asked, why this should be necessary since the individual soul will enjoy its bliss of nearness to God in the Hereafter, the traditional Jewish answer, is that God has His plan for the whole of human society here on earth, and that every good deed will be rewarded not in Heaven but by paving the way toward the messianic future of total goodness.

Waiting for the Messiah is a high traditional virtue. It means that the Jew should wish to see the glorious state in this lifetime, should be the kind of person who hates the evils and injustices that we see around us and should strive for the day when they are no more.

Non-Orthodox Views

In modern times there have been, on the whole, two very different reinterpretations of the messianic idea—Zionism and Reform Judaism. A number of Zionists, basing themselves on the idea of the return inherent in the messianic doctrine, came to hold that Zionism was a kind of secular version of Messianism and that the return of the Jewish people to Palestine was itself the fulfillment of the messianic hope.

This is one of the reasons why many Orthodox rabbis were opposed to Zionism. It seemed to wish to anticipate the redemption by God through His Messiah and generally refused to acknowledge the return as a God-given opportunity for all to acknowledge Him. With the establishment of the State of Israel, all this became largely academic. After all, the State has been brought into being and it flourishes. Yet religious Jews, while accepting in full the implications

Two False Messiahs

The legend that the Lost Ten Tribes, driven in exile in 722 B.C.E., are in the lost kingdom waiting for the coming of the Messiah, when they will be reunited with the rest of Jewry, has persisted for centuries. In the early sixteenth century a strange man appeared, calling himself David Reubeni and claiming to be the brother of King Joseph, ruler over the lost tribes of Reuben (hence his name), Gad and Manasseh in the desert of Habor. Scholars now guess that he really was a Falashan Jew. Appearing in Venice in the year 1523, he announced himself as chief of his brother's army with a mission to the Pope. He eventually had an audience with Pope Clement VII, seeking to persuade the Pope to join forces with him against the Muslims. The Pope, far from dismissing Reubeni's pretensions, gave him letters of support for his venture. In Portugal the Marranos looked upon him as the herald of the Messiah. All these adventures are related in the diary Reubeni kept, which obviously must be taken with more than a grain of salt. Charged with having persuaded Christians to embrace Judaism, Reubeni was imprisoned; he then vanished from the scene of Jewish history.

Solomon Molcho (d. 1532) was born in Lisbon. He was brought up as a Marrano, but when he met with David Reubeni, the other false Messiah of that period, he asked to be formally admitted into the Jewish faith and was circumcised. Together with Reubeni, Molcho went to Emperor Charles V, probably to persuade the Emperor to urge the Jews to fight with him against the Turks. As a Marrano who had reverted to Judaism, Molcho was guilty of a capital offense. He was tried through the intervention of the Emperor and was burnt at the stake. False Messiah though he was, because he was a martyr, Molcho was held in high esteem by the rabbis of his day, including the author of the *Shulḥan Arukh*, Joseph Caro.

Coming of the Messiah

Some Jews throughout the ages have believed that the actual date of the coming of the Messiah is hinted at in Scripture and is conveyed to certain saints. Thus, some engaged (though most of the Rabbis disapproved) in trying to work out the date of the "end." For instance, there was a widely-held belief in the Middle Ages that the Messiah would come at the beginning of the sixth millennium (a nice round number), that is, in the year 5000, which corresponded to the year 1240. Others believed that the Messiah would come 600 years later (in the year 5600, corresponding to the year 1840) because this is hinted at in the 600 years of Noah at the time of the Deluge. Naturally, when these forecasted dates came and went without the Messiah's arrival, there was considerable loss of faith. There were also false Messiahs, like Shabbetai Zevi, who wrought similar havoc with Jewish belief and trust in God.

From Martin Buber

Each of us has to do his or her bit in making the world a better place until the messianic age eventually arrives. Martin Buber recalls that when he was a little boy he heard of the legend that the Messiah waits patiently among the poor in Rome for the day when he will be allowed to come. Little Martin Buber once asked his grandfather, "Grandfather! What is he waiting for?" The grandfather replied: "My child, he is waiting for you."

of Jewish statehood, still cannot see it as the realization of the messianic dream. Consequently, some prefer to speak of the emergence of the State of Israel and its many notable achievements as "the beginning of redemption." Something tremendous has taken place, the "footsteps of the Messiah" can be heard clearly, but the final redemption has still not arrived.

Classical Reform, on the other hand, tended to welcome the new spirit abroad in Europe at the beginning of the last century as itself the heralding of the messianic age. The idea of the return was pushed into the background or rejected entirely. The emergence of the era was to take place in the West. Some declared that Germany was the Messiah and Berlin the new Jerusalem, or America the Messiah and Washington the new Jerusalem. Very few thinkers today would hold such a naive view, because the terrible inhumanity of people to other people which has disfigured this century make it impossible to see in Western society, despite its achievements, the creation of a new higher type of person under the kingdom of God. Most Reform thinkers have, like the Zionists, come to grips with the nationalistic side of Messianism and the idea of the return. But reform places the emphasis not on the miraculous elements of the ancient belief—the rebuilding of the Temple, the restoration of the sacrificial system, and so forth—but on the new age that will dawn.

For the same reason, most Reform Jews believe in the dawning of a messianic age rather than in the coming of a human Messiah. Many Reform Jews still speak of the poetic elements in the ancient dream, such as the coming of Elijah the prophet as the forerunner of the Messiah. They will still sing of Elijah's coming and of the Messiah's, but in the spirit of poetry which uses ancient symbols to express the yearning for a new age, as is typical of the Jew and his hopes for the future.

The Messiah in Judaism and Christianity

The messianic idea had already developed by the rise of Christianity. Jews at that time, under Roman rule in Palestine, looked forward to the fulfillment of biblical prophecy which they understood as referring to the Messiah. The early Christians believed that Jesus was the Messiah foretold by the prophets. (The word *Christ* is from the Greek and means "Messiah," "anointed one"). Apart from the very serious difference between Judaism and Christianity on the question of the divine nature of Jesus—Judaism considers it blasphemy and a form of idolatry to suggest that Jesus is divine and the son of God—Judaism differs profoundly from Christianity on the messianic doctrine.

According to the traditional Christian view, the Messiah has already come in the person of Jesus and we have been living in the messianic age these past 2,000 years. Redemption, in Christian thought, no longer means what it means in the Jewish doctrine of the Messiah (the redemption of Jews and ultimately of all humanity from persecution and oppression) but redemption from sin through belief in Jesus. Here Judaism protests that Jesus cannot have been the Messiah, since there have been wars and hatred and the world is still as bad as ever, even if we see signs of some improvements, such as those in health and social welfare, which have had more to do with secular than with religious thought. Judaism, then, differs from Christianity in still looking forward to the messianic age. It will come one day— we hope very soon, but we are certainly not living in it now. When one of the rabbis in the last century was told that the Messiah had come, he looked out the window and after a few moments declared: "No, the Messiah has not come, because I cannot see that the world is any different from what it was." This is Judaism's attitude: the Messiah has not come; if he had, the world would be very different.

And yet the great Maimonides does see much significance in the emergence and growth of Christianity from the point of view of the messianic doctrine. At the end of his famous code of law, Maimonides has a lengthy passage in which he describes Jewish Messianism. Here Maimonides writes: "Even of him [Jesus] who imagined that he was the Messiah but was put to death by the Court, Daniel had previously prophesied: as it is said: 'Also the children of the violent among thy people shall lift themselves up to establish the vision; but they shall stumble' (Daniel 11:14). Has there ever been a greater stumbling than this? For all the prophets declared that the Messiah will be the deliverer of Israel and their savior, gathering their dispersed ones and confirming the commandments. But he caused Israel to perish by the sword, their remnant to be dispersed and humbled. He induced them to change the Torah and led the greater part of the world to err to serve another beside God.

"No human being, however, is capable of fathoming the designs of the Creator, for their ways are not His ways, neither are His thoughts their thoughts. All these events [relating to Jesus] and even those relating to him who succeeded the one referred to [Mohammed], were nothing else than a means of preparing the way for King Messiah. It will reform the whole world to worship God with one accord. . . . How will this be? The entire world has been filled with the doctrine of the Messiah, the Torah and the Ten Commandments. The doctrines have been propagated to the distant isles and among many peoples, uncircumcised of heart and flesh. They discuss these subjects which contradict the Torah. Some declare these Com-

"Judaism protests that Jesus cannot have been the Messiah since the world is still as bad as ever it was."

Judaism firmly rejected Jesus because he did not fulfill Jewish expectations of the Messiah.

While Jews wait patiently for the Messiah, they continue to build a better world.

mandments were once true, but have been abrogated at the present time and have lost their force; while others assert that there are hidden significations in them and they are not plain of meaning—the King has already come and revealed their hidden significance. But when the [true] King Messiah will in fact arise and succeed, be exalted and lifted up, they will immediately all recant and acknowledge the falsity of their assertions."

Thus, for Maimonides it is not Judaism alone that has prepared the way for the coming of the Messiah. The daughter religions of Christianity and Islam have also had their part to play in the great drama by making people more civilized and more decent and more ready to acknowledge the truth, which at present they see only dimly, but will see and accept in its full splendor in the messianic age.

Life in the Messianic Age

Joseph Klausner, author of a fine book on the history of Jewish Messianism, remarked that all peoples believe in a Golden Age but, whereas most ancient peoples believed that the Golden Age belonged to their remote past, the Jews, whose past as slaves in Egypt was nothing to boast of, projected their Golden Age into the future. Now the concept of a Golden Age is bound to have something dreamlike about it. No one knows what the future will be like, and when Jews speculated about the messianic age they quite naturally thought of it as a time when all their hopes would be realized. The many modern Jews who think of the messianic age in naturalistic terms, although in terms of divine intervention not merely through human progress, think of life in the messianic age as more open to the call of the divine but still not very different from what it is today. Traditional Jews, following the Orthodox position, dwell more on the miraculous and on the differences between life in that age and life today. But Maimonides reminds us that many of the statements, even in the rabbinic literature, are pure speculation and only God knows the details.

A Jewish folk song, for instance, sings of "What Will Be When the Messiah Comes." Drawing on rabbinic statements, it tells of the great banquet that will be held for the righteous. At this banquet the meat of the Leviathan and the Wild Ox (two mythical creatures) will be served as well as wine that has been stored in the vat "from the six days of creation" (the year one was a good year for wine!). Moses will "say Torah" at the banquet, Miriam will dance, and King David will recite Grace After Meals. There is no doubt that in the folk mind, such details might be taken more or less literally. But the more subtle thinkers and the mystics interpreted it all figuratively. For instance, the "wine" represents the heavenly teachings which can be disclosed only in a world more perfect than the present. The Jewish teachers were sufficiently realistic to appreciate that only the spiritually minded could have a nobler vision of what life would be like in the time of the Messiah.

Here is Maimonides' conclusion to the section of his code dealing with the Messiah (and to the code as a whole): "The Sages and the Prophets hoped for the days of the Messiah neither because they would rule over all the world nor because they would have dominion over the nations nor because the nations would admire them and neither because they would eat, drink and be merry but only because then they would be free to study the Torah and its wisdom without being subject to oppression which hinders such study, and all this is so that they might attain to the life of the World to Come [which Maimonides understands as spiritual bliss in the Hereafter]. . . . At that time there will be neither hunger nor war, neither envy nor competition for the good will be found in great abundance and all delicacies as accessible as the dust of the earth. The whole world will have no other occupation than to know the Lord. Consequently, Israel will be great sages, knowing undisclosed matters and grasping the knowledge of their Creator insofar as this lies within man's power, as it is said: 'For the earth shall be full of the knowledge of the Lord, as the waters cover the sea' " (Isaiah 11:9).

27
The Hereafter

Life after Death

The doctrine of the Messiah refers to the state of the Jewish people and of humanity here on earth. But Judaism also believes in "the World to Come" (olam ha-ba), that the death of the body is not the end, but that the soul lives on and, in the traditional version of the faith, the body, too, will be "resurrected," brought back to life. The Rabbis speak frequently of "the World to Come," but in the Middle Ages opinions were divided as to whether it refers to the immortality of the soul (Maimonides) or to the resurrection (Naḥmanides).

Maimonides was, in fact, accused by his opponents of denying altogether the resurrection of the dead. Toward the end of his life, Maimonides wrote his "Essay on the Resurrection" in which he stated that he did believe in the resurrection but that it would not last forever. Maimonides could not imagine that the body would endure forever, so he held that after a very long period the resurrected dead would die once again and only the soul would be immortal. Naḥmanides did believe that the resurrected bodies would live forever, yet felt obliged to state that these bodies, although identified with our present bodies, would be very refined, almost spiritual, bodies. Following the talmudic teachings, which Maimonides quotes in support of his view, Naḥmanides held that after the body has been resurrected it would be so refined as not to require food or drink or any other bodily needs.

Thus, according to the traditional scheme, the future will be as follows: First the Messiah will come. Then, after a lengthy period, the dead will be resurrected, which means that the souls, until then in Heaven, will be rejoined with their bodies. According to Maimonides these, too, will one day suffer death, the soul alone enjoying eternal bliss, while, according to Naḥmanides, the refined bodies will live on forever. Many Reform and some other modern Jews prefer to believe solely in the doctrine of the immortality of the soul, not in the resurrection. According to this view, the soul alone is immortal.

Basically, the two doctrines of the immortality of the soul and the resurrection are incompatible. According to the first doctrine, there is no death at all except of the body—the soul never dies. According to the resurrection doctrine, death ends both body and soul; but the whole person, body and soul, is "resurrected," brought back from the dead to live again. You no doubt have seen artists' impressions of the graves giving up their dead. But over 2,000 years

Our Sages say that this world is like a vestibule to the World to Come.

ago the two doctrines were combined to produce the official, traditional view, namely, that the soul lives on when the body dies and it is reunited with the body at the resurrection. One of the reasons Orthodox teachers oppose cremation is that it interferes with the resurrection by destroying the body completely. Of course, God can reconstitute the body from the ashes, just as from the dust to which it is eventually reduced, but it is held, that people must not themselves destroy the body that is to be resurrected.

Why Not in the Bible?

If Judaism believes in life after death why is there almost no reference to it in the Bible? It cannot be that the biblical writers knew nothing of this belief, since they must have been aware of the pyramids and other evidences that the Egyptians and other ancient peoples held this belief. It has been suggested that the comparative silence of the Bible is its protest against the pagan notions of life in the Hereafter as being bound up with pagan religion and pagan gods. The great classical work of Egyptian religion is *The Book of the Dead* and the task of Egyptian priests was to help the dead in their future existence. Perhaps that is why the Torah forbids a *kohen*, priest, from coming into contact with the dead (see Leviticus 21:1–3). In any case, the belief in a Hereafter did become prominent in postbiblical Judaism and has remained so ever since, though, not all Jews believe in the resurrection of the dead.

"If Judaism believes in life after death, why is there hardly any reference to it in the Bible?"

Judaism: This-Worldly or Other-Worldly?

Is, then, Judaism a this-worldly religion or an other-worldly religion? Does Judaism place its emphasis on life in this world or does it think of this life as a preparation for eternal life? It is difficult to give a simple either/or reply to this question. The English poet Keats describes this world as "a vale of soul-making"—it is the place in which human beings, by their moral living, prepare themselves for eternal life. By living good lives here on earth we "make" our souls, which can enjoy eternal bliss. Judaism certainly looks upon this world as a kind of school in which we learn to love the good so that we can love God and enjoy His love forever.

The Talmud compares this life to the eve of the Sabbath and the World to Come to the Sabbath. Only one who makes adequate preparations on the eve of the Sabbath can enjoy the Sabbath. However, Judaism refuses to see this life solely as a preparation for eternity. This life is good in itself and even if there were no after-life, people would be expected to live worthily and decently. In *Ethics of the Fathers* (4:17) the second-century teacher, Rabbi Jacob, expressed the paradox in this way: "One hour of repentance and good deeds in this life is better than the whole life of the World to Come but one

"Judaism differs in refusing to see this life solely as a preparation for eternity."

A Proverb

Rabbi Israel Salanter noticed a shoemaker working late into the night. When asked why he worked so late, the shoemaker replied: "For as long as the lamp is burning, one must do the repairs." For the rest of his life Rabbi Israel used to repeat the words of the shoemaker as the most powerful reminder to him to strive constantly for self-improvement: "For as long as the lamp is burning, one must do the repairs."

hour of spiritual bliss in the World to Come is better than the whole of this life." "Better" is a word that depends on its context. From the standpoint of worshiping God, one hour in this life is "better" since the Hereafter is the place of reward, not of service. But from the viewpoint of ecstatic bliss in the nearness of God as the reward of virtue, one hour of life in the World to Come is "better" since it is fully possible only in the Hereafter.

Therefore, the answer to the question,"Is Judaism an other-worldly or a this-worldly religion?" is that it is both. It is other-worldly in that it does hold that this life is not the end and that the ultimate purpose of life on earth is to prepare for eternal life. But it is this-worldly in that it holds that this life is a good in itself and that we can acquire immortality only by living a good life here and now.

Bread of Shame

The Jewish mystics try to explain the meaning of the World to Come in this way: People have been created with a stern independence. They do not really want something for nothing. Even if a poor person is given the finest food and the choicest wines daily at a rich person's table, he will, with any self-respect, prefer a morsel of bread he has earned by his own labors. No one wants to eat "bread of shame," always in debt to someone else's bounty. While God is the Source of all goodness and His purpose in creating humanity was to bestow good upon people, He does not give us any unearned good, for that would make us totally indebted to Him and the bliss we enjoy would be a "bread of shame." God places us in a world containing both good and evil, and we by our own free choice can lead the good life. If we do, we make the good our own and it is a good we have earned.

God is the Source of all goodness, but He does not give us any un-earned good, for that would be the "bread of shame."

We have first been placed in this world in order ultimately to reach the place that has been set aside for us.

Actually, the mystics go even deeper. The greatest good is the nearness of God. But if we are brought nearer by God without our prior efforts, we are not God-like, since God is not given the good but it is part of His Being. When we freely choose the good, in spite of all obstacles, we acquire a goodness that is truly our own and come nearer to God.

Rabbi Moses Ḥayyim Luzzatto states it early in his book, *Mesillat Yesharim*: "The foundation of saintliness and the root of true worship is for it to become perfectly clear to man what his duty in life is and to which aim he must direct all his endeavours throughout his life. Now our Sages have taught us that man was created for no other purpose than to find delight in the Lord and bask in the radiance of His Presence. But the real place for such delight is the World to Come which has been created for that very purpose.

"However, the way to reach that goal of our desire is this world. That is why our Sages say that this world is like a vestibule to the World to Come. The means by which man attains to this purpose are the *mitzvot* which God has commanded us and the place in which the *mitzvot* can be carried out is this world. Therefore, man has been placed at first in this world in order to reach the place that has been set aside for him through these means. There he will enjoy the good which he has acquired through these means. . . .

"In order for a man to deserve this good it is right and proper for him to engage in the effort to acquire it for himself, that is to say, he must strive to cleave to God by carrying out deeds which result in this communion with God. Now God has placed man in a world in which there are many things which keep him far from God; these are material desires which, if he is drawn after them, cause him to be remote from that true good. So he is placed, in truth, in the midst of a fierce battle, for all man's circumstances are severe trials. . . . But if he is a hero and wins the battle on every side, he becomes the perfect man who is worthy of cleaving to God. He will then leave the vestibule to enter the palace, there to enjoy the Light of Life."

Some of us may find Luzzatto a little too strong and otherworldly for our tastes. He does seem to be saying that there is no good at all in worldly things except as "trials." But the basic philosophy is surely sound from the religious point of view. It is very hard for religious people to understand why God allows us to depart this life with so much undone and unfinished unless there is an opportunity for further progress toward the knowledge of God in the Hereafter.

Heaven and Hell

Nowadays we speak of the state of eternal bliss as "Heaven." Actually, "Heaven" (*shamayyim*) in Jewish literature is either the name for the sky or the name for God. Nor is *Paradise* (a Persian word meaning "orchard") ever used for the Hereafter. The usual term for it is either "the World to Come" or *Gan Eden*, "Garden of Eden." We speak of eternal bliss in the nearness to God in the Hereafter, but the truth is that this experience is bound to be unintelligible to us, since we live in this world of matter. The Rabbis say that we can have only a "foretaste" of it, say, when we observe the Sabbath and experience the Sabbath delight that is "out of this world" literally.

Maimonides observes that to try to grasp the nature of eternal bliss in the Hereafter while we are still in this world is like a person born blind trying to grasp the nature of color. God alone knows what is in store for the righteous.

Does Judaism believe in Hell? There are certainly many references in the rabbinic sources to *Gehinnom*, meaning "Hell" but here, too, a good deal depends on what we mean by this concept. Many

> *"The experience of the Hereafter is bound to be unintelligible to us, since we live in this world of matter."*

Death, Burial, and Mourning

According to tradition, it is a high mitzvah to give the dead a decent burial. A rabbinic saying has it that this is the most sincere act of benevolence, since one cannot expect from the dead any favors in return.

Originally, the Talmud tells us, the dead were buried in costly garments, and people would be embarrassed if they lacked the means to provide their dead with these. Rabban Gamaliel, prince of his people, left in his will that he should be buried in simple linen shrouds so that people might say, "What was good enough for this aristocrat is good enough for us." It was a great step forward in preventing families from becoming impoverished by a funeral. The Talmud goes on to say that after funerals in the Holy Land, the mourners used to drink a special toast to the memory of Rabban Gamaliel. At a later period, special white shrouds were introduced, the details of which owe much to the Kabbalah. The body is first washed thoroughly so that it may be laid to rest with dignity. This is known as the *taharah,* "the purification." The coffin is usually made from simple planks of wood. Indeed, in the State of Israel, the dead are generally buried without a coffin at all. It is now also the custom to wrap a man's tallit around his corpse. To perform the last rites for the dead is held to be a great privilege. Traditionally there was a "holy society" (*Ḥevrah Kaddisha*) that carried out these services voluntarily. It was considered a great privilege to be admitted into such a society.

It is a mitzvah to escort the dead to their last resting place. The funeral is known as the *levayyah* ("the escorting"). Among traditional Jews, a garment is torn before the funeral of near relatives (father, mother, sister, brother, son, daughter, husband, wife) as a sign of mourning. For parents, this is done on the left side of the garment (near the heart), for other relatives on the right side. When the coffin is lowered into the grave, those assembled say: "May he (she) come into his (her) place in peace."

It is the traditional practice for near relatives to sit in mourning on low stools for a week (hence the term "sitting shiva," that is, for seven days). During this period, prayers are recited for the repose of the soul of the deceased. A light is left burning in memory of the deceased, as it is on the anniversary of the death (the *Yahrzeit*). It is a mitzvah to visit mourners and to try to give them words of comfort and consolation. The traditional greeting to mourners is: "May the Almighty comfort you among those who mourn for Zion and Jerusalem."

simple folk do take it literally to mean that the wicked are punished in fire, but the more subtle thinkers understand it figuratively. According to many Jewish thinkers, Hell is the state of a person who rejects the good and finds, upon dying, that God is still remote.

Maimonides, again, seems to suggest that "Hell" does not mean torment at all but simply that a thoroughly wicked soul is annihilated, feeling no pain but simply passing out of existence so that it cannot enjoy the bliss reserved for the good. One does not hear much of "Hell" in modern Jewish preaching, but perhaps we have gone too far in our sentimentality. Perhaps the idea of "Hell" is intended to suggest that we cannot automatically go to "Heaven" if we have led a bad life and must first suffer the torment of the remoteness from God that our bad life has caused.

The general principle is that we should try to live as good a life as we can and then leave the rest to God, Who will not let a single good deed or thought go unrewarded. Descriptions of Heaven and Hell should be seen for what they really are, pure speculation about a state unlike anything we can experience in this life, but which people have tried to describe as best they can with the language they have. Yet these descriptions have their value. That which we cherish the most we tend to see as being ours in Heaven, which is why the Rabbis, for whom the study of the Torah was the greatest joy, thought of Heaven as the place or state in which God Himself teaches the Torah to the righteous.

Contacting the Spirit World

In comparatively recent years there have been numerous mediums who claim they can contact the spirit world and who hold seances for that purpose. There is even a religious movement known as Spiritualism. In addition, attempts have been made to investigate such phenomena scientifically through what is now known as psychical research. Does Judaism approve or disapprove of attempts to contact the spirits of the dead? Insofar as Spiritualism is a rival religion to Judaism, it is obvious that a Jew cannot be a Spiritualist. But what of attempts to contact the dead in a nonreligious context?

Now on the face of it this, too, is rendered completely taboo by the Deuteronomic law: "There shall not be found among you anyone that maketh his son or his daughter to pass through the fire, one that useth divination, a soothsayer, or an enchanter, or a sorcerer, or a charmer, or one that consulteth a ghost or a familiar spirit, or a necromancer" (Deuteronomy 18:10–12). But these rules, in the context, refer to various magical practices associated with pagan rites, the rabbis explain. Some medieval authorities once permitted two Jews to make a pact that when one of them died he would return to tell the other what transpires after death. So it is not certain that there is an actual law forbidding any attempt at contacting the dead. Still, the weight of opinion among the Jewish teachers is that such things should be avoided entirely. Besides the vast amount of sheer fraud

"Descriptions of Heaven and Hell should be seen as pure speculation about a state of existence utterly removed from anything we can understand."

It is hard to understand why God allows us to depart this life with so much unfinished unless there is an opportunity for further knowledge of God in the Hereafter.

Dybbuks and Ghosts

Belief in the existence of ghosts, evil spirits, imps, demons and werewolves was rife especially in medieval Germany. Even the famous moralistic work, *Sefer Ḥasidim,* accepts these beliefs and they were certainly entertained by the people. There are numerous folk practices based on superstition, which the Rabbis tried to discourage without much success. There are many accounts of *dybbukim.* A *dybbuk* (the word means "one attached") is supposedly a wandering soul which has entered the body of a living human being and has to be driven out. On Purim Rabbi Elhanan Wasserman used to tell his students his eyewitness account of an exorcism of a dybbuk presided over by the Ḥafetz Ḥayyim.

The fear of the evil eye was rife. One way to ward off the evil eye from a child was by tying a red ribbon round its arm. Ḥayyim Tchernowitz, in his autobiography, tells how he and his fellow students in Russia, at the turn of the century, would engage in table-rapping, although the practice is strictly forbidden by Jewish law. In Eastern Europe there was a widespread belief that when a synagogue was closed at night, the dead would gather there to pray. It was said that if a man, passing a synagogue at night, heard his name called he should not enter. The dead, short of a *minyan,* would draw him to their fate. Belief in witchcraft was held even by some rabbis. A Ḥasidic legend tells of a wizard who turned himself into a wolf to terrorize school children, but when the Baal Shem Tov sang Jewish songs with them, the wizard was frightened away.

and trickery on the part of many mediums, it is unhealthy to wish to pierce the veil, to contact the other world. As Judaism sees it, our duty is to concentrate on living worthily here and now, without bothering our heads about the nature of the "Great Beyond." Rabbi A. I. Kook, the distinguished twentieth-century rabbi, mystic, and thinker, was asked by a devout Jew whether it might not be good to contact the dead in order to strengthen faith—if one believes he has spoken with the dead, he will have no doubts regarding the Hereafter. Rabbi Kook replied that while some sort of a case can be made for permitting it, he strongly advises against it. The Jew should not seek to strengthen faith by dubious means.

> *"Our duty in this life is to concentrate entirely on living worthily here and now without bothering about the nature of the 'Great Beyond.'"*

Prayers for the Dead

There are references to prayers for the dead as early as the period of the Maccabees. Since Judaism believes that the dead are not really dead but live on in Heaven and need our prayers, it is customary to pray for their repose at the funeral, on the Yahrzeit (the anniversary of the death), and on Yom Kippur (and in many communities on other occasions as well). The best-known prayer for the dead, the Kaddish, is, however, not really a prayer for the dead at all! Originally the Kaddish was a prayer for the reign of God over all the earth when (in the messianic age) His name will be "sanctified" (*Kaddish* means, in fact, "sanctification" of God's name). When it was later introduced that a son (or a daughter, according to some authorities) recites the "mourner's Kaddish" the meaning is that by reciting in public the

> *"The best-known prayer for the dead, the Kaddish, is, however, not really a prayer for the dead at all!"*

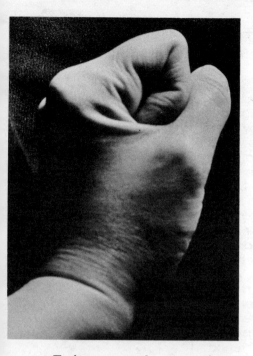

Trying to grasp the nature of eternal bliss in the Hereafter is akin to a blind person's trying to grasp the nature of color. God alone knows what is in store for the righteous.

special prayer of sanctification, one is in effect declaring: "My father (or mother) tried to live as a Jew who sanctifies God's name. My parent is no longer alive to do this on earth, so I will take his place and by reciting the Kaddish show my determination to live Jewishly and sanctify God's name in my life as my father did in his. In this way I shall keep his memory alive, since if it were not for him I would not have come into the world to be able to make this declaration."

It was a custom in some Eastern European communities for the parents of the bride and bridegroom to go to the cemetery and invite their dead parents to the wedding. Even today we sometimes speak of dead relatives as being present at the festivities "in spirit" though not in the flesh.

Reincarnation

It is often asked whether Judaism believes in reincarnation, that a soul, after death, can return to earth to inhabit a different body. A number of Jewish thinkers like Saadiah Gaon reject the doctrine as thoroughly un-Jewish, but in the Kabbalah the doctrine is accepted as true. Some kabbalists even suggest that the reason little children sometimes die in infancy is that the souls in their bodies had been on earth in another existence and had to return for a further short stay to atone for their sins. Most of us are content to look upon this, too, as a matter of speculation without its having any effect on our moral life one way or the other.

The End

The consideration of what happens at the end of time is known as eschatology. We have seen in this brief chapter how much pure speculation there is in Judaism on eschatology. We repeat that the healthiest attitude is not to attempt to pry too deeply into matters we cannot possibly hope to know much about. The important thing, so far as Judaism is concerned, is to appreciate that there is an "end" that is, at the same time, a "beginning." For, as the Jewish thinkers never tire of telling us, eternal bliss in the Hereafter does not mean a static kind of rest that would be a state of utter boredom. Nor does Judaism try to describe the Hereafter in terms of harp-playing or flying about with angels' wings. There is progress in the Hereafter, the righteous going from strength to strength. This thought is no doubt behind the rabbinic saying that Torah scholars have rest neither in this world nor in the next. For who wants "rest" in the purely static sense? George Bernard Shaw defined Hell as a "perpetual holiday." Somehow, Judaism teaches, the righteous in Heaven go on from stage to stage in the understanding of truth and in nearness to God, and since God is Infinite, their progress, their joy, and their increase in knowledge is infinite and eternal.

INDEX

Aaron, 193
Abarbanel, Don Isaac, 6, 44
Abbaye, 58
Abraham, 37, 63, 78, 81, 89, 122, 182, 205–206, 211, 215, 220
Adoption, 219
Afterlife, see Hereafter; Messianic idea
Agag (Amalekite king), 179
Aggadic Midrashim, 63
Aharonim (later ones), 72
Akiba, Rabbi, 22, 50, 57, 58, 86, 171–172, 208
Alfasi, Rabbi Isaac (The Rif; Yitzak Fasi), 70, 193
Alkabetz, Rabbi Solomon, 88
All-knowing God, 17–18
All-powerful God, 16–17
Amidah, 115, 180
Amoraim, 56–58, 64
Amos (and Book of Amos), 47, 48, 175
Amulets, 16
Anger, 209–210
Animals
    cruelty to, prohibited, 133, 175–177
    forbidden, as food, 30, 32, 133
    shehitah and, 133–135
    terefah, 135, 137, 138
    See also Meat
Anti-Maimonists, 81–82
Antiochus (Roman emperor), 111, 133
Anti-Semitism, 149
    See also Holocaust
Apocrypha, 50
Arama, Rabbi Isaac, 104
Architecture of synagogues, 68, 117
Arele, Rabbi, 207
Aristotle, 45, 80
Ark (aron; tevah), 117–118
Asher, Jacob ben, 71
Ashi, Rav, 58, 60
Ashkenazim, 8, 71, 128, 164
Assimilation, Rosenzweig and, 84, 85
Athalta de-geulah (beginning of redemption), 159–160

Atheism, 10
Attar, Hayyim Ibn, 78
Azulai, Hayyim Joseph David, 75

Baal, 11
Baal Shem Tov (Israel ben Eliezer), 37, 141, 200, 237
Babylonian (Bavli) Talmud, 2, 8, 56–58, 60–64
Bacharach, Rabbi Jair Hayyim, 73
Baer, Rabbi Dov (The Maggid), 141, 142
Bahar (to chose), 38
Bahya (man), 146
Bar Mitzvah, 123, 216
Baraitot (outside works), 59
Baruch (Jeremiah's scribe), 46
Bar Yohai, Rabbi Simeon, 88
Belief in God, 10–18
Ben Azzai, 28, 214
Ben Gamaliel, Rabban Simeon, 190
Ben Gurion, David, 163
Ben Lakish, Rabbi Simeon, 96, 103
Ben Pedat, Rabbi Eleazar, 58
Ben Petura, Rabbi, 171–172
Ben Yair, Rabbi Phinehas, 198–199
Ben-Zvi, Yitzhak, 164
Benevolence (gemilut hasadim), 180–183
Berlin, Isaiah, 106
Bertinoro, Obadiah, 68
Bet Din (court of law), 188–190
Bet ha-Knesset (house of assembly), 115
Bet ha-Midrash (house of study), 115
Bet ha-Mikdash, see Synagogue
Bet ha-Tefillah (house of prayer), 115
Bet Yosef ("House of Joseph;" Caro), 71
Bible, the (Tanakh), 1, 11, 19, 46–55
    and biblical criticism, 52–54
    books of, 47–50, 52; see also specific books
    commentaries on, 54–55
    life after death not mentioned in, 231

passages of, on chosenness,
    38–39
study of, 26, 27
translations of, 50, 51
See also Torah
Bimah (platform), 117–119
Binah (understanding), 92
Binah le-Ittim "Understanding the
    Times;" Figo), 75
Birds, types of, forbidden as foods,
    133
Blessings, Sabbath, 100, 102
Blood, prohibition against,
    135–136
Book of the Dead, The, 231
Brit, 215–216
Buber, Martin, 84, 197, 225
Buddhism, 1
Burial, 235
Business practices, fairness in,
    191–192

Cantor (Ḥazzan), 122
Caro, Rabbi Joseph, 70–72, 119,
    157, 225
Character
    actions affecting, 168–169
    ethical, 211
Charity, *see* Tzedakah
Children
    adopted, 219
    circumcision and Bar Mitzvah
        of, 215–216
    first-born, 39
    naming of, 215
    obligations of, to parents, 204,
        217–218
    parental obligations toward,
        216–217
    respectful, 218–219
Chosen people, 38–45, 158
Christianity, 6
    fundamental ethical difference
        between Judaism and, 187
    messianic idea in, 226–228
    Rosenzweig considering
        conversion to, 85
Chronicles, 46, 47
Circumcision, 215–216
Clement VII (pope), 225
Codes, 67, 69–72
Comfort giving, 181–182
Commentaries
    biblical, 54–55
    talmudic, 67–69
Compassion (raḥamanut; rach-
        mones), 174–180
    defined, 174–175
    determining need for, 177
    extent of, 175–176
    expressions of, 178
    and heart of flesh, 179
    importance of, 175

limits of, 178–179
Compromise, justice and, 194, 195
Conflict-of-interest situations,
    love in, 170–171
Conflicting claims, just settling of,
    188
Conservative Judaism, 145–146
    emphasis of, on Israel, 4, 5
    minyan and, 115
    music in synagogue and, 121
    Sabbath and, 99
    in State of Israel, 162
    Torah reading in synagogue
        and, 123
    women in synagogue and, 119
Conversion
    to Judaism, 42
    Rosenzweig considering, to
        Christianity, 85
Cordovero, Rabbi Moses, 89
Courts of law (Bet din), 188–190
Creative work on Sabbath, 99
Crescas, Ḥasdai, 14, 78
Crime and punishment, 188
Crown (taggin) of the Torah, 21, 34
Cruelty to animals, prohibited,
    133, 175–177

Daily services, 122–123
Dairy products, prohibition
        against mixing meat with,
        136–137
Daily life, justice in, 191–192
Daniel, Book of, 46, 47, 52, 227
Darkhe shalom (ways of peace), 45
David (King of Israel), 7, 27, 52,
    54, 63, 179, 221–223, 228
Dead, the
    benevolence toward, 181
    burial of, 235
    prayers for, 8, 115, 237–238
    resurrection of, *see* Hereafter
    Yahrzeit for, 8, 123, 235, 237
    See also Mourning
Dead Sea Scrolls, 53, 128, 164
Deuteronomy, 16, 19, 38, 47, 59,
    124, 126, 129, 136, 168, 175,
    179, 189, 191, 193, 236
Diaspora Jews, State of Israel and,
    162–163
Dietary laws, 30–33, 73, 132–139,
    146, 199
    on health-damaging foods, 138
    meat in, *see* Animals; Meat
    kashrut and, 132–133
    on plants and vegetables,
        138–139
    probability and neutralization
        principles and, 137–138
    standards of observance of,
        133–134
Dreidel, 110
Dress, Ḥasidic, 143

Dreyfus, Capt. Alfred, 149
Dualism of Kabbalah, 94
Duties of the Heart (Baḥya), 146
Dybbuks, 237

Ecclesiastes, 47–49, 52
Ed, *see* Witnesses
Eliezer, Israel ben (Baal Shem
    Tov), 37, 141, 200, 237
Eliezer, Rabbi, 57–59
Elijah, 177, 209–210, 226
Elilim, pagan gods as, 11
Employee relations, fairness in,
    191
Emunah (faith), 8
Encouragement and praise,
    benevolence expressed in, 182
Encyclopedia Judaica, 164
Encyclopedia Talmudit, 164
En Sof, 91, 93, 94
Enlightenment (Haskalah),
    143–144
Envy, 210–211
Epstein, Rabbi Y. M., 207
Eretz Yisrael (Land of Israel),
    157–159, 196; *see also* Israel,
    State of
"Essay of the Resurrection"
    (Maimonides), 230
Esther (and Book of Esther;
    Megillah), 47, 48, 52, 111–113,
    219
Eternal God, 15–16
Eternal light (ner tamid) in
    synagogue, 118
Ethical character, 211
Ethical monotheism, Judaism as,
    18
Ethics, 203–211
Ethics of the Fathers, 28, 29, 35,
    145, 182, 190, 203, 211, 218,
    232
Etrog (citron), 34, 35, 108, 109
Etz ha-Ḥayyim ("The Trees of
    Life;" Vital), 90
Even ba-Ezer ("Stone of Help";
    part of *Shulḥan Arukh*; Caro),
    71
Evil and suffering
    existence of God and, 11–13
    in Saadiah's philosophy, 79
    See also Holocaust
Evil tongue (Lashon Ha-ra),
    208–209
Evolution, 84
Existentialism, 84–85
Exodus, Book of, 19, 38, 39, 47,
    59, 96, 98, 101, 105, 106, 113,
    117, 126, 135, 136, 177, 189,
    190, 205, 208, 219
Eybeschuetz, Jonathan, 75
Ezekiel, Book of, 47, 49, 52, 179,
    212

Ezra (and Book of Ezra), 46, 47,
    52, 157
Ezrat nashim (court of the
    women), 119

Fackenheim, Emil, 151
Falk, Rabbi Joshua, 189
False messiahs, 94, 141, 225
Family (Mishpaḥah), 212
    Jewish home and, 220
    relationship of, to outside
        world, 219–220
    See also Children
Fasting
    on Av, 48
    on Yom Kippur, 110–111
Ferdinand I (King of Naples), 44
Festivals, 3, 30, 105, 199, 202
    working on, 113
    See also specific festivals
Figo, Rabbi Azariah, 75
Filial duties, 204, 217–218
Finkel, Rabbi Nathan Zevi, 40, 182
First-born child, significance of, 39
Fish, types of, forbidden as foods,
    133
Five Scrolls (Ḥamesh Megillot), 47
Foods
    Passover, 8, 105
    Sabbath, 101, 103
    Shavuot, 107
    See also Dietary laws
Foreknowledge, free will and, 14,
    78
Forgiveness, 31
Frank, Anne, 155
Frankel, Rabbi Zacharias, 146
Free will, 14, 29, 78
Freud, Sigmund, 189

Gamaliel, Rabban, 58, 59, 123, 235
Gambling, responsa on, 74
Ganzfield, Rabbi Solomon, 72
Gaon of Vilna, 27, 35
Gehinnon (Hell), 235
Geiger, Rabbi Abraham, 144
Gemara, *see* Talmud
Genesis, 19, 22, 47, 59, 78, 89,
    170, 212
Gentiles, *see* Non-Jews
"Gentleman's psalm," 7
Geonim, 63–64
Gersonides, Rabbi, 14, 54, 78
Ger Tzedek (righteous proselyte),
    42
Gevurah (power), 92
Ghosts, 237
Gift taking (shoḥad) by judges, 189
God
    belief in, 10–18
    concern of, for all of humanity,
        41–42
    in Halevi's philosophy, 79, 80

holiness and presence of, 202
in Kabbalah, 89, 90
in Krochmal's view, 83
in Maimonides' philosophy, 80
in Mendelssohn's philosophy, 82
nature of, 13–14
in Philo's thought, 78
in principles of faith, 5, 6
Reform Judaism emphasis on, 4, 5
in 20th-century philosophy, 84, 85
in Zohar, 89
Golden mean of Maimonides, 80–81
Golem, 94
Gratitude, 193
Guide for the Perplexed (Maimonides), 32, 80

Ha-Am, Aḥad, 163, 187
Habakkuk, Book of, 47
Ḥafetz Ḥayyim (Israel Meir ha-Kohen), 96, 207–209, 211, 237
Haftarot, Sephardim and Ashkenazim, 8
Hagar, 78
Haggadah, 34, 105, 106
Haggai, Book of, 47
Ha-Kadosh, Rabbenu (Judah the Prince), 56, 58, 59, 176–177, 192, 197, 207
Ha-Kohen, Israel Meir (Hafetz Ḥayyim), 96, 207–209, 211, 237
Halakhah, 62–63, 65, 156, 164
Halevi, Judah, 12, 40–41, 79–81, 157
Ḥallot (bread), 101
Haman, 111, 113, 150
Hamesh Megillot (Five Scrolls), 47
Ḥametz (leavened bread), 105
Hand washing, 32
Ḥanukkah, 34, 111, 113
Ḥasidism, 127, 141–144
holiness and, 196
humility in, 206
joy of mitzvot in, 35
tales, sayings, and proverbs in, 32, 168, 200, 202, 207, 208
Haskalah (Enlightenment), 143–144
Havdalah (division), 102
Ḥazal (rabbis of blessed memory), 64–65
Havdalah candles, 199
Ḥazzan (cantor), 122
Health-damaging foods, 138
Heaven and Hell, 234–236
Hebrew alphabet, 50
Heilprin, Jehel, 75
Hekhalot (Palaces) literature, 86

Heller, Yom Tov Lipmann, 68
Helpless, the, taking advantage of, 193–194
Hereafter, 7, 140, 230–238
benevolence and, 183
bread of shame and, 233–234
Heaven and Hell and, 234–236
and life after death, 230–231
Maimonides and, 68
non-Jews performing mitzvot sharing in, 42
not mentioned in the Bible, 231
other-worldly and this-wordly character of Judaism and, 232–233
See also Messianic idea
Herzl, Theodor, 147
Ḥesed, *see* Compassion; Love
Heschel, Abraham Joshua, 84
Hezekiah (King of Israel), 52
Hiddur mitzvah (adornment of the mitzvah), 34–35
Hillel, Rabbi, 58, 111, 167, 215
Hirsch, Rabbi Samson Raphael, 145
Ḥisda, Rabbi, 8, 58
Hitler, Adolf, 149–152
Hod (splendor), 92
Ḥokhmah (wisdom), 92
Holdheim, Rabbi Samuel, 144
Holiness (kedushah), 115, 196–202
Holocaust, 11, 44, 113, 149–157, 172
challenges of, 150–151
effects of, on Jewish unity, 152
mourning for victims of, 151–152
reactionary attitudes due to, 154–156
Holy objects, 196
See also specific holy objects
Holy sparks, 91
Honesty and integrity, 195
Hosea (and Book of Hosea), 47, 48
Ḥoshen Mishpat ("Breastplate of Judgment"; part of *Shulḥan Arukh*; Caro), 71
Hospitality, 182
Ḥukkim (statutes), 31
Human dignity, 203–204
Humility (Shiflut), 142, 205–207
Huna, Rabbi, 58

Ibn Adrat, Rabbi Solomon (Rashba), 73, 81
Ibn Ezra, Rabbi Abraham, 54, 106
Ibn Migash, Rabbi Joseph, 193
Ibn Pakudah, Baḥya, 2, 36, 154
Ingratitude, 193
Isaac, 37, 78, 81, 89, 122
Isaiah (and Book of Isaiah), 7, 8, 41, 47, 50, 52, 53, 100, 197, 222, 223, 229

Islam, 6, 227, 228
Israel, 1, 3–5
  as chosen people, 38–45, 158
  emphasis on, in Conservative
    Judaism, 4, 5
Israel, State of, 113, 148, 153,
    157–165
  burials in, 235
  Diaspora Jews and, 162–163
  ingathering of exiles in, 163–164
  justification for, 157–159
  Karaites in, 141
  Messianic idea and, 159–160,
    224, 226; see also Messianic
    idea
  peace and, 164–165
  role of religion in, 160–162
Isserles, Rabbi Moses, 72
I-Thou philosophy of Buber, 84

Jacob (patriarch), 37, 78, 81, 89,
    122, 210
Jacob, Rabbi, 232
Jaffe, Rabbi Mordecai, 190
Jastrow, Marcus, 66
Jeremiah (and Book of Jeremiah),
    46, 47, 53, 175
Jesus, 226–227
Jethro, 190
Jewish home, characterized, 220
Jewish philosophy
  need for, 77
  20th-century, 83–85
  See also specific philosophers
Jewishness, determination of, 9,
    164
Job (and Book of Job), 12, 47, 48,
    52, 187, 219
Joḥanan ben Zakkai, Rabbi, 45, 58
Joel, Book of, 47
Jonah, Book of, 47
Jose the Galilean, Rabbi, 58, 136
Joseph, 210
Joshua, Book of, 25, 46, 47
Joshua, Rabbi, 57, 58, 103, 123
Joshua ben Levi, Rabbi, 58
Judah the Prince, Rabbi (Rabbenu
    ha-Kadosh), 56, 58, 59,
    176–177, 192, 197
Judaism
  defined, 1; see also God; Israel;
    Torah
  fundamental ethical difference
    between Christianity and, 187
  kept alive during Holocaust,
    153–154, 156
  Maimonides' principles of faith
    and, 5–7
  particularistic and universalistic
    character of, 42, 43, 80, 82
  rabbinic formulation of, 7–8
  role of, in Israel, 160–162
  See also Conservative Judaism;

  Orthodox Judaism; Reform
    Judaism and specific aspects
    of Judaism
Judges, Book of, 46, 47, 52
Judges, court, 190
  gift taking by, 189
Justice, 187–195

Kabbalah, 78, 82, 86–95, 128, 235,
    238
Kabbalistic studies of Torah, 26
Kaddish (sanctification), 8, 115,
    237–238
Kagan, Rabbi Meir Simḥah, 39
Kaplan, Rabbi Mordecai, 84, 125
Karaites, 64, 140, 141
Kashrut, 132–133
  See also Dietary laws
Kavvanah (direction; concentra-
    tion), 35–36
Kedushah (holiness), 115, 196–202
Kehillah (and kehillah kedoshah;
    Jewish community), 119, 197
Keli Yakar ("Precious Vessel;"
    Luntschitz), 75
Kera satan (rend Satan asunder), 16
Kevod ha-beriot (respect for God's
    creatures), 204
Ketubbah (marriage lines), 215
Ketuvim ("The Writings"), 46, 47
Kiddush (sanctification), 100–102
Kiddush ha-Shem (sanctification
    of the name), 44, 45
Killing, see Taking of life
Kimḥi, Rabbi, 54
Kingdom of priests, 39
Kings, Book of, 46, 47, 52
Kisma, Rabbi Jose ben, 28
Klausner, Joseph, 228
Knots
  tefillin, 127
  tzitzit, 126
Kook, Rabbi A. I., 84, 224
Kosher
  defined, 132
  See also Dietary laws
Kotzker Rebbe, 197
Krochmal, Nachman, 83
Kuzari (Halevi), 79, 81

Lamdan (the learned), 66
Lamentations, Book of, 47, 48, 52,
    113
Lampronti, Isaac, 75
Landau, Rabbi Ezekiel, 73, 117
Lashon Ha-ra (evil tongue),
    208–209
Leiner, Rabbi Gershon Henoch, 125
Lekhah Dodi, 88
Leon, Moses de, 88–89
Letter(s)
  Hebrew alphabet, 50
  Torah scroll, 21–23

Letter of the law, going beyond, 192–193
Levayyah (escorting), 235
Leviticus, 19, 44, 47, 51, 108, 166, 167, 169, 176, 177, 194, 197, 208, 209, 231
Levush Malkhut (Jaffe), 190
Lipkin, Isaac (Rabbi Israel Salanter), 32, 146, 177, 207, 211
Life after death, 230–231
 See also Hereafter
Lipschutz, Rabbi Israel, 68
Lishmah (for its sake), 35, 36
Literature, *see* Rabbinic literature and specific works
Lot, 22
Love, 92, 93
 justice and, 187
 thy neighbor (ve-ahavta le-reakha), 30, 40, 166–173
 of Torah, 23; *see also* Torah
Lulav (palm branch), 35, 108–109, 195
Luntschitz, Rabbi Ephraim, 75
Luria, Rabbi Isaac de 90–91, 94
Luzzatto, Rabbi Moses Hayyim, 198, 199, 234
Luzzato, Samuel David, 81

Ma'ariv, 122, 123
Maaseh Bereshit ("Account of Creation"), 86
Maaseh Merkavah ("Account of the Chariot"), 86
Maccabees, 111
Maggid, The (Rabbi Dov Baer), 141, 142
Maggid Mesharim ("Speaker of Upright Words"; Caro), 70
Maimonides, 5–6, 14, 16, 17, 26, 32, 65, 80–82
 adornment of mitzvot and, 35
 on bimah, 119
 chosenness and, 40
 codes of, 70
 commentary of, to Mishnah, 67–68
 dietary laws and, 139
 eight degrees of charity of, 135
 foreknowledge and free will and, 78
 messianic idea and, 221, 222, 227–230
 on mezuzah, 131
 on mourning, 151
 shehitah and, 135
 Sukkot and, 108
Makom kadosh (holy place), 197
 See also Synagogue
Malachi (and Book of Malachi), 47, 49
Malkhut (sovereignty), 92
Mappah (Tablecloth), 73

Marriage
 ceremony of, 213–215
 as duty, 213–214
 out-of-faith, 212–213
 polygamous, 213
Maskilim, 143–144
Masoretic Text of the Bible, 50, 52
Masorites, 50, 51
Mattanot la-evyonim (gifts to the poor), 113
Matzah, 105, 106, 132
Meat
 mixing of dairy products with, 73, 136–137
 and pork prohibition, 30, 32, 133
 salting of, 135–136
 See also Animals
Medini, Hayyim Hezekiah, 75
Megillah (Book of Esther), 47, 48, 52, 111–113, 219
Meir, Jacob ben (Rabbenu Tam), 69, 73, 127–129
Meirat Eynayim (Falk), 189
Mekhilta, 59
Melakhah, *see* Work
Mendelssohn, Moses, 6–7, 82, 143
Menorah, 111, 118
Mesillat Yesharim (Luzzato), 198
Messianic idea, 221–229
 and birth of State of Israel, 159–160, 224, 226
 in Christianity and Judaism, compared, 226–228
 development of, 222–223
 Messianic age and, 228–229
 natural and supernatural elements in, 222–223
 non-Orthodox views of, 224, 226
 Orthodox view of, 223–224, 228
Mezuzah, 30, 34, 74, 129–131, 196, 199
Micah (and Book of Micah), 8, 9, 37, 47
Midrash, 20, 21, 107, 108, 156, 159, 174, 182, 183, 193
 aggadic, 63
 Israeli edition of, 164
 Torah scroll interpretation provided by, 21–23
 tannaitic, 59
Midrash Rabbah ("The Great Midrash"), 63
Mikdash Me'at (Temple in miniature), 116
Mikveh, 164
Minhah, 122
Minyan (quorum), 115
Mishnah, 25, 58, 117, 135, 140, 170, 182, 183, 187, 203
 commentaries to, 67–68
 defined, 56
 Six Orders of, 59–60
 work as described in, 98–99

Mishneh Torah (Yad ha-Hazakah;
    "Second to the Torah;"
    Maimonides), 70
Mishpaḥah, *see* Family
Mishpatim (judgments), 31
Mitnaggedim, 142–144
Mitzvot, 29–37, 43
    adorning, 34–35
    as duties of the heart, 36–37
    joy of, 35
    Kavvanah doctrine and, 35–36
    non-Jews performing, sharing
        in hereafter, 44
    person-to-God and person-to-
        person, 30–31
    positive and negative, 29–30, 33
    rabbinic, 34
    reasons for, 31–33
    taryag, 33–34
    See also specific mitzvot
Modern inventions, responsa on, 74
Mohammed, 6, 227
Molcho, Solomon, 225
Moloch, 11
Money lending, as expression of
    benevolence, 182
Monotheism, Judaism as ethical, 18
Mordecai, 113, 219
Moreh Nevukhey ha-Zeman
    (Krochmal), 83
Moses, 5, 6, 8, 19, 38, 46, 52–54,
    58, 87, 98, 107, 127, 134,
    189–190, 193, 205, 208, 209,
    219, 228
Mourning, 235
    and comforting mourners, 181
    days of, 113–114
    for Holocaust victims, 151–152
Musar (instruction), 146–147, 177,
    182
Music
    and chants accompanying
        Scripture reading, 48
    in synagogue, 121
Musical notations on Torah
    Scroll, 22
Myrtle and willow, 108, 109
Mysticism, 86–95

Nahman ben Isaac, Rabbi, 2, 18, 58
Naḥmanides, 37, 54, 157, 206, 230
Nahum, Book of, 47
Naming of children, 215
Negative mitzvot (mitzvot lo
    ta'aseh, 30, 33
Nehemiah (and Book of Nehe-
    miah), 46, 47, 157
Neighbor, love of, 30, 40, 166–173
Neo-Orthodoxy, *see* Orthodox
    Judaism
Neshamah yeterah (additional
    soul), 96
Netzaḥ (victory), 92

Neutralization principle, 138
Neviim (Book of the Prophets),
    46–49
Noah, 42
Nondogmatic character of
    Judaism, 7
Non-Jews, 42–45
    behavior with, 44, 45
    Torah for, 42
    views of, 43–44
Numbers, Book of, 19, 47, 59, 124,
    125, 183, 205, 212, 220

Obadiah, Book of, 47
Olam ha-ba, *see* Hereafter
Oneg shabbat (Sabbath delight),
    100
Oneness of God, 15, 21
Orah Hayyim ("Way of Life;" part
    of *Shulḥan Arukh;* Caro), 171
Oral Torah (Torah she-be-al Peh),
    19–20, 140
    See also Midrash; Torah
Ordinary mortals, holiness for, 199
Orlinsky, Harry, 50, 51
Orthodox Judaism, 145–146
    biblical criticism rejected by,
        53–54
    burial in, 235
    cremation in, 231
    emphasis of, on Torah, 4, 5
    Kabbalah and, 94
    Messianic idea in, 223–224, 228
    music in synagogue and, 121
    Sabbath and, 99
    Shulḥan Arukh and, 72
    in State of Israel, 162
    Torah reading in synagogue
        and, 123
    women in synagogue and, 119
Otzar Yisrael (Hebrew Encyclope-
    dia), 196
Out-of-faith marriage, 212–213

Paḥad Yitzhak ("Dream of Isaac;"
    Lampronti), 75
Palestinian (Yerushalmi) Talmud,
    56, 60, 62–64
Pappa, Rabbi, 58
Pardes Rimonim ("Orchard of
    Pomegranates;" Cordovero), 89
Parents, *see* Children
Particularistic character of
    Judaism, 42, 43, 82
Passover (Pesaḥ), 8, 47, 105–106,
    113, 183
Peace
    State of Israel and, 164–165
    ways of, 45
Pentateuch, *see* Torah *and
    specific books of* Pentateuch
Person-to-God mitzvot, 30–31
Person-to-person mitzvot, 30–31

Pesah (Passover), 8, 47, 105–106, 113, 183
Pharisees, 141
Philo, 77–78, 97
Philosophical studies of Torah, 26
Philosophy, *see* Jewish philosophy
Plants and vegetables, 138–139
Polygamy, 213
Pork prohibition, 30, 32, 133
Positive mitzvot (mitzvot aseh), 29–30, 33
Potocki, Count Valentine, 42
Practice and study of Torah, 25
Prayers, 126
  for the dead, 8, 115, 237–238
  Hasidic, 143
  during Holocaust, 153
  house of (Bet ha-Tefillah), 115
  of Jewish Saint, 154
  as person-to-person mitzvot, 30
  reasons for swaying during, 199
  for recovery, 181
  in synagogue, 115–116, 120–121
Principles of faith, 5–7
Probability principle, 137
Prophets, 48–49
  See also specific prophets
Prophets, Book of (Neviim), 46, 48, 49
Proverbs, 46–48, 52
Psalms, 7, 27, 47, 48, 52, 54, 131, 157, 208
Punishment
  crime and, 188
  rewards and, 5, 6
Purification (Taharah), 235
Purim, 47, 111–113

Rabbinic literature, 45, 67–75
  codes as, 67, 69–72
  commentaries as, 67–69
  intellectualism in, 75–76
  other types of, 74–75
  responsa in, 67, 72–74
Rabbinic mitzvot, 34
Rahamut (rachmones), *see* Compassion
Rashba (Rabbi Solomon Ibn Adret), 73, 81
Rashi, Rabbi (Solomon ben Isaac), 54, 68–69, 127–129, 173, 207
Rational mitzvot (mishpatim), 31
Rava, 58
Ravina, 58, 60
Reasoning, truth discovery by, 79
Reform Judaism, 144–145
  emphasis of, on God, 4, 5
  hereafter in, 230
  Messianic idea in, 224, 226
  music in synagogue and, 121
  in State of Israel, 162
  Torah reading in synagogue and, 123

  wedding ceremony in, 214
  women in synagogue and, 119
Reincarnation, 238
Rekhilut (talebearers), 208–209
Respect, 203–205
Responsa, 67, 72–74
Resurrection of the dead, *see* Hereafter
Return, Law of, 164
Reubeni, David, 225
Revelation, 2, 6, 79, 82
Rewards and punishment, 5, 6
Righteousness, *see* Tzedakah
Rimmonim (pomenagrates), 34
Rishonim (early ones), 72
Rosenzweig, Franz, 84–85, 105
Rosh Hashanah, 31, 60, 109–110, 113, 121, 221
Rosh Hodesh, 106
Rossi, Azariah de, 65, 77
Rozin, Rabbi Joseph, 27
Ruah (wind), 51
Ruah ha-kodesh (holy spirit), 196, 198
Ruth, Book of, 47, 48, 52

Saadiah, 79, 139, 238
Sabbath, 3, 73, 88, 96–104, 199
  celebrated during Holocaust, 153
  in Conservative Judaism, 146
  as foretaste of hereafter, 232, 235
  as gift, 104
  Halakhah and Aggadah in observance of, 62, 63
  Havdalah on, 102
  importance of, 96–98
  Karaites and, 140
  keeping, as person-to-God mitzvah, 30
  Kiddush recitation on, 100–102
  music on, 121
  observance of, in State of Israel, 162
  oneg shabbat and, 100, 105
  in Reform Judaism, 144
  Torah reading on, 123
  work on, 19, 98–99
Sabbath candles, 32–33, 199
Saducean movement, 140
Safrai, Samuel, 116
Saint, prayer of Jewish, 154
Salanter, Rabbi Israel (Isaac Lipkin), 32, 146, 177, 207, 211
Salting of meat, 135–136
Samuel (prophet; and Book of Samuel), 46, 47, 52
Samuel, Rabbi, 48, 223
Samuel ben Hophni, Rabbi, 58, 65
Sanctification, *see* Kaddish; Kiddush
Sarah, 78
Saul (King of Israel), 179
Savoraim, 63–64

Schechter, Rabbi Solomon, 146
Secular Judaism, 1
Seder ha-Dorot ("Order of the Generations;" Heilprin), 75
Sedey Ḥemed ("Fields of Delight;" Medini), 75
Sefer Ḥasidim, 237
Sefer Torah, 19, 20, 22, 26, 34, 71, 77, 117, 123, 196, 199, 202
Self-denial as sin, 200
Self-control (self-discipline) freedom and, 29
    holiness and, 197–198
Self-defense, taking of life in, 172–173
Sephardic Jews, 8, 71, 121, 128, 164
Septuagint, 52, 77
Sermons, 121–122
Servants, family relationship with, 219
Shaḥarit, 122
Shalom Aleichem (song), 100
Shammai, Rabbi, 58, 111, 215
Shavuot, 47, 106, 107, 113
Sheelot u-Teshuvot (Questions and Answers; Responsa), 67, 72–74
Sheḥitah (kosher killing), 133–135
Shekhinah (Divine Presence), 115, 116
Shem ha-Gedolim ("Names of the Great;" Azulai), 75
Shema, 15, 21, 24, 59, 191
Shemini Atzeret (Eight Day of Assembly), 109
Shiflut (humility), 142, 205–207
Shishah Sedarim (Orders of the Mishnah), 59
Shofar blowing, 31, 110, 196
Shulḥan Arukh ("Arranged Table;" Caro), 70, 71, 99, 119, 122, 157, 181, 225
Sick, the, visiting, 181
Sifra (Torat Kohanim), 59
Silver, Rabbi Abba Hillel, 145
Simeon, Rabbi, 57, 58
Simeon ben Lakish, Rabbi, 58
Simeon ben Shetaḥ, Rabbi, 45
Simḥah (joy), 105, 142
Simḥat Torah, 23, 109
Simlai, Rabbi, 33
Six Orders of Mishnah, 59–60
Sofer, Rabbi Moses, 207
Solomon (King of Israel), 49, 52, 189, 221, 222
Soloveichik, Ḥayyim, 183
Song of Songs, 24, 47–50, 52
Spiritualism, 236–237
Study
    of Bible, 26, 27
    holiness and, 199
    house of (Bet ha-Midrash), 115
    of Kabbalah, 95

of Talmud, 61, 66
of Torah, 24–28, 96, 100, 182–183, 202, 204, 229
Sukenik, E. L., 53
Sukkah, 34, 103, 108
Sukkot, 34, 48, 106, 108–109, 113, 195
Superiority, chosenness and, 40–41
Synagogue, 115–123, 197
    architecture of, 68, 117
    ark in, 117–118
    bimah in, 118–119
    cantor's role in, 122
    choosing a, 116–117
    daily services in, 122–123
    eternal light burning in, 118
    melodies sung in, 121
    praying in, 115–116, 120–121
    rabbi and sermon in, 121–122
    Torah reading in, 115, 123

Tabernacle, 117–118
Taggin (crowns) of Torah, 21, 34
Taharah (purification), 235
Taking of life, 170
    of animals, *see* Animals
    saving one's life by, injunction against, 172–173
    in self-defense, 173
Talebearers (Rekhilut), 208–209
Tallit, 124–126, 131, 196
Talmid ḥakham (disciple of the wise), 66
Talmud, 19, 20, 25, 27, 86
    Babylonian, 2, 8, 56–58, 60–64
    commentary on, 67–69
    cures in, 65
    as final authority, 64
    Israeli editions of, 164
    life after death in, 232
    mitzvot and, 31, 32, 34, 35; *see also* Mitzvot *and specific mitzvot*
    non-Jews in, 42
    Palestinian, 56, 60, 62–64
    Savoraim and Geonim and, 63–64
    study of, 61, 66
    and synagogue, 115, 116, 119, 122
    Tannaim and Amoraim and, 56–58, 64
    and ways of peace, 45
    See also Rabbinic literature
Talmudic rabbis of blessed memory (Ḥazal), 64–65
Tam, Rabbenu (Jacon ben Meir), 69, 73, 127–129
Tannaim, 56–58, 64
Tannaitic Midrashim, 59
Tarfon, Rabbi, 58
Taryag mitzvot, 33–34
Tefillah, *see* Prayers
Tefillin, 126–130, 196, 199

Tekhelet (blue thread), 125–126
Ten Commandments, 3, 33, 107, 118, 195, 204, 217, 218, 227–228
Ten Sefirot, 91–94
Tevah (the ark), 117–118
Terefah prohibition, 135, 137, 138
Theism, 10, 11
Tiferet (beauty), 92, 93
Tiferet Yisrael (Lipschutz), 68
Tish'ah B'av, 113–114
Tomer Devorah ("Palm Tree of Deborah;" Cordovero), 89
Torah, 19–29, 43, 46, 47
  aim of, 37
  as blueprint, 23
  chosenness and, 41
  copies of, 50, 51
  love of, 33
  meaning of, 19
  mitzvot and, 33, 34; *see also* Mitzvot *and specific mitzvot*
  Oral, 19–20, 140; *see also* Midrash; Talmud
  Orthodox Judaism emphasis on, 4, 5
  in Philo's philosophy, 77, 78
  principles of faith and, 6, 7
  reading of, in synagogue, 115, 123
  Saadiah and, 79
  study of, 24–28, 96, 100, 182–183, 202, 204, 209
  weekly reading from, 48
  worship of, prohibited, 24
  in Zohar, 88, 89
  See also Bible, the; Talmud
Torah Scroll, 20–23
Tosafot (additions), 69
Tosefot Yom Tov (Heller), 68
Traditional mitzvot (hukkim), 31
Truth, 207–208
  reasoning and discovery of, 79
Tur (Arba'ah Turim; "The Four Rows;" Asher), 71
Twelve, Book of the, 47, 52
Tzedakah (charity; righteousness), 29, 45, 180–181, 183–186
  determining amount and qualifications for, 163–164
  eight degrees of, 185
  gentiles and, 43, 44
  and gifts to the poor, 113
  order of priority in, 185
  in praise of, 185–186
Tzitzit, 124–126, 130, 131, 196
  tekhelet in, 125–126

Uniqueness of God, 15
Universalistic character of Judaism, 42, 43, 80, 82

Vegetables and plants, 138–139
Vegetarianism, 139
Ve-ahavta le-reakha (love thy neighbor), 30, 40, 166–173
Vital, Rabbi Hayyim, 90

Warsaw Ghetto uprising (1943), 155
Washing of hands, 32
Wasserman, Rabbi Elhanan, 237
Wellhausen, 54
Will of God, 8
Wise, Rabbi Isaac Mayer, 144, 145
Witnesses (Ed), 21
  in lawsuits, 190
Women
  called to Torah, 123
  in minyan, 115
  in synagogues, 119
Work
  on festivals, 113
  on Sabbath, 19, 98–99, 113
World to Come (Gan Eden; Garden of Eden), *see* Hereafter; Messianic idea
Written Torah (Torah she-bi-Khetav), *see* Torah

Yaarat Devash ("Forest of Honey;" Eybeschuetz), 75
Yahrzeit, 8, 123, 235, 237
Yadin, Yigal, 53
Yehiel, Rabbi Asher ben, 26
Yesod (foundation), 92
Yihus (family pride), 212
Yitzhak, Rabbi Levi, 35, 213
Yom Kippur, 31, 109–111, 113, 121, 123, 199
Yom Tov, *see* Festivals
Yoreh De'ah ("Teaching Knowledge;" part of *Shulhan Arukh;* Caro), 71

Zaddik, 142–143
Zalman, Rabbi Shneur, 66, 184
Zangwill, Israel, 39
Zechariah, Book of, 47, 190
Zeitlin, Solomon, 53, 115
Zephaniah, Book of, 47
Zera, Rabbi, 2
Zevi, Shabbetai, 94, 141, 225
Zionism, 145, 147–148, 224, 226
Zohar, The ("Illumination"), 87–90, 121, 126, 199, 202
Zunz, Leopold, 83
Zusya, Rabbi, 208

PICTURE CREDITS

The sources for the illustrations in this book are shown below by page number. Unless otherwise noted by an asterisk (*), all pictures were provided by Art Resource, New York City.

3 Bill Aron*; *4* Jeanne Hamilton; *6* Bill Aron; *7* Jacqueline Gill; *9* Bill Aron*; *10* New York Public Library Picture Collection*; *11* Library of Congress*; *12* Marion Bernstein; *13* Raimondo Borea; *15* Michelangelo, "Creation of Adam." Alinari; *16* photographer unknown; *17* Ch'i-P'ei, "Bird on Flowering Branch." Sotheby Parke-Bernet; *19* Jasper Johns "Target with Four Faces," 1955. Encaustic on newspaper over canvas, 26×26". Collection: The Museum of Modern Art, New York*; *20* photographer unknown; *21* United Israel Appeal*; *22* Bill Aron*; *23* source unidentified, The Jewish Museum; *27* Fairchild; *29* From the collection of Arthur Kurzweil*; *30* Bill Aron*; *31* Caravaggio, "The Card Cheaters." Alinari; *33* Leonardo da Vinci, "Vitruvian Man," Alinari; *36* Jan Lucas; *41* source unidentified, "Stoning Jews in Lent."*; *43* (left) Raphael and Giulio Romano, "Building of the Ark." The Jewish Museum;* (right) Ben Shahn, "Allegoria Terza." Scala; *44* Peter Hellman*; *45* source unidentified*; *48* Jan Lucas; *49* Auguste Rodin, "The Kiss." Alinari; *50* Bill Aron; *53* The Israel Museum, Jerusalem*; *57* Joint Distribution Committee*; *58* Israel Office of Information*; *61* source unidentified*; *62* Canadian Consulate General*; *65* Religious News Service*; *67* source unidentified*; *69* Michael Dobo; *70* United Israel Appeal Photo Archives*; *72* The Central Archives for the History of the Jewish People, Jerusalem*; *73* Jan Lucas; *75* Bill Aron; *76* Phyllis Friedman*; *79* Charles Gatewood; *80* Victor Loredo*; *83* Bill Aron; *84* Tower Newsphoto; *85* Bill Aron; *87* Brueghel, "The Garden of Eden." Scala; *89* Laimute Druskis; *90* Andrew McKeever; *91* Bill Aron; *92* source unidentified; *93* Shabbetai Horowitz, "The twenty-eight lights (fingers) issuing from the ineffable name (hands)," Paris Bibliotheque Nationale*; *94* Michelangelo, "Ezechiel," Sistine Chapel. Alinari; *96* Wide World Photos*; *97* (top) Ted Feder; (bottom left) Laimute Druskis; (bottom right) photographer unknown; *98* (left) Roger B. Smith; (right) Andrew McKeever; *99* Bill Aron; *101* Doug Magee; *102* Herman Struck, "Man Making Havdalah." The Jewish Museum; *103* Isidor Kaufman, "Friday Evening." The Jewish Museum; *105* Paris Bibliotheque Nationale from The Photographic Archive of the Jewish Theological Seminary of America, New York*; *106* source unidentified, The Jewish Museum*; *108* Bill Aron; *109* (left) Bill Aron; (right) Yivo*; *111* Jan Lucas; *112* The Jewish Museum*; *113* United Israel Appeal*; *115* Consulate General of Israel*; *116* Bill Aron; *119* photographer unknown, *Keeping Posted;* *120* Jim Smith; *123* Bill Aron; *124* The Jewish Museum; *127* Michos Tzovaras; *129* Paris Bibliotheque Nationale*; *130* Bill Aron*; *131* The Jewish Museum*; *132* photographer unknown; *133* Jan Lucas; *134* Paris Bibliotheque Nationale*; *135* Alain Keller; *137* (left) Jacqueline Gill; (right) Charles Gatewood; *138* H. Roger Viollet*; *142* Bill Aron; *143* Bill Aron; *144* Bill Aron*; *145* Miner-Baker Studio,

Indianapolis; *146* Bill Aron*; *149* Michos Tzovaras; *150* Broktorfy, "The Expulsion of the Jews." The Jewish Museum; *151* Daniel S. Brody; *152* (top) Sipa Press; (bottom) Nachum Tim Gidal, Zionist Archives*; *154* Bill Aron; *157* Jewish National Fund*; *158* Claude Michaelides*; *161* Jewish National Fund*; *162* The Jewish Museum*; *163* Oskar Tauber*; *166* Bruce Anspach; *167* Bill Aron; *168* Jan Lucas; *170* Andrew Sacks; *171* Dan O'Neill; *175* Laimute Druskis; *177* Ann Chwatsky; *178* photographer unknown; *181* Raimondo Borea; *182* Laimute Druskis; *184* Doug Magee; *185* The Jewish Museum*; *189* Bill Aron*; *191* Joan Sydlow; *192* Marion Bernstein; *194* (top) Judy Rosemarin; (bottom) Michos Tzovaras; *197* photographer unknown; *198* Bill Aron; *199* Jan Lucas; *200* Daniel S. Brody; *201* Bill Aron; *202* Jan Lucas; *204* Raimondo Borea; *205* Judy Rosemarin; *206* J. Whitaker; *209* Ellen Levine; *210* Andrew Sacks; *213* Charles Gatewood; *214* (top) The Jewish Museum; (bottom) Bill Aron*; *217* Laimute Druskis; *222* William Finch; *223* Jan Lucas; *227* Tower Newsphoto; *228* Charles Gatewood; *231* Daniel S. Brody; *232* Laimute Druskis; *233* Doug Magee; *234* Raimondo Borea; *236* Michael Dobo; *238* Marion Bernstein